Body Under Siege

Two very different, but two very connected stories—Multiple Sclerosis, life at the edge, and The Vidalia Onion, a marketing success story.

By: Danny S. New
(706) 860-2756

With medical information edited by Dr. David C. Hess, MD.

www.thevidaliaonionstory.com

© 2002 by Danny S. New. All rights reserved.

No part of this book may be reproduced, stored in a retrieval system, or transmitted by any means, electronic, mechanical, photocopying, recording, or otherwise, without written permission from the author.

ISBN: 0-7596-4334-2 (ebook)
ISBN: 9-7596-4335-0 (Paperback)
ISBN: 1-4033-7492-9 (Dustjacket)

This book is printed on acid free paper.

1stBooks – rev. 10/16/02

DEDICATION

"This book is dedicated to my wife Vivian and to my son Swain, who have lived through the nightmare of a transition from scattered thoughts to a finished book."

CONTENTS

Schedule of Multiple Sclerosis Information
(Edited by Dr. David C. Hess, M.D.) vii

Introduction ix

Chapter 1   The Vidalia Onion Story 1
Chapter 2   The Battle Begins 35
Chapter 3   The Business and Multiple Sclerosis Progress 51
Chapter 4   Going Public 75
Chapter 5   The Beginning of the End 93
Chapter 6   Starting Over 110
Chapter 7   The Battle Rages 119
Chapter 8   Medical School—More Than a Dream 134
Chapter 9   Gross Anatomy 137
Chapter 10 Multiple Sclerosis—The Basics 145
Chapter 11 The MS Story Continues 155
Chapter 12 The Search Continues 166
Chapter 13 Second Time Around 172
Chapter 14 Adrift in Self-Pity 177
Chapter 15 Searching for Peace 181
Chapter 16 Questions from MS Patients — A Sprinkling of
            What I Missed 191
Chapter 17 Introspection 199
Chapter 18 The Attack Continues 204
Chapter 19 Putting It All Together 207
References 216
Glossary 230

MULTIPLE SCLEROSIS INFORMATION

(Edited By: Dr. David C. Hess, M.D.)

1. Hearing Loss 37
2. Diplopia 39
3. Optic Neuritis 43
4. Diagnosing Multiple Sclerosis 48
5. Corticosteroids 60
6. Fatigue and Multiple Sclerosis 66
7. Effects of Heat, Cold, and Exercise on MS 73
8. Ataxia 101
9. Scotoma 102
10. Nystagmus 102
11. Cerebellar Symptoms 103
12. Cognitive Impairment - (cont. on page 122) 104
13. A Warning About the Danger of Cognitive Impairment in MS 108
14. Impaired Information Processing (See pg. 210 for More Details) ... 108
15. Impact of Relapse on Cognitive Impairment 108
16. Cognitive Impairment - Part 2 122
17. Short Term vs Long Term Memory 128
18. Epidemiology of Multiple Sclerosis 148
19. Demyelination 149
20. Chronic-Progressive vs Relapsing-Remitting Disease 151
21. Evidence that Axons are Also Damaged in MS 154
22. Pain 159
23. Where the Plaques Are 161
24. MRI's Showing Brain Atrophy 162
25. Epilepsy 171
26. Stress 193
27. Dysphagia 194
28. Paroxysmal Symptoms 196
29. Relapse Rate 197
30. Prospect of Remission 198
31. Impaired Information Processing (Cont. From Page 108) 210
32. Treatments Aimed at Altering Course of Disease 214

INTRODUCTION

Body Under Siege is an account of my adult life and will include many things—life with multiple sclerosis, the Vidalia Onion story, taking a company public, attending medical school, and experiencing both success and failure. To a degree, it will be an accounting. But more than this, it will be the story of a struggle to preserve hope.

Writing this book was not a choice for me. It was as though my life could never be really validated unless and until I recorded it.

Body Under Siege includes many side sagas that could be, or should be, books in their own right. The Vidalia Onion story is one of these. The Onion didn't just happen on its own; it resulted from many years of perseverance and hard work. My brother and I planned it in detail. We made it happen.

But this book is much more than the Vidalia Onion story. It is a chronology of a life with multiple sclerosis, complete with the heartache and destroyed dreams that accompanied it. Told is the story about a struggle for admission to medical school, and the difficulties caused by multiple sclerosis.

I should be thankful for the diversity of living I have experienced. I have known wealth and I have known poverty. I've experienced the youthful sensation of immortality and strength and good health, and I've known the ravages of disease. I have experienced 20-20 vision and I have been confronted by blindness. I have looked at the world through the eyes of an "intelligent" person, and I have witnessed the dark shadows that haunt the intellectually impaired. I have known complete happiness and I have felt utter despair. My life has run the gamut from one that would satisfy most people's dreams to one that would dwarf most people's nightmares.

Writing this book forced me to reach into the depths of my intellect, to recount unpleasant as well as pleasant moments, and to see people and life in ways that had heretofore alluded me. The victories and the tragedies have made me a far different person. I can understand and relate to a much wider range of people.

The onset of MS and the resultant loss of my business convinced me that the world was a conspiracy against my success—an attitude that was not without empirical support. I did for a time seem to go from one tragedy to the next. But this book is not about tragedy. It is about transformation—about getting to the other side.

I erred in my early judgment of life. God dealt me a set of cards that I didn't want, but it wasn't my hand to deal. And maybe "a little" tragedy is necessary to see the virtue in life.

My goal now is to squeeze every drop of emotion, whether bitter or sweet, from these experiences and to record them in an understandable way. Hopefully,

I can locate order in disorder and can find meaning where there is disarray. I believe that *Body Under Siege* has done that.

CHAPTER 1

The Vidalia Onion Story

* 2001 2
* Early History of Georgia Onions 2
* Pinky McRae 5
* Vidalia—The Town 5
* Genesis of the Modern Day Vidalia Onion 7
* Alligator in the Melon Patch 8
* The Vidalia Farmer's Market 10
* The Georgia Onion Flounders 11
* Testing the Waters 11
* The Invisible Onion 12
* The Death of Kenneth New 14
* The Name 15
* Spreading the Name 16
* The Decision to be Farmers 17
* Getting Started 19
* Our First Harvest 22
* Onion Plants 23
* Early Promotion 26
* Migrant Workers 26
* Processed Foods from Vidalia Onions 27
* The Vidalia Onion Niche 31
* Hi Swain 34

2001

As I sit in my wheelchair and view the world through a never-ending haze, I ponder the dream life God had given me, but I had lost.

Multiple sclerosis altered every area of my life. Now my subconscious divides everything into before MS, and after MS. It was not a smooth transition from one life to the next.

Nineteen is a young age for anyone to be cast into the pits of free enterprise. But I wasn't cast in; I jumped in. In 1973, an unquenchable fire of aspiration engulfed me. I had to make my mark in life and business was my calling—or so I thought.

Getting rich in business was never the aim—at least not the sole aim. I wanted to bring to life something that didn't heretofore exist, or if not to make something from nothing, at least to resuscitate something nearing death. In the end, finding what I looked for required little searching. Destiny chose a path for me that I could not avoid. All markers pointed to the Georgia onion. I couldn't see the end of the road, but I knew that this was the road I must take.

But everything was not smooth sailing. Life prepared plenty of turbulence to muddy the water. And life delivered me to an end-point that was a strange place with no markings of familiarity. I expected the entrepreneurial battles that a life in business guarantees. I had prepared myself for them. But I didn't expect and I was not prepared for the physical assault that lay in waiting for me. And I didn't foresee the many sharp turns that would change my direction and send me to places unimaginable in my younger days—places without standing in the world that my mind had engineered for me.

Well, I'm getting ahead of myself. Maybe I should slow down and regress to the beginning—wherever that is.

Early History of Georgia Onions

Now I will go forward with what, in many respects, is a very confusing story. Many states grow onions, and often these are very good onions. And, on a more global scale, many places in the world have successfully penetrated the "sweet onion" niche. But none as successfully as Georgia—with its Vidalia Onion.

To say only this, however, misses the mark. The end and the middle and the why's of the story will not be easily comprehended without first revealing the complete past—if, indeed, they ever can be understood.

Some historians narrate important events, even when the importance is only marginal and borders on unimportance, with a slant toward drama rather than fact. I hope to dispel any fear of that possibility early, thus assuring the reader that this volume will contain only what I know is true, and without exaggeration.

Knowing when this story reached its end was easy. Finding the beginning was more difficult. I was born in 1953, but this stage was set in the forties, maybe even the thirties. The Georgia onion industry was a roller-coaster ride from the beginning, and virtually disappeared for a lot of years. The Onion lay nearly dormant for much of my youth. Because of the tremendous impact this vegetable had on me, I am compelled to begin My story with The Onion's story. The two are inseparable.

World War II spared no part of society. It touched everyone and everything, including agriculture. But farmers still farmed, produce distributors still distributed, and most businesses adapted, and actually prospered. World War II, as terrible as it was, ended The Great Depression. In this setting, onions made their commercial debut in Georgia. Although Georgia produced a very small quantity of onions in the thirties, it was not until the forties that production with any commercial significance began. In 1940, approximately 2000 acres of onions were grown in the Toombs County section of Georgia. These were mostly yellow and white Bermuda type onions, primarily marketed in the East.

But there were a few onions grown in the 30's, too. Mose Coleman, a Toombs County farmer and an often-heard name in the early history of Georgia onions, grew and pedaled a small quantity of Georgia onions then. The Dashers, Kicklighters, and Olivers—in Tattnall County—grew and sold Georgia onions in the 30's. Glenville had the advantage of a farmer's market, built in the thirties, primarily as an outlet for tomatoes—an important cash crop in Glenville then. The farmer's market developed into a centralized marketing center for Georgia onions grown in the Tattnall County area.

All of these men sold their onions primarily in Georgia, and not as a unique item. They were just a "good" onion; a commodity. No unique qualities were attributed to these onions. In fact, it was a substantial effort to overcome the inferior qualities of the Georgia onion—the short shelf-life, the difficulty shipping long distances, and the short season. Nevertheless, these men helped to start a new Georgia onion industry. But developing the name "Vidalia Onion" had to wait on the talents of others. Gerry Achenbach started the ball rolling regionally; Danny and David New made the name "Vidalia Onion" a household word nationally, with their Vidalia Sweets Brand—Vidalia Onions.

Lots of men, to greater or lesser degrees, were instrumental in the early development of the Georgia onion. When the Tanner-Brice Company became financially involved with the Rockefeller family, onion production expanded. This was primarily, if not completely, the result of Phil Friese—who was sent by the Rockefellers to Vidalia. His job was to expand the local production of onions. He did that; unfortunately, he couldn't make buyers buy them. In 1940, the stench from thousands of bags of rotting onions engulfed Vidalia, and Phil Friese ran for his life.

In 1946, Othal Brand and three of his brothers in Atlanta added Georgia onions to the expanding line of vegetables marketed by the Brand Brothers. Othal and his brothers founded Griffin and Brand, Inc.; eventually, with no help from the Georgia onion, Griffin and Brand became one of the largest produce companies in the world.

I asked Othal, who was Mayor of McAllen, Texas from '77 to '97, "When did you start growing onions in Georgia?"

Othal said, "I started in the 40's, when I came back from the war. Earlie Jordon went to work for me and we started growing onions over there (around Vidalia)."

Earlie lived near Vidalia, and influenced the start-up of the Georgia onion deal. I asked Earlie about onion farming back then. He said, "I grew onions, but I also sold onion plants to most of the other farmers." Farmers then didn't like growing the plants, so Earlie was recruited in 1944 to travel to Texas to purchase plants.

I asked, "What were the onions called in the 1940's?"

Earlie said, "They were just a Bermuda onion."

The Brand Brothers continued marketing Georgia onions through the late forties and early fifties.

Traditionally, farmers in this country have been trailblazers; they are risk-takers by habit, if not by nature. In 1940, talk by Phil Friese of a new money crop found a large and interested audience. The Phil Friese fiasco cooled interest in onions for a time, but a new farmer's market built later in the forties re-fueled the interest. The Brand Brothers helped to provide an outlet for the onions. Soon, production in Toombs County increased again. Georgia, at that time, was not much of a factor in the onion markets. The buyers disliked Georgia onions; the reason soon made itself obvious. Othal Brand said, "It was sweet, but its reputation was that it wouldn't carry any great distance after it was ripe. We only had about three weeks that we could ship them. We used the old yellow granex, a very mild onion. It was a semi-flat onion with large cells. It was tender, and we'd let 'em get big like they wanted them. But it wasn't a very long season. We moved out to Texas because we had longer seasons out there. We could ship onions out of Texas from March to July."

I spoke with several onion growers from the forties. They told horror stories about growing onions during that time, in Georgia. One farmer said, "Eventually, all the sane farmers backed away from growing onions in Georgia."

I asked one of the older farmers, "Why did you quit?"

He said, "I grew onions for five years. There was always a problem. The season was too short. The onions wouldn't hold up in shipment. The stores didn't like them because they didn't have the shelf-life that the western onions did. For several years, it seemed like we threw away more than we sold. In good years when we had a large crop, we couldn't sell them. Most of the buyers preferred western onions because the quality was generally better. In the 1950's, the Georgia onion became basically a local retail deal.

Pinky McRae

In the mid-fifties, a Toombs County native, by duration if not by birth, purchased a tract of farmland from a colorful gentleman named Mac New. A farmer with particular talents, Mac New had a special flair for growing onions, and was one of the earliest onion growers in Georgia.

Pinky McRae, the buyer of this land and an important player in the Georgia onion saga, decided to produce onions in Toombs County on this land he had acquired from Mac New. As a condition of the transaction, Mr. McRae negotiated an employment agreement with Mac New to grow sweet onions on this farm. "My agreement with Mac when I bought the place from him was that he would stay there with me for at least three years and plant onions," Pinky said. "That's when I really got into the onion business."

Pinky recharged the Georgia onion deal. "Of course, as you well know, I never called them Vidalia Onions," said Pinky. "We called them Toombs County—Georgia Sweet Onions."

Vidalia—The Town

Vidalia, set apart from the rest of the world, bustled with its tobacco farmers and tobacco warehouses, factory workers, and an assorted array of "downtown businesses." These were owned and operated by a colorful lot of "downtown businessmen," whose sole calling was "to serve Vidalia," —as though "Vidalia" was every bit as organic as any of its 10,000 occupants.

I never considered another spot in the world suitable for a Vidalian to live in, and certainly not me. My family roots ran deep in Toombs County, going back at least four generations, and probably more. As one native Vidalian liked to boast, "The only reason for other towns to exist is so Vidalians can visit them occasionally. Savannah and Augusta and Macon were built so Vidalians would have a place to go shopping at Christmas."

But Lyons, just five miles away, was different. True Vidalia "blue-bloods" in the fifties and sixties knew Lyons to be a primary resource for potential brides and grooms. All of the high school kids from Vidalia and Lyons knew that any serious relationship would probably start in the other town. I guess it was "the grass is greener on the other side of the fence" syndrome. At an early age, I suffered all of the acute symptoms. Eventually, my condition advanced into a chronic stage, and, fortunately, I could find no cure. Vivian Griffin's hair was thick, straight, the color of coal. Her big brown eyes sparkled when she smiled. There was much kindness in her. I started dating Vivian when I was fifteen, we were married at nineteen, and we had our 27th anniversary in 2000. Various eccentricities interacted to make Vivian, Vivian. When she disagreed with me, she looked up at her angel, pleading for help.

When she detected an untruth, or even a slight fabrication, her brown eyes flashed dangerously, as a warning to the beholder that white-water was near. And her twinkling little face left no doubt that she was serious. Her face bore a strange contrast. There was childlike innocence, but also a confidence that provided all the protection that Vivian needed.

Metropolitan Vidalia—with maybe 12,000 within the city limits, and that many twice over in the outlying areas—had the customary sprinkling of "rural suburbia." Cedar Crossing, Norman Town, Johnson Corner, Oak Park, and other spots I likely overlooked, served as accepted landmarks for intracounty directions. Locals assumed that any person not immediately familiar with each of these places could not possibly be a native, and likely drifted in to visit a third or fourth cousin.

Estroff's, Max Smith's, Bailey's, Shuman's Grocery, and other small independents are all gone now. A generation of businessmen unique in time and place owned and operated these establishments. That time and those people represented an entirely different view of what life should be. Walmarts, chain grocers, shopping centers, and a redefined work ethic have replaced them all. Maybe it's just nostalgia or growing old or something, but I liked the way it was.

A landmark edifice in Vidalia during my youth was Jack's Drive-In. It's gone, too, but its mark on the teenagers of Vidalia in the fifties and sixties isn't gone. Owned by Jack and Louise Gibson, this curbside and sit-down eatery stood as a monument to the world's best hamburgers and French fries—and maybe the world's greasiest, too. At a time when franchised fast-food restaurants only existed in some plutocrat's mind, or maybe were only an aberration of some distant entrepreneurial spirit, Jack's Drive-In stood as Vidalia's premiere gathering spot for everyone under 20.

Traveling as a youth, I encountered many perceptions about Vidalia. "Oh yeah, Vidalia. That's near the Altamaha River. Right?" Or, "Plant Hatch is near Vidalia, isn't it?" But not once did I hear Vidalia referred to as "The Onion City." It was not until the seventies that Vidalia's identity was redefined with the new slogan, and then only after a lengthy battle that pitted farmer against farmer and town against town.

But eventually Vidalia did become "The Onion City." Now I will tell how that happened.

Genesis of the Modern Day Vidalia Onion

In the early fifties, providence delivered me to the town of Vidalia, in the county of Toombs, in the state of Georgia, and it is by birthright that I claim this as home. Today, the name Vidalia conjures images of endless acres of onions that possess some magical constitution bestowed by the enchanted soil around this otherwise ordinary country town.

As I grew up in this small town, where strangers were uncommon and secrets were non-existent and life was a community effort, even in this culture I lived unaware of onions in Georgia by any name, although my father was in the produce business. The onion endeavor in Vidalia in the 60's was hardly visible and only involved a very small number of people, maybe two or three, and onions were an insignificant sideline for even these few farmers.

Pinky McRae continued through the 60's as the most public onion merchant in Toombs County, selling his Toombs County—Georgia Sweet Onions. No organized marketing effort had evolved and the business of selling Georgia onions drifted aimlessly.

In the late sixties and earlier, Piggly Wiggly Southern continued aggressively marketing Georgia onions. They set the stage for what the New Bros. later did. It is likely, or it is possible, that there would be no onion industry in Georgia without the efforts of Piggly Wiggly, through their President and, for all pragmatic purposes, founder—Gerry Achenbach. Gerry Achenbach threw the ball. David and I caught it and ran.

This was the state of the Georgia onion industry in 1972 when David and I arrived on the scene. And this was the year that circumstances fell into place assuring the genesis of the modern day Vidalia Onion industry. I was nineteen, recently married, and in college at the time. Our father survived a heart attack in that year. Motivated partly by a sense of responsibility to our father, and partly by an innate desire to be in business, David resigned his employment, I quit college, and we became equal partners with our father in his small produce and trucking company.

For many years, commercial onion production in Georgia had stood still. In the early 70's, most of the onions came from Tattnall County and went into bags labeled "Glennville Sweets" or "Tattnall County Sweets," marketed by Gerald and Robert Dasher; or were sold to New Bros., Inc. and packaged under their private Vidalia Sweets Brand; or to Piggly Wiggly Southern who marketed them under their "Pride of Piggly Wiggly Brand Vidalia Onions," and sold in their Georgia stores.

Danny S. New

Alligator in the Melon Patch

I asked David, "How many potatoes do we have in the warehouse?"

He said, "Counting the load that just came in, somewhere around 2000 bags." That was enough to last through the weekend. "There will be another trailer load Monday, but that one goes to Piggly Wiggly," David said.

Potatoes were an important part of our business. Our trucks took Chinese vegetables to a family chain of Chinese restaurants in New York City and brought potatoes back from Long Island. Profits from the potatoes and Chinese vegetables kept our head above water in the winter months, when our cash flow was the lowest. With David and me now in the business, it had to support three families instead of one.

The Company could only afford to pay us $75 a week at first, but we had confidence that we could come up with something to make the business support us all. Expanding our Northeast watermelon business to the Midwest was on top of the list of possibilities. Dad had business in the Northeast, and David and I had made some promising contacts in the Midwest. A watermelon business was not our ultimate goal, but we knew it could serve as a stepping stone to finance our way into the onion business. We knew that was where we wanted to go.

In keeping with the general nature of youth, we wanted to operate the watermelon business a little different from the way Dad did. Dad bought watermelons by the trailer load, with the grower providing all the labor. Labor was always a headache for farmers, so David and I felt that we could increase our profit by taking this burden off of the farmer's back. We would assume all the risk of harvesting.

David said, "Kenneth Durrence has 25 acres of Charleston Greys near Reidsville. Let's go look at 'em."

Kenneth Durrence was one of Tattnall County's larger tobacco farmers. We found at Kenneth's farm one of the best watermelon fields we had ever seen, and we had seen a lot of watermelon fields in our lives. We grew up in the watermelon business; it was second nature to us.

Kenneth met us at the field. He asked with an exaggerated southern draw, "What do ya'll think? It's sandy land, but the rain has been perfect."

I said, "They look good, but they need a home pretty quick."

Kenneth said, "I understand you fellows will buy the melons in the field, and do the harvesting yourselves. I'd be very interested in that kind of deal. I really don't have time to fool with labor."

What he really meant to say was, "I don't have anyplace to sell them." This wasn't unusual in farming, especially vegetable farming. Marketing was an afterthought for many farmers back then. Things have changed a lot. Now, most farmers are more sophisticated and more strategic in their business planning.

Survival of the fittest forced a more professional approach. Farms with poor business plans failed, and were sapped up by the more efficient operations.

I asked, "How much do you want for the melons, Kenneth?"

He said, "Give me $2,500 cash and they're yours." We expected to pay more; we wondered if we had missed something. David and I looked at each other and with no words spoken we came to a complete meeting of the minds. This was the start of a relationship that became so fine-tuned that sometimes we needed only a glance to certify even complex business decisions.

I said, "Okay Kenneth. We have a deal."

We were anxious about our first transaction as partners in the business, but our problems had only just started. The next day, headlines about an independent trucker's strike covered newspapers. Over the next couple of decades, other trucker's strikes hit the nation, but we felt the sting of the first one. Independent truckers carry almost all of the nation's produce.

We had our labor lined up, but that wouldn't do any good without trailers to put the melons on. We estimated 25 trailer loads on the first two clippings. David said, "I saw some piggybacks at the rail-yard this morning; we'd better find out if we can get some."

Piggybacks are trailers carried by the railroad on flatcars. It takes longer by rail, and the railroad is rougher than trucks. But it is cheaper, and, in any event, we didn't have a lot of options. We made arrangements to have 25 pigs delivered to Vidalia.

At sunrise the next day we were in the field with two pigs and a full crew. The field was on high ground, but a low basin, almost a swamp, surrounded it. David and I were surveying the situation when we heard someone from the crew yell, "Gator! Gator!"

David looked at me and said, "What did they say?"

I said, "It sounded like they yelled alligator; there aren't any alligators around here."

David asked, "Even if there was, what would he be doing in our watermelon field?" But sure enough, there was an alligator, and he was chasing the crew. He didn't catch anybody, but he did put the fear of the swamp in them. We finally chased the alligator out of the field, but hours passed before we convinced everybody that it was safe to go back. Rattlesnakes we expected. But alligators?

It took about ten days to bring our first transaction as business partners to a close. The pigs worked great, and the truckers' strike actually made us money. It made watermelons scarce in the North and Midwest, but we got ours up there. In less than two weeks, we made a profit of over $25,000 on a $2,500 investment. We were ready to take on the world.

Danny S. New

The Vidalia Farmer's Market

In Piggly Wiggly Southern, David and I first took notice of Georgia onions. Piggly Wiggly marketed them as an unusually sweet onion. The concept of marketing an onion as a specialty food item intrigued us.

We noticed an increasing number of inquiries about local sweet onions. "Why all the interest in onions?" I asked Dad. Our father knew most people connected with produce in Georgia, and many people in other parts of the country, too. At that time, the early seventies, our office and warehouse were one-half of the old farmer's market in Vidalia, and was located on U.S. 280—the main and busiest road through town.

Dad said, "Growers first packed Georgia onions on this farmer's market back in the forties. In fact, the State built it for that purpose."

I said, with a degree of surprise, "There must have been a lot of onions being grown around here for the State to invest so much money in a farmer's market in a little spot in the road like Vidalia." I was born and grew up in Vidalia. Maybe if I had seen just a little activity in onions the notion of the State building a farmer's market exclusively to promote onions wouldn't have surprised me.

Dad explained, "This deal started in the thirties. The acreage grew substantially in the forties. After a devastating marketing failure in the early forties, four brothers from Atlanta, the Brand brothers, restored confidence in the onion market for local onions, and the onion industry took on new life.

Bill Brand approached Senator Herman Talmadge, a prominent State Senator, about building a farmer's market in Vidalia so that the farmers would have a place to pack onions. The Brands were savvy politicians. They convinced the Senator that Vidalia needed a farmer's market. After the market was built, the onion acreage increased dramatically. The Brand brothers marketed many of the onions."

I asked, "What happened? Why did the onion deal die down?"

Dad explained, "Well, more farmers started growing onions—too many onions. The Georgia onion had a reputation for being a sweet onion, but it wouldn't carry any distance very well. The shelf-life was nothing compared to onions grown in Texas and other western states, and the grocery stores didn't want to buy them. I remember one or two years when growers flooded this farmer's market with onions they could not sell. They hauled off thousands of bags to the dump. This discouraged farmers, and most quit growing onions."

The Georgia Onion Flounders

By 1955, the onion deal had almost disappeared in Toombs County. Pinky McRae had been successful in resurrecting it. From there and from Piggly Wiggly Southern the inquiries reached us.

People stopped and asked, "Do you know where we can get a bag of the Toombs County sweet onions?" They asked about an unusually mild onion grown in the general area of Toombs County. Over the following few months, David and I spoke incessantly about onions.

Georgia onions had limited recognition in 1972; Pinky McRae sold his Toombs County—Georgia Sweet Onions; a handful of growers in the neighboring Tattnall County marketed theirs as Tattnall County Sweet Onions, or Glenville Sweets; Piggly Wiggly continued with their Pride of Piggly Wiggly brand.

David asked, "Dad, with so much interest in Georgia onions why hasn't anyone been more aggressive in marketing them? Why haven't you?"

Dad said, "After the disaster with the onion deal in the forties and fifties, farmers had little interest in growing Georgia onions. The onion deal became more of a local retail deal. My business was mostly in the Northeast, and Georgia onions would not ship well. Western states produce twice as many bags per acre as Georgia does; we can't compete with them on price—Growing onions in Georgia costs too much. For the same reasons that the Brand brothers left, I saw little potential in it."

Testing the Waters

David and I didn't see the onion deal in the same way that Dad did. We both saw an untapped reservoir of business potential slumbering with the Georgia onion. In April of 1973, we pondered the vegetable as though it was a hidden bounty waiting to be discovered, and we were the only ones with a map to the treasure.

Farmers grew only a handful of onions in Toombs County in 1973. Wade Usher grew a small acreage for Piggly Wiggly, Pinky McRae and Vann Lewis grew a few, and that was about it. Tattnall County had more onions, but not many.

We wanted to test the Georgia onion business that year, but we couldn't find any onions. "Why don't we poke around Tattnall County and see what we can find?" I suggested. Most farmers plowed up onions around the first week in May back then. Georgia had too few onions to do any serious business in 1973, but the possibilities dazzled us. It was a special product being marketed in a very unspecial way. We were determined to change that.

Danny S. New

During the winter of 1974, in anticipation of aggressively testing the Georgia onion deal, we had an onion sack printed. Across the top, in large letters, we put the name of the city we lived in—Vidalia, Georgia. The names heard more often than others were "Toombs County Onions," as Pinky McRae called his, or "Glenville Onions," as most of the few Tattnall County growers called theirs.

Near the end of April, a friend contacted us. "I hear you're looking for some onions," he said. "I know a man near Cobbtown with about three acres."

By the end of the decade, three acres would only last us a few hours, but in 1974 it seemed like a major find. We purchased the three acres of onions in Cobbtown, Ga. from Dickey Collins. We quickly discovered how little we knew about the farming end of the produce business. Our background was in marketing, but we were determined to learn everything about the onion business.

Fortunately, Dickey shared with us his knowledge on harvesting onions. Dickey was a quiet man with strong Christian convictions. A good man. He provided us with desperately needed tips.

The agrarian lifestyle soon addicted us. When we plowed up the onions and laid them on top of the rocky soil, and the smell of the freshly moved earth filled the air, I was certain that, for then at least, this was the direction my life had to take. For the next twelve years, second thoughts didn't exist. Now I knew where I was going. We plunged ourselves into the onion business; we changed agriculture in Georgia forever. Any fledgling concerns about finishing college, or other intellectual pursuits disappeared, or were placed in the mind's cold storage for retrieval in some future time.

The harvest was not well orchestrated; our ignorance of the task confronting us caused more than a few snags. We supposed, I think, that our youthful energy could manufacture solutions to every problem. Today, in 2001, onion-grading machines are everywhere in the area around Vidalia; it wasn't so in 1974.

Frank Fountain—the produce buyer for Piggly Wiggly, a close friend of our father, and an expert on Georgia onions—told us that Piggly Wiggly had a small, outdated potato grader that would also grade onions. "It doesn't have a sizer, but at least it has a conveyor to grade on, and bag hangers," Frank said. Frank loaned us the machine, we set it up at our warehouse, and soon we were bagging onions—although very slowly.

The Invisible Onion

David said, "Okay, we found onions. Now what? I called Morris Hudis in Philadelphia. He said that his customers thought he was joking. He said, "You might can sell Georgia onions in Georgia, but they laugh in Pennsylvania. All my customers said that they weren't going to be the first kid on the block to try 'em."

Body Under Siege

We took turns calling our produce accounts in the Northeast. We heard little that was positive, but there was no shortage of skepticism about our Georgia onion. Everyone was satisfied with their Western suppliers. The produce buyer for one major chain laughed and said, "Georgia doesn't grow onions." Relative to the onion industry as a whole, he was right. Georgia was really not important in the onion business. But David and I were determined to change that.

Our claims of unusually mild onions fell on deaf ears. We had long-standing relationships with many of these accounts, but they were reluctant to handle onions from Georgia.

I said, "Maybe we should stick to our Georgia business for now. Everybody north of the state line thinks we're joking."

David said, "I think you're right. Fortunately, we have less than two thousand bags to sell. That should be easy."

Actually, it was easy. The local interest created a limited retail market. We put signs up on Highway 280 in front of our warehouse, and sold several hundred bags in about two weeks.

Pinky was our main competition. He had built a loyal following with his Toombs County—Georgia Sweet Onions; however, we sold our few easy enough. But we realized that outside of the state the Georgia onion was invisible. It would be up to David and me to breathe life into "The Onion." We were convinced that we could do that.

Danny S. New

The Death of Kenneth New

    The early days in business with my Father and my Brother had been the most satisfying time of my life. It's customary and natural, maybe even expected, that young men and women revere and admire their Dads. I idolized mine. He was one of the few people I knew that became friends with virtually every person he met, and had no enemies—at least none that I knew.
    He was a short, chubby man with a gleam in his eyes, a perpetual smile, and a general demeanor that always suggested, or insisted, that everything was right in the world, or that if problems existed they would not find a resting-place in his heart. He wore his pants up high, as though there main purpose was to warm the belly-button, giving him a round, but pleasant, jolly appearance. Above all other things in the world, he liked to eat. But the most appropriate way to characterize Kenneth New is simply to say that he loved life and he loved people.
    If the day had been particularly bad, or uncertain in its result, or troublesome in some ill-defined way, then just the presence of my Father and all the worries vanished like vapor, as though they were not allowed in his presence. The purveyor of troubles knew this, and didn't waste his time trying to manipulate Dad, knowing that such efforts would be fruitless in their intended result.
    That is not to say that troubles were never a part of my Dad's life. They were. But he lived the good times and ignored the bad ones, bringing happiness

and hope to whatever forlorn creature had the good fortune of stepping in his path.

The pressure of any business in its infancy, or a new venture in an existing enterprise, surpasses the imaginings of the uninitiated. These earliest days of the Vidalia Onion bulged with pressure, and I have no doubt that The Onion contributed in more than a small way to the death of our Father. On May 7, 1974 of our second year in the Georgia onion business, even before settling on a name, our Father had a heart attack and died.

This day started well ahead of the sunrise. Our days usually did. I made a delivery of onions to Douglas, Georgia. When I returned, Frank Fountain met me. I knew something was wrong. Frank said, "You need to go to your Mother's house, Danny. Your Father is dead." I was numb.

Dad's third heart attack brought to a close the life of one of Vidalia's favorite people. I couldn't escape the thought that maybe I had contributed to his death. Stress was everywhere during onion season, and my ambition maintained it at a higher level than it deserved.

Dad always said that when his turn came he wanted to just go to sleep and not wake up. He got his wish. The Onion started with a huge investment by the New Family. For the moment, our interest in onions vanished.

The Name

A constant flow of inquiries from consumers around the state bombarded us. We discovered that general knowledge of Georgia onions was even more limited than we had thought. Everyone loved The Onion when they tasted it, but it needed a name. David said, "We've had seven calls today about onions. Mostly they just ask about 'those sweet onions.' Nobody knows what to call them." Some asked about "Tattnall County onions." Some about "Glenville Sweets." Most of the callers asked about "Toombs County Sweet Onions," or just "Georgia Sweet onions."

I said, "You know, we really need to decide on a promotable name, if an onion business is to be in our future. We need a clear direction. A shot-gun approach will fail." We printed VIDALIA GEORGIA in big letters on our bag, but just the name of a town missed the mark. We knew the importance of selecting the right name. In marketing, something as simple as "ear appeal" can mean the difference in success and failure.

The problem of supplies complicated the process of choosing a name. Most farmers that knew how to grow onions lived around Glenville, in Tattnall County. We depended on others to produce the onions—we were not farmers, yet. Marketing we knew. Farming we didn't.

I said, with a genuine belief that we were under attack, "The Tattnall County growers have formed the Tattnall County Onion Growers and Distributors Association. One grower told me that the main purpose was to stop Tattnall County onions from going into a bag with Vidalia written on it." They didn't like Tattnall County onions going into Piggly Wiggly's bag, and they disliked New Bros. bag even more; Piggly Wiggly only distributed to their own Georgia stores, but it was clear that our market was the United States. And Piggly Wiggly and New Bros., Inc. both made it clear to the consumer that our businesses were in Vidalia—not Glennville.

We planned to buy some of our onions in Tattnall County; a few grower commitments were in place. But we felt targeted by the new association. No quality difference existed between Tattnall County and Toombs County onions. I said, in support of our resolve to call New Bros. onions, Vidalia Onions, "Everything about our business says VIDALIA."

David and I agreed that the name for our onions would be "Vidalia Onions." The name had "ear appeal."

A feud developed between the Toombs County growers and the Tattnall County growers over nomenclature. Tattnall County had the advantage; their volume was substantially higher than Toombs County. And the Toombs County growers were divided. Pinky McRae and Vann Lewis stuck with "Toombs County—Georgia sweet onions." We liked the name we had picked. We had a vision, and the "Vidalia Onion" was it.

Spreading the Name

With the decision on name out of the way, we began the job of building a business with The Onion. Gerry Achenbach and Piggly Wiggly Southern had done an exceptional job of promoting the Georgia onion. Our job now was to introduce The Onion to other areas and to promote the name we had chosen.

Our problem was supply—not demand. David said, "I've talked to farmers all over Toombs County. They have little interest in growing onions; horror stories about the onions lost in the forties and fifties still linger."

In 1974, there were no more than 75 acres of onions in Toombs County. Most farmers considered onion production to be a foul subject, not deserving of serious regard, with much the same level of sobriety as raising ostrich, or perhaps rice farming in Georgia. At that time, our agrarian pursuits centered around marketing produce. We were not farmers, and I'm not sure we wanted to be. We liked marketing, but we needed a dependable supply of onions to market. That looked uncertain.

We spent the winter of '74 marketing "Vidalia Onions" as though an unlimited supply would be available. We needed to test the concept. We had to convince ourselves that we were right about The Onion. We knew that building demand outside the state would take a lot of sweat, patience, and perseverance. Still, we were sold on the Vidalia Onion and confident in our ability to make it work.

We couldn't afford much paid advertising, so we sent press releases to target markets. It worked. When the 1974 season hit, the orders drowned us. We rationed our limited supply. If a customer ordered eight hundred bags, we might only send two hundred.

Only three wholesale produce houses in Atlanta sold Georgia onions in 1974. Ours weren't the first Georgia onions to show up on the Atlanta Produce Market, but they were the first ones with "Vidalia" written on the bag. Cerniglia Produce sold "Glenville Sweets" for the Dashers, and Green & Milam and Burnett Produce sold "Vidalia Sweets" for us.

After struggling for months with various names, we chose "Vidalia Sweets" as our trademark. Our orders exceeded 25,000 bags in 1974. We made deliveries on no more than 5,000.

Wholesale produce is an early morning affair. The markets bustle with business by four A.M. A wake-up call from one of the markets became a daily occurrence for David and me. "Where are the rest of my onions? I have people waiting. Put another truck on the road," snarled the disappointed buyers.

In 1974, we shipped the first trailer load of Vidalia Onions to ever leave Georgia (Piggly Wiggly distributed only to their Georgia stores). Red Foods in Chattanooga, Tennessee bought it. We knew now that we had a winner. Consumer demand took the decision making process away from the produce buyers. Soon, all we had to do was answer the phone and take the orders.

The battle over the name raged for several years, but it eventually ended with Vidalia the clear winner. Now we had a very clear goal—make the name "Vidalia Onion" a household word. Our premeditated plan worked.

For many years, we put virtually all of our profits back into the business. Promoting the name "Vidalia Onion" became a compulsion. By the end of the seventies, New Bros. had prevailed and the name Vidalia Onion was safe.

The Decision to be Farmers

By the end of the 1974 season, we knew that we had chosen the right name. We felt success in the air. Now only one serious obstacle stood in our way—how could we get enough onions?

The few Tattnall County growers considered it heresy to put the name Vidalia on the bag. Some even suggested that it was illegal. "Onions grown around Glenville are Glenville onions, and around Vidalia are Vidalia Onions," said many of the Tattnall County growers.

Danny S. New

A loose, informal division evolved by County—Glenville being in Tattnall County and Vidalia in Toombs County. Vidalians believed that putting an onion grown in Tattnall County into a bag labeled with the Vidalia name misrepresented the product. Unfortunately for us, there were few onions grown in the immediate vicinity of Vidalia, and farmers had very little interest in changing that. Only one solution existed—we had to grow them ourselves. In the fall of 1974 we made the quantum leap—we became onion farmers.

The Onion quickly claimed a life of its own. Like a jealous child, it demanded all of our time, and brooded when our deliberations meandered in other directions. Any endeavor that sidetracked us was somehow vanquished from existence, or otherwise diminished to insignificance

Children, as they maneuver through childhood and then adolescence, craft aspirations, or maybe fantasies, of what they hope themselves to be if and when they actually achieve adulthood. My excursions into this fabled land took me through many realms and callings, but never once did I suppose myself a farmer. Had I experienced that life in my younger days farming may very well have been my first desire.

Nevertheless, I didn't, with premeditation, choose this direction; a scion of circumstance and necessity chose for me. I never considered farming to be anything more than a transitory life for me, or maybe a stepping stone to another destiny, or I think I didn't consider it at all, but rather moved without conscious thought, perceiving that this new life was somehow preordained.

Most, if not all, of the many purviews of agronomy foretell an arduous life, albeit a rewarding one. Onion production is an extreme of these difficulties, on the fringes between "Why is life so hard?" and "I can't take any more!" The more traditional crops, corn or soybeans for example, are planted in the spring and harvested in the summer or fall, and thus grown in temperate weather for a reasonable period of time; not so with onions.

Farmers plant onions in late summer or early fall; they harvest eight months later in the spring. Thus, the onions must survive the winter—which they very often fail to do. The onion grower constantly fights inclement weather. He fights an army of insects. And he fights a formidable array of microorganisms, too.

Onion production is the agrarian marathon of vegetable farming. I know of no crop, vegetable or otherwise, that demands as much—both economically and emotionally—as the production of short-day onions. (A small piece of horticultural trivia—long-day onions are varieties that require long days to mature and short-day onions mature before the days get long. Thus, a spring harvest as opposed to a summer harvest).

David and I began this adventure in total ignorance. We knew lots about marketing produce. We knew nothing about how to grow it. We didn't even know the difference in a bottom plow and a harrow—yet we were staking our future on this pursuit. If we had known the sacrifices required of us, we would probably have ended the journey here; nevertheless, for better or for worse, we would soon add farming to our expanding repertoire of experiences.

Getting Started

Our youth had convinced David and me that everything fell into the realm of possibility for us. All we needed was a direction, and now we had it. So we didn't know the difference in a bottom plow and a harrow—somebody knew, and we could find out; anything we needed to know we could find out. With this cavalier attitude we set out to be farmers.

We started this venture completely from scratch. We had to rent the land; we had to buy the equipment; and we had to learn how to use it. New equipment was not an option. Even a small Massey Ferguson tractor would cost over $20,000, new. The harrow, bottom plow, fertilizer distributor, planters, sprayer, and irrigation equipment cost more than we could handle unless we bought them used. Before long, we felt at home on the farm equipment auctions. Onion season had ended and we enjoyed the change of pace, even if we didn't know what we were doing.

We inspected the equipment on the auctions as though this was routine for us. We looked at the Massey Fergasons and the John Deeres and the International Harvesters, and told ourselves that we had this game all under control. After several trips to auctions and after inspecting dozens of tractors, David came across one that looked different. He said, "I've never seen an EBRO before. It looks good. It must be some kind of foreign tractor." This was a used equipment auction, but this was a new tractor. We eyed the machine with skepticism.

I said, "Let's ask Ray Thompson and see if he knows what it is." Ray was a friend that made a living buying and selling used farm equipment. He lived at the auctions.

Ray said, "I've only seen one of them in my life, but I know what they are. When FORD quit manufacturing the old Ford Major in the United States, they sold it to a company in Spain. All of the parts are interchangeable."

We bought the EBRO for $4,000, only a fraction of what it would have cost with FORD written on it. Then we bought four Planet Junior planters, a broadcast fertilizer distributor, a sprayer, harrow, and a John Deere four-bottom plow. With this limited arsenal of agricultural equipment we were ready to be farmers.

Now we needed land to grow the onions on. "Why don't we talk to Bob Cato?" I suggested. Mr. Cato was one of the largest farmers in Toombs County, and a man that could be trusted to do what he said—a characteristic that we were finding rare in business. A written contract was not necessary with Bob Cato. A handshake sufficed.

Bob Cato had the land we needed and soon we were ready to start growing onions. Onions can be grown directly from seed, or they can be grown from transplants. It is more expensive per acre to grow onions from plants, but the yield is higher, and the overall risks less. But nobody grew any plants in Georgia in 1974.

The few Tattnall County growers bought their plants in Texas. We reasoned that if a Texas onion is hotter than a Georgia onion, then a Georgia onion grown from a Texas plant might be hotter than a Georgia onion grown from a Georgia plant. We decided to use transplants, but to grow them ourselves. On September 20, 1974, we took our EBRO tractor, our Planet Junior planters, and our 300 lbs. of Yellow Granex onion seeds, and, like a couple of kids with a new toy army, we set out to conquer the world. "You can take the first shift driving," David said. We had asked dozens of farmers hundreds of questions and were convinced that we knew all we needed to know about tractors and farming and everything even closely related to the business of agriculture. We had turned and leveled the land, treated the seed, and had the Dacthal ready to go (Dacthal was the only herbicide approved for onions in 1975).

I jumped onto the tractor and headed down the field. I looked straight ahead and drove like I had been doing this all of my life. There is nothing to this; it's a

PACKING LINE ON DIRT FLOOR - 1974

Body Under Siege

ONION FIELD – 1974

piece of cake, I thought to myself. When I arrived at the end of the first row I looked back in shock. It looked as though I had been navigating an obstacle course. "Maybe you need to do the driving," I suggested to David.

The onions soon broke the dirt. Free time quickly became part of the past. When the onions needed watering, David and I "toted" the pipe. We sprayed. We plowed. We spread the fertilizer. We hauled the labor to pull the weeds. And we handled the rest of the never-ending problems that came with farming.

But we found that the most difficult task was to do all the worrying. The questions ricocheted between us. "Why are some of the onions in the plant bed dying? Why hasn't the Malathion killed all the thrips? Should we spray Bravo, Manzate or Dyrene this time? We have cricket moles in the beds. Is it too late to spray Diazanon? Some of the tops are turning yellow. Why didn't we send off the soil sample? Do you think the pH might be too low? If the pH is too low, is it too late to do anything about it now?"

The list went on and on and on. But even with the problems, we loved this new life.

Our First Harvest

By the spring of '75, we saw the results of all the long days and short nights. The tops were green and succulent, and the bulbs were swelling the ground right on schedule.

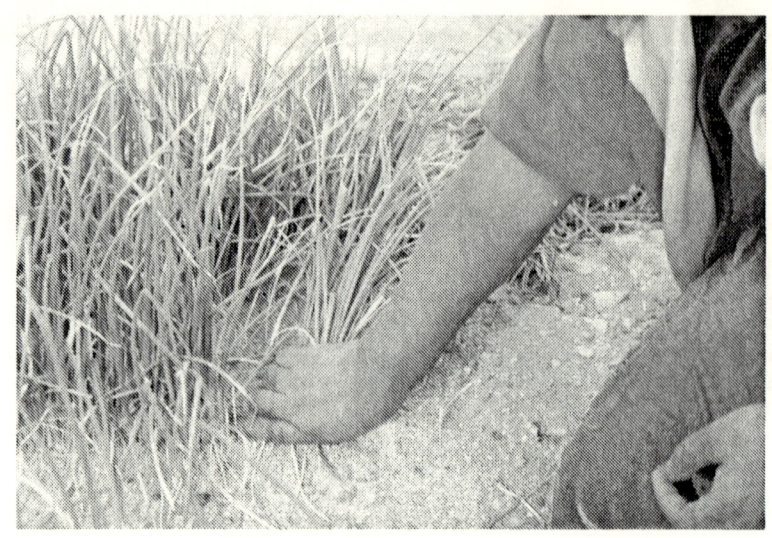

ONION PLANTS BEING PULLED

ONION PLANT BED

During the winter, we had purchased a new onion grader, and had relocated our warehouse. Several years earlier, the state had given the old farmer's market to the city of Vidalia. The city chose to tear it down, and to replace it with a recreation park.

We bought the old American Legion property across the street. The ten acres that came with the building gave us all the room we needed for expansion.

Time restricted improvements for the 1975 onion season. We threw up a makeshift shelter for the packing line, and rented a pneumatic tire forklift that could operate on the dirt floor.

Finances restricted the size of our work force. Harvesting required more than 100 manual laborers; we cut expenses where we could—but not there. Other positions we lumped into an ill-defined "non-essential" designation that David and I worked into our schedule. We harvested the onions during the day, graded them at night, and did the bookkeeping in the early morning before things got started on the farm. During the day, we took turns making short trips from the farm to the pay phone to sell the onions and to find trucks to haul them.

On a night when we slept four hours, we felt like we had been on vacation. The onion yield was great, demand was even better, and we literally named our price. No price within reason seemed too high.

Onion Plants

The shortage of onions probably helped in the long run; it is human nature that people want what they can't get. But we knew that unless we solved the supply problem, competition would develop and solve it for us. We couldn't ration onions another year without hurting ourselves.

Choosing the name Vidalia Onion was decisive; it was catchy, descriptive, and promotable. Our brand name, "Vidalia Sweets," we protected. We continued fighting for the name Vidalia Onion over other names that occasionally resurfaced, but we never claimed, or wanted, any proprietary rights to the name. Owning the name "Vidalia Sweets" served our purpose.

Soon, people quit asking about Georgia onions, or Toombs County onions, or Glenville onions. They asked for Vidalia Onions. Chain grocers in the southeast lost the option of handling or not handling Vidalia Onions. The consumer demanded them. In 1977, New Bros., Inc. sold 90% of Georgia onions carrying the Vidalia Onion name. The demand far exceeded supplies.

David asked, "Why don't we grow the plants? I think we will see more interest from farmers if we can supply the plants." Growing the plants is the most costly and riskiest part of producing onions.

"I think you're right. It is too late to grow the plants when most farmers finally make a decision. And by then, the main supplier of plants is Texas." We

Danny S. New

believed that Texas plants grew hotter onions than Georgia plants; therefore, we only handled onions grown from Georgia plants. In the fall of 1976, we increased our onion production to 150 acres and added 50 acres of onion plants. That was enough to grow nearly 500 acres of onions.

150 MILLION ONION PLANTS is a lot of plants, but this is the number Danny New (left), and David New (center) expect New Brothers Produce Co., of Vidalia, to provide from their beds this year. Here they observe as Garret Warnock ships onion plants all over the United States. (Photo by Kitty Peterson)

(Photo by Kitty Peterson)

The Vidalia Advance, 1980

Body Under Siege

— BILL DURRENCE/Special
Danny New (left) and his brother, David, have faith in the Vidalia onion but have trouble finding labor for the harvest

Overwhelmingly onionish

Bumper crop has smell of success in Vidalia

"New Brothers Produce will spend more than $100,000 this year to promote Vidalia onions with television commercials, in-store promotions, and other devices geared toward marketing the Vidalia Sweet Onion, according to David New."

"Harvesting onions, according to Toombs County agricultural extension service director Eston Daniels, requires mostly hand labor." "This year for the first time, New Brothers brought in about 200 migrant workers, mostly Mexicans from South Texas, to help with the harvesting."

Early Promotion

We lacked the patience to wait for society to discover on its own the novelty and the attributes of the Georgia onion; we also lacked the resources to buy media coverage. We had confidence in The Onion, but we knew the consumer had to be persuaded and enlightened before a business could survive. Over the next few years we solicited what free media coverage we could get. This worked. The media liked the story, and David and I kept the news flowing.

We pursued free publicity. We placed a propaganda sheet in every bag of onions. We supplied the buyers with point-of-sale material. We hired an ad agency to do press releases about the Vidalia Onion and about every new twist that David and I came up with concerning onions. We placed as much paid advertising as we could afford. We did in-store demos enticing people to try, "The onion that you can eat like an apple."

The reputation of The Onion spread at an exponential rate. Even with our own production and that of many contract growers, we still had problems meeting the demand. Rationing continued through the seventies. We doubled and tripled our supplies every year, but we never caught up with the demand.

Migrant Workers

As our production grew, the problem of finding enough harvesting labor grew with it. Soon, local labor was not an option; unfortunately, harvesting onions is strictly a hand operation, and mechanization, if it came, would be in the distant future.

Machinery people with success stories about mechanical harvesters could be found, but they only had stories; the manual laborer with a pair of onion shears was all the industry had. There were plenty of local workers out of jobs, but fieldwork was usually not a job that they would consider. It is difficult to produce onions in Georgia, even under the best of conditions. But producing them and then losing a substantial portion because of too few workers was heart breaking.

Today, the South Georgia onion belt is crowded with migrant farm workers when the onion bulbs reach maturity. But it wasn't so when David and I started. As early as 1975, we saw a major problem developing—and local labor would never solve it.

We had a particularly severe labor shortage in 1976. That year I received a call from Miguel Rodriquez. With broken English that required serious decoding, Miguel said, "Mr. New. This Rodriquez. I told you need clippers." We managed to carry on a linguistic exchange, with rudimentary resemblance to actual conversation, for at least ten minutes.

Miguel had little trouble holding my attention. We had plowed up all of our onions, and only twelve local hands showed up. We needed 50 just for the fieldwork—and we needed more help on the packing line, too.

Miguel said, "I have the help in Florida; I can bring 50, but I'll need an advance."

Eventually, we did make a deal, and Miguel was true to his word. With some difficulty, we arranged housing for them.

This was the beginning of a new culture for Vidalia and the surrounding counties. But the community handled it, and the industry grew. Migrant workers, mostly from Mexico, solved the labor problem.

Processed Foods from Vidalia Onions

Everything went right for New Bros., Inc. in the seventies. Our brand was known nation-wide, we had fine-tuned our knowledge of how to grow onions, and we had been right on target with our marketing strategies.

But David and I weren't totally at ease with our situation. Farming is an uncertain business under the best of circumstances; fortunately, the seventies turned out to be the best of circumstances. But we knew it could turn around at any time.

New Bros., Inc. was the largest grower and shipper of Vidalia Onions in 1978, but we were not a diversified company. Our only source of income was The Onion. Our company was in good shape financially, but two straight years of bad weather could wipe us out. We were too dependent on the fresh onion.

We transplant onions in November and harvest them in May; and thus, they must survive the winter, which they often fail to do. We saw how exposed we were to the whims of nature. We remembered the old economic tenet that in business profits tend to eliminate themselves. This refers to a supposition that in most new industries, more and more competition will erode the profit for businesses in that industry. Future dealers in The Onion would not have to spend the small fortune that David and I had invested to promote the name. To shield ourselves, we felt that we had to diversify.

By the late seventies, we had established the fresh Vidalia Onion business. But we saw more opportunities and wanted to keep going. I said to David, "The enthusiasm about The Onion goes beyond imagination. Let's take advantage of the name recognition and produce some products made from The Onion."

David's pragmatism surfaced; this usually kept us out of a lot of trouble. He said, "We don't know anything about the food processing business. But it is a tempting idea."

We knew as little about food processing in 1978 as we had about farming five years earlier. I said, "It can't be as hard to learn as farming." Still, it was clear that we had a lot to find out if we wanted to go into the food processing business. We already knew the business of marketing farm products when we decided to be farmers; all we needed to learn was how to grow it. We didn't know the technical end or the marketing end of the food business. But, as with farming, we knew that we could learn.

Over the next few weeks, we studied the various categories of the food business in search of options that meshed with the specialty nature of the Vidalia Onion. We looked at the equipment requirements and the regulatory requirements for each alternative. We needed a product that was easy to make, part of a significant category, and would command added value because it contained Vidalia Onions.

We considered a meat product that included whole Vidalia Onions, but regulation of products containing meat was much tougher than regulation of non-meat products. We weren't ready for that. Eventually, we settled on a Vidalia Onion relish for the test. We went through an extensive trial-and-error process. We used old family recipes, looked at other published sources, and eventually settled on a formula with the uniqueness to be a winner. We adapted the recipe to commercial production. Then we worried about equipment.

We took the miserly approach on this unproved venture. We had to be certain that there was a business in processed Vidalia Onion products out there somewhere. We believed there was, but sometimes, maybe most of the time, the consumer thinks in a way different from the way the businessperson does.

David said, "Why don't we just buy some inexpensive cookers for now, and pack it manually?" I agreed, and we started our processing business with six stainless steel pots and six commercial gas cookers. It wasn't impressive, but it was functional. We could only pack fifty cases of Vidalia Onion relish per day, but that was enough to gauge the market.

No commercial means of storing Vidalia Onions existed in 1979. This limited production time to only two months each year. But in this short time, in 1979, we knew that the processed business could be as big as the fresh business—maybe bigger.

The 1979 season gave us the confidence needed to make a more substantial investment in food processing. Our production capacity limited sales the first year, and solving this problem became a priority. Processing equipment is expensive, and, although we were not afraid of risk, we had our conservative side, too; therefore, as we did when we started farming, we looked for auctions and used equipment dealers. We found an Elgin single piston filler, a Resina capper, a 150-gallon steam jacketed kettle, and a small steam boiler.

Body Under Siege

DANIEL, LEFT, DAVID NEW MEET WITH GOV. HARRIS
After Announcing New Vidalia Sweets Product Line

New Bros. To Introduce Range of Vidalia Onions

New Bros Inc will introduce a line of fresh and refrigerated salad dressings to be marketed in the produce section of grocery stores beginning in mid-October, it was announced today.

The six salad dressings, made with the famous Vidalia onion, are the latest addition to the New Bros. line of processed foods, also made from "The Onion" according to Danny New, president of the Vidalia based company.

"We think public demand for fresh Vidalias, coupled with the tremendous popularity of fresh and refrigerated salad dressings, will make our dressings a great success." New said

The salad dressings, which include Ranch, Blue Cheese, Thousand Island, Creamy Italian, French and Vidalia Onion, will be available in the produce section of grocery stores in six southeastern states beginning in mid October. National distribution is scheduled for early 1984

Ads depicting the new dressings as "Sweet Things from The Onion" are scheduled to run throughout the southeast beginning in October.

In addition, the company announced that corporate headquarters on Highway 280 are being expanded and renovated. Former retail space will be remodeled to accommodate the company's expansion and management staff additions

Joe S. Zuba also was named Plant Manager and head of product development for New Bros. Inc. Zuba was formerly with Ragu, Rainbo Foods, and Beatrice Foods.

Thursday, Oct. 20, 1983
Lyons, Georgia
The Lyons Progress

Danny S. New

The Vidalia Advance/May 29, 1980/Page 4b

FACES

By Janet Rodekohr

VIDALIA—Those Vidalia onions have the sweet smell of success about them. Nobody promotes them beyond a few signs and word of mouth, nobody searches out new markets and nobody's arguing that the economic picture looks pretty glum for most other businesses.

But onion growers in the four-county Vidalia area sell all they grow, no matter how much they plant. DAVID and DANNY NEW of Vidalia just keep planting more onions. Says Danny, "I think the future looks pretty bright for Vidalia onions. The demand seems to double or triple every year."

But the smell of success can turn sour when people try to cash in on a good thing. The situation is ripe for those willing to run the gamble. The Vidalia onion is the same onion they grow in Texas called Granex, but when you plant Granex in Georgia, it matures into a sweet onion mild enough to eat like an apple. That same onion planted in Texas comes out hot. It also comes out cheaper. Because of differences in yields and expenses, it costs about half as much to grow the Texas hot onion as it does to grow the Georgia sweet onion.

They look alike and they have the same name, but if you think you're buying a sweet Vidalia onion for half price, you may have a hot surprise waiting for you. That's the problem that the growers like the New brothers are facing as people rebag Texas onions under the Vidalia name.

Danny says, "I don't really want to clobber somebody and keep them out of business, but rebagging outside onions is fraud. We've talked with our legislators and they're working on legislation for next session that would require that a bag tells the territory the onion came from and the grower's name and address. They've done that in Florida with some of their fruit and it works just fine down there."

Some other possibilities are to tightly control the bags with the Vidalia name by having one person or association sell official bags to the growers for a small fee and let that fee go for research, education and promotion. Another suggestion has been to clamp a seal on the string of the bags, similar to certified seed, to guarantee to the customer that the product is the true Vidalia onion.

The New brothers have even put in a toll free hot line—1-800-342-9658 for Georgia and 1-800-841-1102 nationally—so people can call to find out the nearest legitimate Vidalia onion distributor.

The New brothers have seen a future in onions, and to back up their prediction they've gotten into the business in a big way. They started out as brokers for the onions, but they didn't like to rely on everyone else for the growing, grading, sorting, sizing and bagging before it got into their hands. So they're in on every phase now, supervising the planting and harvesting, processing and selling.

They say, "It costs $1,200 an acre if you grow your own plants, and as much as $1,500 if you transplant. It's an expensive crop and the risks are high, but you can make it."

Onion growers can just about set their own prices because of the demand, but when you think about the risk involved, they almost deserve that right. For instance, since little research has been done on onions, they have no herbicide designed for their crop, they have some insect and disease problems, a freeze at the wrong time can wipe them out, they must irrigate, and harvesting requires expensive hand labor. On top of all that, if it rains during the two week harvest, all is lost.

With those kind of risks, you wonder why people get into a business like that. The New brothers are just doing what their father, Kenneth, liked best—selling onions.

By 1980, our production reached 150 cases per day—still low, but going in the right direction. Our product line expanded quickly. First, we added Vidalia Onion pickles; and then, Vidalia Onion barbecue sauce. Consumers loved the concept and the product. We could not come close to meeting the demand. As in the past, we continued to over-market.

The Vidalia Onion Niche

When we started selling processed Vidalia Onions we assumed that capturing a fair share of the existing market in any particular category was the best we could hope for. We were confident that the popularity of The Onion would give us an advantage over our competitors in any given market.

But we soon learned that we didn't need a share of the existing market. The Onion expanded the size of the market instead of carving-up the existing market in a different way. People bought our Vidalia Onion relish as an impulse item; relish was not on their shopping list. The same thing happened with Vidalia Onion pickles, Vidalia Onion barbecue sauce, and Vidalia Onion spaghetti sauce.

Eventually, we expanded our product line to include frozen Vidalia Onion rings and a line of refrigerated Vidalia Onion salad dressings. If we put Vidalia Onions in the product and made certain the quality was good, the demand always followed. We had complete control of a product line with high name recognition, a high profit margin, and no competition. When people saw the name Vidalia Onion and New Bros., Inc., they assumed quality. Our job was to make sure it was there. That we did.

MERCHANDISING DISPLAYS

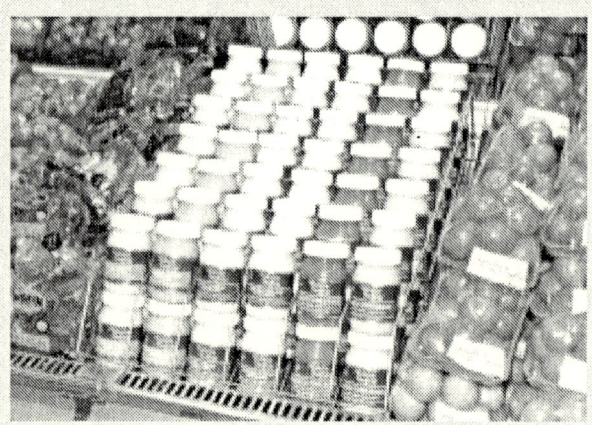

REFRIGERATED SALAD DRESSINGS

Body Under Siege

Danny S. New

Hi Swain

Although I had nine months to prepare for it, I wasn't prepared. Suddenly, six pounds and eight ounces of "what life is all about" were thrown into the mix with Vivian and me. Swain had his mother's olive complexion, and a full head of black hair. He spoke volumes with his big brown eyes. On May 3, 1980, I knew that the world would never be the same again. The many years of endless hours of work made sense, now.

Swain, holding a freshly pulled onion, was a vision. And he was a vision anew with each trip to the onion field. His hair was thick and black, like his mother's. The sensation of Swain's little hand holding mine as we crossed the onion field lives with me. The touch of his trusting, utterly dependent little hand brought life into focus. The business was doing well, David and I knew where we wanted to go and we knew how to get there. Now the vision of Swain's and Britt's (David's son) involvement in the business added more than a sprinkling of purpose.

CHAPTER 2

The Battle Begins

* The Hearing Loss—Day 1 36
* The Route Trucks 37
* Double Vision—Day 33 38
* Day 34—July 25, 1980 39
* Day 35 40
* Day 36 40
* The Search for a Diagnosis 40
* Blurred Vision 42
* The Paradox 45
* Mass General Hospital and the Answer 45

Danny S. New

The Hearing Loss—Day 1

The 1980 Vidalia Onion season was a textbook example of business at its best. Everything went right. Murphy was nowhere around. The harvest came and went with no problems. Vidalia Onion relish and pickle production went along like a dream. With Swain's birth, near the beginning of onion season, 1980 seemed like a really good time to be alive.

Early one morning in June, I was strolling around the plant as I often did, more as an observer than as a person with a particular goal in mind. I heard my name howl from the intercom. I picked up the nearest phone set with my right hand, as I was accustomed to doing.

"Hello...Hello!" I heard nothing. I hung up and assumed that someone unfamiliar with our new system was having trouble. Soon my name blared over the intercom again. This time I had a cup of coffee in my right hand so I answered with my left, naturally using my left ear. This time I heard a clear and sharp voice.

Donna transferred the call. In the middle of the conversation I set my coffee down and changed hands. There was silence. I switched ears. I heard fine out of my left ear. I switched ears several times and realized that I could not hear out of my right ear.

I called Vivian to confirm the phone test results. Vivian was my front-line defense against any unexpected attack by any of life's uncertainties. At 25, Vivian's beauty radiated and filled any space she occupied. Her long, jet-black hair accented her tall, slim frame, and her presence demanded notice. Vivian was strikingly beautiful, but didn't know it. With the phone squeezing my left ear I said, "What time are you coming to eat?"

Vivian said, "As soon as I get Swain dressed."

I heard fine. I switched ears and said, "Where are we going?" There was silence.

Hearing Loss

Bilateral hearing loss (in both ears) in MS is unusual, but unilateral hearing loss (in one ear) may not be. In a study by Fischer et al of ten patients with hearing loss (1), 80% had unilateral hearing loss and 20% had bilateral. It is unusual, but hearing loss is sometimes reported as the first symptom of the disease. About 6% of people with MS have complained of hearing impairment. Usually, hearing loss is seen with other symptoms that suggest damage to the brainstem, such as vision and balance.

Tinnitus, a subjective ringing or tickling sound in the ear, or vertigo, are common with hearing loss. In Fischer's study, seven had tinnitus and five had vertigo. Deafness is usually followed by remission.

Hearing loss due to changes in tone frequency are sometimes found (2). This might explain occasional accounts in MS of difficulty in hearing speech with conventional audiometry (3). Usually, symptoms of hearing loss improve.

The Route Trucks

We liked our product line in 1980, but we always looked for the weak link in our game plan. Marketing and sales were our strengths, but we knew that increased competition was inevitable—both in fresh onions and processed.

We were reaching most of the chain grocers, but had missed many of the independents. Sales were not a problem for us, and our concerns were probably unjustified. But David and I wanted to try putting route salesmen on the road. We knew that maintaining our monopoly in the processed Vidalia Onion business required that we saturate the market fast, and the obvious place to start was Georgia. When onions were available, we put eight salespeople on the road with trucks and product.

Figuring out that this was not a cost effective way of marketing our kind of product didn't take long; the high costs of operating the trucks, combined with sales commissions, quickly ended our new distribution system. The route trucks were an expensive experiment.

Double Vision—Day 33

This blistering hot July day in 1980 started not much different from others. The Vidalia Onion season had ended and the business made its annual shift from Vidalia Onions to watermelons, and Cordele, Georgia became our summer retreat. I loved the business with such depth that I overlooked the long hours. I overlooked the heat. I overlooked the Georgia gnats. And I overlooked a whole roster of problems by most standards.

The close of the day in any produce season was always special. Like the final play in a big sports game, win or lose, you could relax, because the game was over and nothing more could be done until the next game. An end of the day routine had evolved for David and me; we went out to eat, sat and talked about the day's successes and failures, and then went to bed. But this day ended differently.

As we spoke, an uneasy feeling came over me. David's face seemed distorted, and I saw two of him. I looked outside for some assurance that I hadn't lost my sanity. I found an eerie metamorphosis; now everything had a twin.

I am not prone to panic, and I believed that sleep would probably make everything normal again. Perhaps, I thought, this was the consequence of a spoiled trifle from our earlier dinner. Or possibly time enfeebles the body with such potency that it rebels and refuses to function properly. Or maybe it was runaway imaginings, or perhaps a dream.

In all events, I knew it would be morning before I could do anything about it. I figured the passage of the night would likely vanquish whatever grim fate my brain had supposed. If a dream caused this, I would awake at some point and smile at my unjustified fears. If too much work and too much worry caused it, then perhaps the night's rest would make the problem disappear.

I am an optimist at heart; I was too busy with life to consider any unwanted changes in my design for it.

> ### Diplopia
>
> Persistent diplopia, or double vision, in an otherwise healthy young adult is most likely the result of multiple sclerosis. A study by Kurtzke (10) indicated that 19% of MS patients have this symptom at some time during the course of the disease. Other studies indicate a much higher percentage. A U.S. Army series (11) reported diplopia in 22% of patients at the onset.
>
> Diplopia that persists is usually the result of internuclear ophthalmoplegia (INO), which is always due to an intraaxial (within the brainstem) lesion of the pons or midbrain. A feature of an INO is that the internal rectus muscle (one of the muscles that moves the eye) may not act on lateral gaze but will on convergence (12).
>
> The prospect for recovery from diplopia, and other symptoms that are probably the result of "small" lesions—optic neuritis, vertigo, or cranial nerve lesions in general—is much better than the prognosis for symptoms caused by larger lesions (13).
>
> Initially, most neurologists suggest covering one eye with a patch and a course of steroids. If the problem persists, diplopia can sometimes be alleviated with eyeglasses containing prisms.

Day 34—July 25, 1980

The morning brought little comfort. The diplopia (double vision) worsened and my concern multiplied. I saw the first doctor I could find.

The diplopia alone was not a sufficient reason for the level of concern that I felt. But there were other, more subtle changes—changes that almost escaped definition, or at another time I would have blamed on the long hours, or hectic pace, or some other non-description. For one thing, I had a noticeable awkwardness in my movements. Also, I sensed more than a small concern by the doctor. And what about the hearing loss in my right ear? It was still there. Now I suspected that the double vision and the loss of hearing were connected in some way.

I didn't leave the doctor's office very comforted. Our society bestows on doctors an omnipotent character that they may or may not want, and often cannot live up to. I expected an immediate explanation for my problems, but he offered none.

My imagination ran wild. I convinced myself that I had a brain tumor and would soon be dead. The human mind is an unpredictable instrument. That night I walked for hours down a railroad track behind the motel. I was only 26 years old. Why was this happening to me, I wondered? I had a three-month-old son. Who would teach him to fly a kite and to play baseball?

For the next 48 hours the diplopia worsened dramatically. My right eye would not move past the mid-line, rendering a morbid appearance that made me ultra self-conscious around anyone. My imagination continued with the brain tumor scenario. I do not know why my mind had selected this medium for my ruin, but it had, and only positive proof to the contrary would annul its decision. It would be awhile before such proof was provided.

Day 35

The doctor in Cordele referred me to a doctor at Memorial Medical Center in Savannah, where I had full confidence an answer would be found.

None was. The trip started a lengthy attempt to put a name with the condition. At Memorial, Doctor Ensanipor did a general examination. I felt deep concern, but no answers. Dr. Ensanipor made me an appointment with a neurologist for the next day.

With each non-answer, my apprehension multiplied.

Day 36

Dr. Roberts, a young neurologist fresh out of residency, was the third in a series of doctors to "inspect" me since the diplopia started. They all seemed to know, but didn't know, or knew, but lacked the degree of confidence needed to make the revelation.

Dr. Roberts, now charged with the diagnostic challenge, had most, or all, of the virtues required to carry out his office. He was compassionate, motivated, and highly intelligent. What he lacked was experience.

Nevertheless, I soon accepted his knowledge and talents as sufficient for the task, and I allowed the pressure to dissipate, a little; still, no answers.

The Search for a Diagnosis

Soon began a long series of tests that were heretofore unknown to me—an ignorance that I was completely content with. "What kinds of tests are you going to do?" I asked Dr. Roberts.

He said, "After we do a CT scan, I would like to do a series of tests called evoked potentials, and I'd like to do a few other tests."

I asked, "Can all of this be done as an outpatient?"

Dr. Roberts said, "No. I'd like to admit you for one night."

David and I were making plans for the onion crop we would start planting in a few weeks, and I didn't like the idea of spending a whole day in the hospital.

"What are evoked potentials?" I asked. I was accustomed to a world of simple medicine where the patient describes the problem and the doctor immediately writes a prescription for the remedy, part of which had to be at least one day in bed, if it was a serious problem."

Dr. Roberts said, "These tests MIGHT rule in or out some of the possibilities."

The one day in the hospital went by fast. Dr. Roberts added several more tests to the list. This seemingly inclusive barrage of medical inquisition would surely reveal everything that could be known about my problem. But it didn't.

After my discharge, Dr. Roberts said, "We still can't be sure. On a positive note, however, I am sure that you do not have a brain tumor. Let's just watch it for a few weeks and see what happens."

I concluded that my condition must be unknown to modern medicine and only by some freakish mischance would the true nature of this malady be revealed. Yet, society had instilled in me a genuine awe for the adequacy of modern medicine, and at my core I believed that eventually these skilled men would fathom this mystery and would reveal its secrets, and would provide the appropriate pill to neutralize whatever poison this fiend had administered.

In retrospect, I realize that the skilled physicians knew exactly what they were looking for and had a fair notion of what they expected to find and were reasonably sure of what their response to me would eventually be. Still, at the time, the experience seemed nothing more than randomized tests born from a confounded intellectual system groping in the dark. My analysis gained support by the fact that, after all these efforts, still, no diagnosis—not even an educated guess.

Whatever the essence of the beast that threatened me I knew that I had to soon learn its identity and its nature, or my sanity would be short-lived. There was something destroying me little by little and I did not know where it would take me.

The relief from the brain tumor scenario only lasted a short time before my overly zealous imagination provided an ample supply of replacement horrors. Nothing short of a definitive answer would quiet these spirits.

Blurred Vision

After a few days, a relative calm settled over my world. But it didn't last and soon the attack began again. I still saw two of everything, but now they were both blurred. My attitude changed, too. Indignation replaced fear.

The fight caused no fear any longer, but I wanted to know what I was fighting, and the doctor's inability to figure it out frustrated me. Even dying didn't scare me anymore, but I wanted to know the killer's name. The apparent helplessness of the doctors against this enemy, which I did not know of and could not see, overwhelmed me.

The next day I went back to Dr. Robert's office. After his exam he said, "The optic nerves are pale. You have optic neuritis. This is an inflammation of the optic nerve. The problem will probably disappear in a few days and might never return."

The name "optic neuritis" didn't sound particularly threatening. I needed a benign explanation and this one worked. My fantasy of tragedy lurking in the shadows seemed like an overreaction now.

Armored with this new information, I took up where I had left off with life. For now, I put all thoughts of malady into a mental cooler and directed my attention back to the business.

Dr. Roberts prescribed steroids and said, "This should make it clear up faster." I knew that this was the magic bullet I had been waiting for. That night, for the first time in days, I slept.

Optic Neuritis

Optic neuritis is inflammation of the optic nerve, usually resulting in blurred vision. This nerve transmits visual images and light from the retina to the brain. This condition is also known as retrobulbar neuritis, because the nerve is behind (retro) the globe.

About 55% of the people with MS will have this symptom sometime during the course of the disease. Often this is the first symptom.

Many studies show that over 50% of the people who present with isolated optic neuritis will eventually develop MS (14, 15). Researchers reporting in the New England Journal of Medicine have indicated that treating first-time optic neuritis patients with a combination of intravenous and oral steroids cuts in half their chances of developing MS within the next two years.

Pain is common in optic neuritis, usually preceding visual symptoms, but can be at the same time or after they appear. It varies in intensity and sometimes is felt only when the eye is moved.

The maximum loss of vision is usually from 3 to 7 days after the onset of symptoms (16).

The blurred vision is often described by patients as a haze or mist over the eyes. The "heat haze" effect, like steam rising from hot, wet asphalt, is common.

Bright flashes, known as movement phosphenes (17), sometimes are noticed when moving the eyes in the dark. These usually occur during the acute stage of optic neuritis, but may occur during recovery.

Visual field defects, especially a central scotoma or a generalized impairment of the whole field, are very common. (See Scotoma on page 103)

The degree of loss in visual acuity can vary from none to total loss of perception of light. A pale disc is always present with severe, permanent visual loss, but there is no close association between optic nerve pallor and visual acuity.

Usually visual acuity returns to normal following an initial attack of optic neuritis. Earl and Martin (18) found that optimal acuity occurred after a mean of two months from onset. No more improvement can be expected after six months (19).

Slight dulling of the visual image is common, even after recovery of normal visual acuity (20). A perceptual change in the qualitative brightness of colors is common. Better vision at dusk (21) and an intolerance to bright light are occasional observations.

Temporary blurring of vision can sometimes be induced by exercise, heat, emotional disturbance, eating a hot meal, and smoking, according to one study (22).

The occurrence of bilateral optic neuritis, involvement of both optic nerves in rapid succession or simultaneously, is atypical, but does occur.

The Paradox

This reprieve lasted only a few days and then logical inconsistencies in the doctor's conclusion, or my naive interpretation of it, tarnished my drive toward normalcy. I wanted to believe that nothing serious was wrong, so I jumped on the optic neuritis explanation without even one question to the doctor—such as, what can optic neuritis have to do with hearing loss?

Superficially, and from a lay person's perspective, optic neuritis seemed like a plausible, innocuous explanation. Being in the market for a plausible, innocuous explanation, I latched on to this one. But the more I considered this the more I questioned the completeness of the conclusion.

I consulted medical dictionaries and did some basic research at Georgia Southern University in Statesboro. Optic neuritis is an inflammation of the optic nerve, which is the second cranial nerve. Inflammation of this nerve would not cause double vision. That would most likely be caused by a third, fourth, or sixth nerve palsy. The hearing loss was probably caused by problems with the eighth cranial nerve. Optic neuritis could only explain the blurred vision. Obviously, there was an underlying problem much more serious than just optic neuritis.

The next day I told Dr. Roberts that I wanted a second opinion. He recommended a neuro-ophthalmologist he knew at Mass General Hospital in Boston, where he had done his residency. "She is one of the world's leading experts in this area," he said. But I was still ignorant of what "area" he referred to.

Dr. Roberts made the arrangements and in a few days Vivian and I left for Boston.

Mass General Hospital and the Answer

I've spent considerable time in the Northeast, particularly in large cities, so no cultural revelation awaited me. Vivian was different. She had never been in a city like Boston, and Vivian was Southern to the core. Something as insignificant as saying good morning, or ordering breakfast, held the attention of everyone within listening range. And I spoke fluent Southernese myself.

Our motel was within walking distance of Mass General. This was more than just a convenience. I was concerned about my very attractive, 26-year-old wife being alone in Boston, if I had to stay in the hospital. But mainly, I could tell that Vivian was nervous. Actually, the proximity of the motel seemed quite distant to her.

I met with Dr. Wray the first day. She was a quiet, soft-spoken, middle-aged woman. A neuro-ophthalmologist is a neurologist who has carried the specialty one step further. As the name implies, she is an expert in neurological problems that concern vision. After Dr. Wray reviewed my records, she did a limited physical exam. Dr. Wray said, "I would like to admit you tomorrow."

With the rest of the day free, Vivian and I miraculously metamorphosed into tourists. I said, "Let's take a walk on the Harvard University campus." At times I wished that I had continued in school. I felt I had missed an important part of living by swapping college for business; nevertheless, I was content with my life.

But I'm not sure Vivian agreed. We looked at housing at the University of Georgia before we got married. She and I assumed that I would finish school there, and go on to be a doctor, or lawyer, or something with a title; then Vivian would have been the wife of a doctor, or lawyer, or something with a title. But an onion sidetracked me.

I was born with the curse, or the blessing, of seeing some grand possibility behind every opportunity, and all that was needed to bring it to fruition was enough hard work combined with enough hard thinking. I saw life as complex and I analyzed everything in order to discover its peculiarities. But Vivian lived a much simpler life in her mind. She saw only what the eyes could see and had no desire or motivation to go beyond that. She was passionately concerned with little, or if there was passion, it was stored deeply within her, beyond her perception or mine. She had no goals, in Vidalia, that I was aware of, but she was not bored with life. She was content. Ambition had not left its scar on Vivian. She was the perfect, beautiful, southern wife. She knew no other life and she wanted no other life. She saw today and now; life was a snapshot. But there was a contrast, too. Vivian succeeded at what she did, a habit that earned her a management position at a bank in Vidalia.

On August 18, 1980, I was admitted to Mass General Hospital. It was close to capacity and a private, or even semi-private, room was not possible. They put me in a section more like a barracks than a hospital. But I didn't care. I didn't plan to be there very long.

First, they did a spinal tap; analyzing the makeup of the cerebrospinal fluid (CSF) is helpful in diagnosing or eliminating certain conditions. A formidable number of exhaustive tests followed.

On my second and last day at Mass General, I asked Dr. Wray what the purpose in all the tests was. She said, "We want to rule out all the possibilities we can."

With the involvement of the first, the sixth, and the eighth cranial nerves, by process of elimination, I believed that they must have been close enough to at least make an educated guess.

"It is probably a demyelinating disorder," said Dr. Wray. Big deal! They continued camouflaging what they really thought with medical jargon. I, along with a few million other people, knew nothing about "demyelinating" disorders. Eventually, I realized that this was a doctor's way of not telling you by telling you.

I wanted, as I would in any uncertain venture of significance, a list of all the possibilities and the odds of each being the actual culprit. I knew the doctors had this kind of information, but were withholding it. By their reckoning, this silence shielded me. But it was driving me crazy. I wanted the field narrowed down to three or four possibilities, and I was convinced that this had already been done in their own minds.

En route to my last test a nurse handed me a sealed envelope and said, "Danny, give this to Dr. Johnson when you get to radiology."

Since it was my money paying for all of this, I asked, "What's in it?"

She looked at me as if to say, "What business is it of yours?" What she really said was, "It's your medical records for the last two days." They rolled me to a waiting room. Ages passed. The envelope had little interest at first—just internal red tape of some kind, devised by the hospital bureaucrats, I concluded. Still, it just sat there staring at me. As time passed, I became more and more curious. Whatever the envelope contained was about me, and, therefore, I figured it belonged to me. Finally, I couldn't stand it any longer and I opened the package. I was totally unprepared for the words I read. "The most likely diagnosis for this patient is multiple sclerosis."

It was like being stabbed with a dagger. Vivian and I were sitting in a waiting room with strangers. I didn't even know for sure what multiple sclerosis was, but I knew it wasn't good. Where was my doctor? I had questions to ask. They should not have allowed me to find this out on my own in such an impersonal way.

My pain soon turned into anger. After the next test, I insisted on seeing Dr. Wray. What is multiple sclerosis? Why didn't you tell me? What happens next? I fired a seemingly endless barrage of questions for several minutes.

I didn't like the way I found out, but at least I knew now what was wrong. After a time, I actually felt relieved. At least I wasn't fighting a ghost any longer.

Diagnosing Multiple Sclerosis

MS can initially be a very difficult disease to diagnose definitively. There are no test or clinical findings specific for MS. However, most neurologists have accepted a set of clinical criteria that must be met to infer a clinical diagnosis (63). There must be evidence of involvement of at least two parts of the central nervous system white matter that are connected with two or more episodes of worsening lasting at least 24 hours, or a slow progression for at least six months. These clinical criteria should be substantiated by magnetic resonance (MR) scans, evoked potentials, and analysis of cerebrospinal fluid (CSF) proteins (64).

MR scans are positive in approximately 90% of MS patients. Although MR scans are very sensitive, they are not specific. MR scan abnormalities are sometimes found in people with no disease and no symptoms. MR scan abnormalities indistinguishable from MS plaques have been found in other conditions such as systemic lupus, migraine, hypertension, metastatic tumors, trauma, leukodystrophies, and more.

Evoked potentials can measure slowed or blocked conduction along central nervous system pathways. This can be caused by demyelination. Additionally, evoked potentials are sensitive enough to detect clinically silent lesions, thereby providing objective evidence of multiple lesions in early MS (65). Unfortunately, evoked potentials are also non-specific. Slowed or blocked conduction can also be caused by many disorders including Friedreich's ataxia, B12 deficiency, neurosyphilis, and tumors.

CSF analysis can be helpful, but it too is non-specific. White cell counts and protein levels may be moderately increased in MS patients. CSF IgG synthesis rate is elevated and oligoclonal bands are present in about 90% of MS patients. Myelin basic protein is sometimes elevated in the CSF within weeks of an acute attack, indicating demyelination. However, none of these abnormalities are exclusive to MS.

There are many diseases that can cause multiple lesions in the CNS, further complicating the diagnostic process. Sometimes they even follow a relapsing and remitting course, as has been reported with systemic lupus (66).

Primary Sjogren's syndrome can occur with central nervous system disease, according to Alexander et al (67, 68) and can have a striking resemblance to MS. Only a minority of cases of Sjogren's syndrome involve the central nervous system, but being a relatively common condition, it must be specifically excluded when making a diagnosis of MS.

Behcet's disease can, uncommonly, resemble MS. In one study, disseminated lesions occurred in 13.6% of patients with this disease (69). Behcet's disease is usually progressive, but partial remissions may occur (70). Confusion with MS is often caused by involvement of the optic nerve and spinal cord.

Acute disseminated encephalomyelitis (ADEM) usually involves multiple lesions of the brain, spinal cord, and/or the optic nerve. ADEM is an immune mediated, inflammatory, demyelinating disease of the central nervous system. Unlike MS, however, ADEM is typically a monophasic illness with all lesions developing in the same phase—as opposed to the progressive nature of MS. A history of a viral infection or a vaccination USUALLY precedes the onset of ADEM by a latent period of several days or weeks. There are cases of ADEM in which patients present predominantly with variable focal neurological deficits clinically similar to MS. In these patients, MR scans (71) and CSF abnormalities may be indistinguishable from those in MS. Clinically, MS can be differentiated by a history of relapses and remissions, or chronic progression. However, in a first attack of MS it may be difficult to differentiate between MS and ADEM. To further complicate the clinical picture, some cases of ADEM may follow a relapsing or progressive course (72, 73). ADEM, unlike MS, occurs predominantly, but not exclusively, in children.

Lyme disease, caused by the tick-borne infection with the spirochete borrelia burglorferi, may mimic MS in certain respects in the early stage, when the central nervous system is sometimes severely involved (74). White matter and periventricular lesions may be seen on MRI and CT scanning (75, 76, 77). The diagnosis of Lyme disease is usually based on serologic tests for antibodies and, thus, any confusion is usually short-lived.

Spinal cord tumors, sometimes benign and sometimes curable, are rarely, but occasionally, mistaken for multiple sclerosis.

The literature contains various references about EEG's as a diagnostic tool for multiple sclerosis (78, 79, 80, 81), but the general consensus is that this technique is of little value in the diagnostic process.

Symptoms induced or worsened by exercise or heat are common at the onset of MS, but MRI has generally eliminated the "hot bath" technique as a diagnostic tool for this disease.

Because of the difficulty in diagnosing MS, elaborate criteria have been developed to reflect the degree of certainty of the diagnosis. Prior to MRI, the diagnosis was based purely on clinical findings and CSF analysis. Now it is generally accepted that the clinical examination, as well as other imaging techniques, are not nearly as sensitive to MS lesions as MR imaging (82, 83).

The widely used Bartel criteria establish the diagnosis as "possible," "probable," or "definite" (84). "Definite" MS must meet the following three criteria; (1) history of neurological symptoms with relapse and remission or progression for at least six months; (2) evidence of two or more anatomically separate lesions in the central nervous system; and (3) a demyelinative spinal fluid profile supporting immunologic disturbance involving the central nervous system. MS may be considered "probable" when there is evidence of two separate lesions in the CNS and one of the two remaining essential criteria are indicated.

"Possible" MS is the appropriate diagnosis when there is a single lesion or clinical deficit and one or both of the remaining essential criteria are satisfied. MRI is often useful in establishing the certainty of a diagnosis by detecting lesions in neurologically silent regions of the brain.

For unknown reasons, there is a propensity for MS plaques to develop in certain regions of the white matter: the periventricular region, the brainstem, the optic nerve, and the spinal cord. About 50% of MS plaques are periventricular (around the ventricles).

CHAPTER 3

The Business and Multiple Sclerosis Progress

* Accepting Multiple Sclerosis 52
* Integrating the Business and MS 53
* Counterfeit Vidalia Onions 55
* The Trade Shows 57
* The Computerized Consumer Pack Machine 59
* More Visual Problems 59
* Labeling Vidalia Onions 61
* Fatigue and Multiple Sclerosis 66
* Grabbing at Straws 67
* In-line Onion Dryers 67
* The First Cold Storage for Vidalia Onions—1983 68
* An Alternative Storage System 69
* The 1982/83 El Nino 69
* Results of the Freeze 71
* Operating in the Big Leagues 72
* Heat and MS 72

Danny S. New

Accepting Multiple Sclerosis

The journey to Boston divided my life into two very distinct segments—before MS and after MS. I don't believe that an investigator analyzing the personage in each of these parts would recognize him as the same being. Eventually, I didn't even recognize myself.

People tend to believe that things they can do today will likewise be possible tomorrow and the next day and forever thereafter—or if we relinquish any ability in life, the effects will be of little consequence. It is this propensity to take things for granted that leaves us unprepared for change, especially unwelcome change.

After returning from Boston, I wasted no time in reestablishing my presence in the business. I needed to get lost in something, and New Bros., Inc. felt like home, and was home. I was comfortable there and sensed a shield between me and the disease that was literally eating away at my nervous system.

I supposed, perhaps, that my familiarity with the squeaky old chair at my desk, or the rusty rafters in the old edifice that was our warehouse, or the cranky old cat that strolled by occasionally, that somehow an empathetic kindred spirit from these animate and inanimate objects would banish from our territory any uninvited intruders—including MS. By such formidable intervention the malady that threatened my future would lose all its decaying influence over me, and for as long as I remained in those corridors nothing foreboding would befall me.

At first, the difficulty with MS was more one of adjustment, or should I say acceptance, than one of limitation. I could do little before that I couldn't do now—from a purely pragmatic standpoint at least. Still, everything was different. Now a cloud hung over my future. Things I had taken for granted all of my life were brought into question.

For the first time, I realized that no certainties existed in this life, and assumptions from the past had no meaning now. And many had been proven wrong. What I thought were very stable and secure relationships, especially on the business end of the spectrum, turned out to be very fragile. The more I learned about MS the more uncertain the future seemed.

I recognized that my approach to this new situation had to change; I had to quit expecting difficulties, and I had to just take one day at a time. Soon after we returned from Boston it was time to plant onions. The land had to be prepared, field crews were arriving, and everything started to resemble normal.

I couldn't wish away the disease, so I knew I had to accept it—unconditionally. I was falling and I had to find something to hold onto. I was living a life more within my thoughts than in the more appropriate world of friends and colleagues and family. Providence had placed me in a world that seemed remote from everything I was accustomed to, and I had to find the way back.

It is man's nature, I think, to seek out and identify with and consort with other souls of similar circumstance. Not me—not at this time in any event. Although I wanted to learn everything I could about MS, I insisted on using medical literature to provide the information. I had no desire to socialize with other people with MS. It was as though I believed that by not being around them I could prevent their fate from being my fate.

I was wrong in every way. It only took a short time to realize this. Seeing the reality of my circumstance was not a contagion that could in some way have a negative impact on my fate. What destiny had planned could not be changed by denial. I sank into these doldrums for no more than a brief time and soon climbed back into the mainstream of life.

Like most people my age, I never considered that health would ever be a problem. I thought I could assume good health until some older age, or if it ever were a problem for someone my age, it would be somebody else and not me.

Still, I wasn't going to let it destroy me. I was content with my life and with my accomplishments. After all, not everybody gets to make an onion famous. I quickly decided that MS would not rule my life. I was only 26, but they had been good years. I had my business, my wife, my son, and my brother. Whatever MS had planned, I could handle it.

Integrating the Business and MS

I quickly adjusted to life with MS and rejected self-pity. I never missed work just because I felt bad, although I qualified for that privilege on a lot of days.

But there were limitations. I could not accomplish as much in a day now as I could before; consequently, it seemed appropriate, conservative, and expedient that we hire more management people.

Taking risk never bothered me, but I always tried to dilute the risk with reason. I didn't know how bad MS would be, but I knew that it was unpredictable. Although I knew not to dwell on the problem, I also knew that I couldn't hide from it. I asked David, "What do you think about hiring a sales manager? This will give us more time to spend on product development and production."

Neither of us particularly liked sales, and we didn't have time to do everything anymore. I said, "We can train Fletcher and Ronnie to handle the job." Fletcher Jones and Ronnie Smith were our two best salespeople from the routes. Ronnie had been a route salesman for Lay's potato chips; Fletcher had been a wine salesman. Both were good salesmen and good people. Their fine-tuned sense of humor kept things in perspective—especially for me. I had developed the bad habit of taking business, life, and myself much too serious. Fletcher and Ronnie had learned to strike a healthy balance. The business needed that.

Next, we added a production manager, a farm manager, and an accounting and financial expert. Learning to delegate authority in what was a rapidly moving and fast changing business was an absolute necessity. Soon I felt confident that we had a team that could handle anything that came along, regardless of what MS did to me.

Counterfeit Vidalia Onions

"Did you read the morning paper?" I asked David. "They finally convicted Nelson Smalley (not his real name) of rebaging Texas onions into Vidalia bags."

David said, "Yeah, I read it. It said they fined him $5000. He probably made a half million and they fined him $5000. What a joke."

Our most damaging competition were western onions mislabeled as Vidalia Onions. The huge spread between the price of Vidalia Onions and the same variety grown in other production areas made crooks out of "almost" honest people. And for that population of naturally dishonest people the illicit opportunities connected with the Vidalia Onion were apparently irresistible.

Sometimes Vidalia Onions sold for $15 to $20 per bag while Texas or California onions, of the same variety, sold for $3. Their taste did not compare, but they looked similar; only an experienced onion dealer could tell the difference, and then only if he had considerable experience with Vidalia Onions.

Taste provided some empirical evidence that an onion was or was not a Vidalia Onion, but this was a long way from "legal" proof of where an onion was grown. Georgia produces a milder onion than most grown in western states, but there are exceptions. These exceptions properly eliminate taste as ratification of authenticity. With the development of new varieties in western states, the distinction grows smaller. In fact, some of the western varieties today and some of the imported onions, such as the Nicaraguan onion, rival the Vidalia Onion.

David said, "What the counterfeiters are doing should be a felony, not a misdemeanor. How can we compete against these people? We've had two loads canceled today. In both cases, the buyers had been quoted a price $7 under the market. It's uncontrollable now. As long as it has misdemeanor status, it won't be stopped."

I said, "Texas onions are $3 a bag. Legitimate Vidalia Onions are $25 a bag. That's a potential profit of $22,000 on one trailer load. The slimes dripping off the trees in Vidalia Onion country."

The problem was getting out of control. To David and me this crime exceeded simple fraud. It smacked of heresy. "This is serious," I said. "The Vidalia Onion is becoming nothing more than a Texas onion in a Georgia bag. Let's talk to Mose Coleman and get his opinion on a political solution."

Mose Coleman, a friend and community leader active in local politics, was one of the earliest growers of onions in Toombs County. We discussed the problem with him.

Mr. Coleman said, "I'll be glad to ask Congressmen Hugh Gillis and Tommy Clifton to meet with us if you would like."

The next week we all met at our office. The Congressman from Glenville (Tommy Clifton) said, "Passing a law that protects something undefined will be difficult. What is a Vidalia Onion? Where can it be grown? Are onions grown in Tattnall County Vidalia Onions?"

The Congressman asked good questions. Excluding Tattnall County was never our purpose. Many of our growers farmed in Tattnall County. But protecting the name "Vidalia Onion" was our purpose. Generally speaking, we had won the nomenclature war, and by 1980 almost everyone accepted the name we had chosen. Still, holdouts existed in both counties. We quickly realized how politically naive we were. More and more people agreed on the name "Vidalia Onion," but no one agreed on the boundaries.

Most people around Vidalia wanted to exclude Tattnall County. The Vidalia Chamber of Commerce started promoting what they called "The Yellow Tag Program." Through this program, a dealer could buy a "certification tag" from the Chamber. The packer attached the tag to each bag of onions as "proof" of authenticity.

But the tag could only be attached to onions grown in Toombs County. David and I disagreed with the Chamber.

In 1980, the State was not ready for a political solution. That would come later.

The Trade Shows

By the end of 1980, we had established our line of processed Vidalia Onion products in Georgia and had exposed the product to most of the Southeast. But we needed to increase our penetration into other areas. I said to David, "Maybe we can do a tie-in special with the processed onion products and the fresh Vidalia Onion. We could do a major roll-out of everything at the United Fresh Fruit and Vegetable Convention in November."

This convention attracted thousands of produce buyers and executives. Most of the chain grocers were represented. This was a national show, and I wanted to introduce our Vidalia Onion products to that part of the nation outside of the Southeast.

We didn't want our products to get lost on the grocery shelf. Marketing them in the produce department would eliminate that problem. Only a handful of processed items find space in produce, and most of these need, or claim to need, refrigeration. Unquestionably, refrigeration allowed us to improve the taste in ways that would not otherwise have been possible. They were all thermally processed and preserved by controlling the pH, a measure of the acidity of the product. We added preservatives for a little extra margin of safety.

The shelf-life of our products would have normally relegated us to "the jungle," the trades euphemism for the grocery shelf. But by tying them to the Vidalia Onion, we convinced most accounts to market the Vidalia Onion pickles, relish, and barbecue sauce in the produce department. This worked especially well during onion season, when the stores displayed the fresh Vidalia Onions and the processed products together.

Putting our products in produce made sense for the grocer, too; the mark-up is generally higher in the produce department. It has to be, because of the perishable nature of produce. But our processed products were not perishable. Sometimes this pitted the grocery buyer and the produce buyer against each other. Usually the produce buyer lost. More often than not, "the jungle" became our home.

Nevertheless, attending the produce industry trade shows proved to be a good move. Even though our stay in produce was usually temporary, the exposure was invaluable. When the stores pushed our products out of produce, and they usually did, they almost always found a home on the grocery shelf. Although this was like moving from the suburbs to the inner city, it was better than not having a home.

DANNY NEW, 1981 PMA (PRODUCE MARKETING ASSOCIATION) SHOW

1982, UNITED FRESH FRUIT AND VEGATABLE SHOW

DANNY AND DAVID NEW, 1983 UNITED FRESH FRUITS AND VEGATABLE ASSOCIATION TRADE SHOW

The Computerized Consumer Pack Machine

The problem of mislabeling engulfed the industry. It seemed unstoppable. Identifying the villains helped very little; the people with authority to do anything about the problem considered the matter unimportant. It wasn't a major social problem, and the number of registered voters effected by it was small.

We needed a package that could not be reused and offered a marketing advantage. David said, "A prepack machine like the Affeldt or the MakFil can do that."

A black market in empty bags of legitimate dealers developed. "Bootleggers" re-bagged western onions into these bags and sold them as Vidalia Onions. The value of the bag paralleled the reputation of the name on the bag. We found New Bros. bags selling for as much as $5 each.

At a cost of $75,000, we figured we would probably have a couple of years before anybody copied us. The onion industry used pre-pack equipment; it wasn't new. But it was new to the Vidalia Onion industry, and being the first kid on the block with anything new had its advantages.

In 1981, New Bros., Inc. installed the first pre-pack machine ever to be used for Georgia onions.

More Visual Problems

For several months after returning from Boston, my condition remained stable. I even considered that maybe the doctors had made a mistake; however, this reprieve was short-lived.

As I observed a truck fertilizing one of our onion fields, a small piece landed in my right eye. I discovered that with my right eye covered I was almost blind.

The next day, Vivian and I went to see Dr. Roberts. He dilated my eyes and looked with his ophthalmoscope.

"What did you see, Doc?" I asked.

"The optic nerves are inflamed and the discs are pale," he said.

You're having a typical exacerbation of MS. Optic neuritis is a very common symptom of this disease. It will probably resolve partially in a few days or weeks. I'm going to prescribe prednisone."

Prednisone is a steroid that suppresses the immune system and has anti-inflammatory characteristics.

Dr. Roberts said, "It has no effect on the overall course of the disease, but it might shorten the relapse (also called exacerbation)."

MS is often marked by relapses followed by remissions. Unfortunately, the remissions are usually not complete and the damage to the central nervous system generally increases with each relapse.

High doses of steroids sometimes result in a condition described as "moonface." The name tells the story. Fortunately, the "moonface" is only temporary, if it occurs at all, and it usually doesn't.

The world is full of people with less than perfect vision. The blurred vision didn't bother me; the uncertainty of what would come next did. The blurred vision just served as an incessant reminder that something was wrong.

Corticosteroids

Doctors routinely use corticosteroids to manage acute relapses of MS. These medications have an anti-inflammatory effect in the central nervous system and help to close the blood-brain barrier, which is often damaged during acute MS attacks.

Most neurologists now believe that a short-course of high dose intravenous methylprednisolone is more effective than oral steroids (such as prednisone) in treating acute relapse of MS. Results in optic neuritis have been especially impressive (92)

Unfortunately, use of these agents has not proven effective in chronic disease.

Labeling Vidalia Onions

Pre-packs did little to discourage consumer fraud, but it was a great marketing tool. Within a few years, everyone in the business had a pre-pack machine. But most of the stores continued selling bulk.

We needed another innovation. I remembered that the citrus industry labeled their product. Why couldn't we? I wondered. A label on every onion might be the answer. I closed my eyes and saw our Vidalia Sweets brand stickered on every onion in massive displays.

But the problems with labeling onions on a production line were major compared to labeling smooth-skinned fruit. Still, if it worked, misrepresenting Vidalia Onions would be difficult, or at least expensive.

We found a company that specialized in equipment to put pressure sensitive stickers on citrus. I called Florida Label and spoke with Yumi Schleifer. "Have you ever put labels on onions?" I asked.

Yumi said, "We've put them on melons, bananas, citrus, apples and other things, but never on onions. I think we can do it, but I see some problems. Orienting the onions under the labeling heads and doing it at a production speed that keeps up with your conveyor is the first one. But I'm confident we can build something that will work."

I asked, "What other problems do you see?"

Yumi said, "I'm not aware of anyone in the world who has ever labeled onions. This will be a first, and we won't know all the problems until we try it on a production scale. Stickers are usually put on permanent surfaces. The outside skin of an onion is not very permanent. Obviously, when the onion husk dries and the outside skin flakes off, the label is going with it. I don't know what percentage of onions will still have labels at the end of the conveyor. It will be an expensive experiment."

"How expensive?" David asked.

"Probably $100,000," said Yumi.

For several weeks David and I knocked the idea around. We didn't want to spend that kind of money on something that might not even work. If it didn't work, we would lose $100,000. If it worked, all of our competitors would eventually put in the same equipment and there would be no marketing advantage. This was not a patentable idea.

Nevertheless, we knew that if something wasn't done to protect the reputation of The Onion, then eventually there would be no industry to protect.

The financial risk was high, but we had to take it. In the winter of 1981, we signed a contract with Florida Label to design and build the first labeling system for onions, and 10 million labels to go with it.

The results were not perfect, but with time the outcome improved. Eventually, labeling Vidalia Onions became an industry standard.

VIDALIA ONION LABELING

Danny S. New

JOE McTYRE/Staff

A label on every one

So you won't have to wonder where its onions come from, New Brothers Produce in Vidalia has purchased a new $100,000 machine that will paste a label on each of the $5 million worth of onions it expects to sell this year. Labeling began this month with the harvest. The company claims to market 50 percent to 60 percent of Georgia's Vidalia onions. The Georgia Legislature failed this year to pass a law that would have set an exclusive geographical area for Vidalia onions. Nevertheless, New Brothers believes their onion labeling machine will offer protection against pirates who market their out-of-state onions as Vidalias.

Body Under Siege

....THE ATLANTA CONSTITUTION, Thurs., April 21, 1983   ...37-A

Labeling expected to end Vidalia onion confusion

By Katheryn Hayes
Staff Writer

In the latest battle of the Vidalia onion wars, a commercial distributor has armed itself with a $100,000 labeling machine that will leave no further doubt about the authenticity of its products.

"It's the first time it has ever been done with an onion," said Fletcher Jones, vice president of New Brothers Produce in Vidalia, which expects to sell $5 million worth of onions this year. The onion labels will be similiar to those that appear on bananas and citrus fruits, and will probably add about 50 cents per 50-pound bag to the cost of packaging — a cost the company plans to absorb without passing it on to consumers, Jones said.

"After we do it this year, it will probably become a standard in the industry," Jones said. If his prediction is accurate, it will mean protection for growers of the premium-priced Vidalias against alleged pirates who are believed to have trucked in out-of-state onions and sold them under false pretenses.

The Georgia Legislature tried to face the issue this year, but then backed away at the last minute from a bill that almost passed. The proposed bill would have set an exclusive geographic area where real Vidalia onions could be grown. But legislators could not agree on what that area should be.

New Brothers — which Jones said markets 50 to 60 percent of Georgia's Vidalias — will take the matter into its own hands with an adhesive decal. The label will be a half-inch in diameter, and will bear the words "Certified Vidalia Sweets grown by New Brothers Produce." The inscription will encircle a smiling sun face used on other New Brothers products, which include pickled onions, onion relish and frozen battered Vidalia onion rings.

"I think it's going to be a lot simpler for consumers to find Vidalia onions this year and be satisfied with what they are getting," Jones said.

The labeling will begin in May when the onions are harvested. The all-important machine will be assembled during the next week, Jones said.

Explaining how the machine will work, he said, "These little funnels will line the onions up and then after the onions come through a little arm comes up and puts the decal on the onion."

Danny S. New

Fatigue and Multiple Sclerosis

As time passed, I became less and less like my old self. It was as though a giant leech was sucking all the energy out of me.

The mornings were okay, but as the day went forward my energy level declined. And sometimes it didn't wait for the day to progress, but disappeared early.

I took more and more breaks. Everyone eventually gets tired, but "tired" doesn't fully describe what happens in MS. The all-encompassing weakness that happens does not have an English word to describe it.

It happens suddenly, with incapacitating fierceness. After walking a short distance, I developed a limp; after walking a long distance, I neared collapse.

Fatigue

It is well established that fatigue is one of the most common and often disabling symptoms of MS. Researchers are attempting to differentiate fatigue experienced by the MS patient from that experienced by people without the disease.

One differentiating factor is the adverse effect of heat and exercise on MS-related fatigue. McDonald & Sears (5) believed that the inability to conduct trains of impulses might be a contributing factor in the rapid onset of fatigue experienced by many MS patients with exercise.

In a study by Freal (6), 78% of the patients had this symptom.

In a study by Krupp (7) it was found that fatigue was not related to depression or degree of disability.

A trial of amantadine (8) found this drug to be marginally helpful. This was thought to be the result of increased release of noradrenaline. Overall, the results were not impressive.

Lassitude is a special type of fatigue often experienced by MS patients. This can occur in the morning or later in the day and is independent of the degree of exertion. This type of fatigue sometimes responds to pemoline (Cylert), fluoxetine (Prozac), and amantadine (Symmetrel).

Body Under Siege

Grabbing at Straws

I searched for any off-the-wall treatment that offered hope. I found literature on snake venom, hyperbaric oxygen, special diets, and other pseudo-treatments with little or no scientific foundation.

I forewent the really bizarre stuff, but a rest-exercise program that one doctor proposed, and a low fat diet from another, seemed harmless, even if they proved useless.

I stayed faithful to these routines for a time, but the lack of change convinced me that, although a healthy lifestyle, the impact on MS would likely be non-existent. Many "street cures" only find life because of the hopelessness often perceived about this disease.

In-line Onion Dryers

The short shelf-life and the difficulty in shipping a long distance continued as the major problem with The Onion's struggle to gain world fame. By 1982, we were shipping onions to every part of the country—but not without significant problems.

In dry years, we managed the problems okay, but Georgia's fame gained more from peanuts and peaches than from dry weather; onions grew better in the dessert Southwest.

One California onion grower, amazed at our bravery as evidenced by our determination to grow onions in such an inhospitable climate, said,

"We can add water when it's dry; we just open gates off of canals fed by the Colorado River. But you can't take the water off the land when it rains too much."

He was right. Growing onions in Georgia was a nightmare. The dryer Southwest got higher yields and grew onions cheaper than us. But our reputation was not cheap onions—it was sweet onions. And on that point we quashed all challengers.

We had occasionally, in desperation, dried onions in tobacco barns; a labor intensive and impractical solution at our current level of production. David said, "Haines Equipment in New York builds an in-line dryer for onions. Let's call Harry Sharpe and get some details."

In 1982, we installed the first in-line onion dryers ever used in Georgia. This improved the shipping quality of the onion dramatically, and diminished the risk from wet weather.

We had eliminated one more flaw in the Vidalia Onion's journey toward greatness. We were systematically pecking away at the problems.

Danny S. New

The First Cold Storage for Vidalia Onions—1983

By 1983, processed foods from the Vidalia Onion represented the largest part of our business—and the part that David and I liked the best. We had less control over the farming end of the business; the weather had most of the control there. But the availability of raw materials for only a couple of months each year made operating a food processing business difficult.

We felt compelled to keep our best employees all year, although the seasonal nature of the business worked against this. Keeping our expensive equipment idle for much of the year likewise bothered us. We had to find a way to store the raw material—the Vidalia Onion.

David and I flew to Binghamton, New York looking for a solution. In New York, growers stored onions in 1000 pound bins placed in a low humidity cold storage at a temperature a little above freezing. If this system would work for us, it would solve a lot of problems; not only could we process for a longer period, but we could also sell Vidalia Onions out of storage, thus extending the season by several months.

David said, "But their onion is so different from ours; what works for them might not work for us."

Georgia onions resembled western onions more than they resembled New York onions, but they didn't store onions in the west. They didn't need to; onions for the markets they went after could be grown in so many different locations, and for so much of the year, they didn't need long term storage.

But we could only grow the Vidalia Onion in a relatively small area of Georgia, and The Onion was only available for a very short time. We desperately needed a way to store onions.

Ronald Krupski met us at the airport in Binghamton. Ronald, one of New York's largest onion producers, said apologetically, "You didn't pick a very good time to visit upstate New York. We've had eight inches of snow in the last three days. But it's clear now, and the plows have most of the roads open. We're not far from our main storage. We'll take a look at that one first."

Ronald showed us a huge storage. "How many onions can you store in this building?" I asked.

Ronald said, "We have a total of 20,000 square feet of refrigerated space here. It is divided into five, 4000 square foot rooms, each 20 feet high. Each room holds about 1,000,000 lb. of onions."

I asked, "What kind of conditions do you try to maintain in the storage?"

"We try to keep the temperature as near to 32° Fahrenheit as possible, and the relative humidity around 70%," said Ronald.

I asked, "Do you have any sprouting problems with the onions?"

Ronald said, "We control sprouting with MH 30. This reduces the yield marginally, but we couldn't store onions without using it."

MH 30 retards growth, and thus sprouting.

Going home, David and I debated the pros and cons of building such a storage. We knew that MH 30 was not approved for use in Georgia, and therefore sprouting might be a problem; nevertheless, we felt strongly that this was a chance we had to take.

Before the 1983 onion harvest, we finished construction of a 5000 square foot, low humidity cold storage. This was the first commercial attempt in Georgia to store onions.

Our success was mixed. We kept onions in the storage for more than six months, but with substantial losses. Now we knew that long term cold storage of Vidalia Onions was possible, but the technology needed a lot of research. Fortunately, Doyle Smittle, with the University Of Georgia Extension Service, involved himself deeply in the development of a Controlled Atmosphere system to store Georgia onions.

An Alternative Storage System

Storing onions for the fresh market would be a bonus; but storing onions for processing was an absolute necessity. If the cold storage worked, we could use the onions for either purpose. But we needed an option in case it didn't work.

Joe Szuba, our new production manager, had extensive experience in the pickle industry, with a background at Beatrice Foods and Vlasic Pickles. Joe said, "I'm going to experiment with the technique we used to preserve cucumbers at Vlasic Pickles. We can't use that system to store onions for the fresh market, but I think it is the solution for our processed foods."

"How does it work?" I asked.

Joe said, "The vegetable is stored in a low pH brine solution. I'm convinced it will work for onions as well as it does for cucumbers."

We told Joe to test the system on onions from the '83 crop. Everything went well.

The 1982/83 El Nino

Before my life as a farmer, my interest in the weather ended with my daily selection of what clothes to wear. But now I was intensely aware that my future was profoundly tied to the temperament of Mother Nature. Our business could die or prosper by a bad or good turn of the clouds. The weather report became as much an integral part of our morning as did our cup of coffee.

Danny S. New

On a particularly cold winter morning in December of 1983, I arrived at the office after hearing a weather report that I assumed must have been from some faraway place in the North—but surely not Georgia.

I asked, "Have you heard the weather report yet?"

David said, "I did, but I assumed that I heard it wrong."

"You didn't," I said gloomily.

Temperatures of five degrees were predicted for that night. Freezes that severe were unheard of in Georgia.

We used cultivation practices to harden the onion plants, thus increasing their chances of surviving the winter. We used transplants and avoided direct seeding. We planted early enough to give the onions time to develop a root system before cold weather hit. We made the plants tougher by withholding large amounts of nitrogen. All of this improved the odds of survival, but for an onion to survive five-degree temperatures would require a miracle.

ONIONS BEFORE THE BIG FREEZE

Body Under Siege

ONIONS AFTER THE BIG FREEZE

We feared it was our turn for a weather disaster, since we had escaped devastation from the '82/'83 El Nino visit to South Georgia. Although the damage in '82 was substantial, we survived it.

I stayed awake that night. At midnight, the temperature had dropped to 18 degrees. By two A.M., it had dropped to 12 degrees. By six A.M., I saw five degrees in Georgia for my first time.

The next morning we made a tour of the onion fields. We spoke little. No words were necessary. We knew that the overall damage to the industry would be substantial, but held out hope that some of our onions would survive. It was a waiting game now. For two more days, the temperature never got out of the teens.

Results of the Freeze

It appeared that once again we had dodged a bullet. The freeze only reduced our yield by about 15% overall. Some fields were devastated, such as the one shown above. Others were less damaged.

Unfortunately, yield only told part of the story. The real nightmare would not unravel for months.

The 1983 freeze was a major factor in unsuccessful efforts to store onions from the 1984 crop. We failed to predict what five-degree temperatures would do to the quality of stored onions.

Operating in the Big Leagues

Operating at the level we were now, and against the older, larger, and better financed food companies required certain adjustments in our marketing techniques. The packaging and quality of a new product are not the only factors that assure distribution. Now we had to contend with slotting allowances. We had to spend money on introductory deals. We had to handle the costs of coupons. And we had to budget a large amount for advertising.

The slotting allowance was nothing more than buying shelf space. This was fine for General Foods and Proctor & Gamble, but we were still a small company. But, like it or not, we were in a bigger game now and had to play by the new rules.

Our sales system also had to be revamped. It was no longer practical to use an in-house sales force exclusively; there was too much territory to cover. It wasn't enough to sell a chain, ship to their warehouse, and assume that everything was okay; somebody had to follow-up at the store level. For this, we needed food brokers. We had no way of knowing if our expensive, four-color point-of-sale material was being used to help sell the product or, instead, to help fill the trash cans. It was the broker's job to be in the stores and to know that we were not wasting our money on promotions that were implemented with only half-effort.

Heat and MS

Our busiest season happened in hot weather, and heat made everything about MS worse. I limited my excursions into fields as much as I could, but there was no way to be in the onion business and completely avoid the heat.

I didn't understand what heat had to do with MS, but it clearly made the symptoms worse. My energy and visual acuity declined as temperatures went up.

Effects of Heat, Cold, and Exercise on MS

Heat can cause a worsening of symptoms for many people with MS. Even small increases in temperature in the central nervous system (CNS) slow impulses in nerve pathways. The reason is well understood.

When sodium ions move across nerve-cell membranes they produce electrical energy. It is this energy that drives the impulse. As the temperature increases, the ion movement across the membrane is faster, and the creation of electrical energy is less efficient.

Any movement, from walking to smiling, adds heat to the body. This heat is either stored or released to the environment. If too much of the heat is stored, it will result in heat stroke or heat exhaustion.

The body loses this heat by conduction, radiation, or convection. Conduction is the flow of heat by direct physical contact, from hot to cold. Convection involves the movement of air to carry heat away from the body. Radiation involves the direct emission of heat into the surrounding environment.

When the ambient temperature is above the normal body temperature, these mechanisms don't work, and the body relies on evaporation of sweat for cooling. In MS, sweating and increased blood flow to the skin—the body's way of bringing heat to the body surface so it can be lost—may be less than normal. (200)

Medical professionals have long recognized a worsening of MS symptoms as a result of exercise or a change in environmental temperature. Uhrthoff (23) first described transient visual deterioration resulting from exercise. In a fundamental sense, this can be explained by what we know about demyelinated axons. Conduction in both peripheral and central nervous system myelinated axons is saltatory—jumping from node to node. This conduction is slowed or stopped by demyelination. On a computer model, the thinner the myelin sheath, the lower the temperature at which conduction is blocked (24).

Strength is also diminished by heat (25). This effect is very rapid, occurring within 30 seconds of getting into a hot bath (26) and sometimes resulting in the patient falling in a hot shower

(27).

Exercise will not improve strength when the muscle is weakened as a result of slowed nerve transmission. A limb dragging during exercise is a result of fatigue, and rest restores function. This is a temporary condition and should not discourage exercise.

Things that have very trivial effects on body temperature, such as a hot drink, can have a negative effect on visual acuity (28), and probably other symptoms as well.

In a small minority of patients, it has been reported that cold can also cause a worsening of symptoms, an observation that has been confirmed (29, 30). One explanation (30) is that temperature changes adversely affect conduction in partially demyelinated fibers.

CHAPTER 4

Going Public

* The Decision to Go Public 76
* Finding an Underwriter 78
* The Prospectus 79
* The Underwriter Goes Belly-Up 82
* Strike Two 85
* The Homerun 85
* Wall Street at Last 88

The Decision to Go Public

The future looked limitless in 1983. New Bros. Inc., had problems, but we managed them. David and I didn't agree on everything, but we understood and trusted each other—above all else, we trusted each other.

On a cold morning in January, we met for our weekly management meeting. As usual, we arrived ahead of the rest of the group, but the doughnuts and coffee were there and I had some business to discuss that had been keeping me awake. The potential for New Bros., Inc. was no longer in question. This was a major company waiting to happen.

Sales were great for the processed foods, but our small plant could not keep up with the demand. I said, with a strong sense of necessity, "I don't think we can count on our monopoly lasting in the processed deal much longer; too many big names are getting interested in what we're doing. We have 100% of this market right now, but if we are going to keep it, we need to do something drastic; we'll be eaten alive if we stay small. I think it's time for a major national roll-out of all the products, but we can't do it without a substantial increase in our production capacity."

Murmurs about interest in processed Vidalia Onions by some of the high rollers in the food industry were getting more common. We heard Campbell's Soup Co. mentioned often. Companies with their level of resources would flatten us unless we stayed one step ahead of them. In business, it is difficult to reach and maintain a level of homeostasis; a constant flux demands action and if that action is slightly off mark, results can be devastating.

I said, "I've put a lot of thought into it, and I believe that now is the time for an equity offering. New issues are doing well, and with all the interest in Vidalia Onions I think we can make it work."

David agreed with the concept of going public. The founders of many small businesses dream of this, and our prospects convinced me that we were on the brink of becoming a major corporation.

"Now is not the time to be timid," I remarked.

David agreed.

I had read a lot about public stock offerings, but David and I really knew very little about the subject. Still, my studies of finance convinced me that I knew the right questions to ask, and I had some idea of where to direct them.

C. M. Jordan, a local businessman, showed considerable interest in New Bros., Inc. Mr. Jordan was a retired banker, a good friend of a good friend, and a man that we respected. "Why don't we talk to Mr. Jordan and get his opinion on taking the company public," I suggested. Mr. Jordan dropped into our office several times a week, more socially than business. We liked Mr. Jordan. We valued his opinion, especially on matters of finance.

Body Under Siege

Mr. Jordan was in the plant and I asked him if he had a few minutes to chat. "Sure, I'll drop by your office before I leave," he said. Joe Szuba was showing Mr. Jordan some of his new ideas for maximizing our limited production capacity. Everyone knew that Mr. Jordan was a confidant of David and me, and he was free to move about as he pleased in the plant.

David and I were in the conference room when Mr. Jordan came in. "Mr. Jordan, I'm sure you've noticed that our small production line can't keep up with sales; and even if it could, it's too labor intensive. We are considering a public stock offering to modernize and expand the plant. We'd value your opinion on this."

Mr. Jordan didn't say much at first, but he listened with much more than the interest of a casual observer. It was obvious that his interest went far beyond that of just an advisor.

In his younger days, Mr. Jordan had founded a small town bank. Eventually, Savannah Bank and Trust, a larger regional bank, purchased his bank and paid for it with stock. Through several mergers and acquisitions, Mr. Jordan became a very wealthy man.

Mr. Jordan said, "Is your financial statement strong enough to get the interest of an underwriter? You know you will have to have your books audited. Going public won't be easy, but if you can, it will open a lot of new opportunities for you. Do you mind if I take your financial statements and study them for a few days?"

We didn't mind. In fact, Mr. Jordan's interest encouraged us.

In one or two weeks, Mr. Jordan called and asked to see us. Later that day we met. We had only asked Mr. Jordan for advice, but his interest clearly went deeper than that. We felt more like a salesman was calling than just a friend. Still, we respected Mr. Jordan and valued his counsel.

"Hello Mr. Jordan. Thanks for stopping by," greeted David.

Mr. Jordan said, "I've put a lot of thought into what you asked me. I think you really have something here; I always have thought that. But I see some problems with your financial set-up; your cash position is too weak, and your assets to liabilities ratio is too low. I think you will have problems going public unless you can improve these items on your financials.

"Well...okay," I replied. "What do you think we can do?"

"If it were me," said Mr. Jordan, "I would sell the plant and office complex, and reduce my debt with the funds. A sell-leaseback will improve your cash position. I think it is the only way that a stock offering will work."

David and I had already considered that move, but thought that finding a buyer would take too long. This was commercial property with an appraised value of 1.2 million dollars. We needed a buyer now or the stock sale could not close in time to have the new production line in place by the 1984 harvest.

I said, "If we can't do this fast, there probably isn't any point in doing it."

Mr. Jordan was clearly holding something back. David and I looked at each other with a probing glance. We knew that Mr. Jordan had something on his mind that went far beyond friendly counsel. We sensed that some kind of proposition was in the air.

After a few moments, Mr. Jordan took the lead. "You know, I have a lot of confidence in you two, and in your business. I might be willing to purchase the property and lease it back to you, if we can work out the details. I think the opportunity here is tremendous and I would like to be part of it. You fellows have put the City of Vidalia on the map, and it is obvious to me that you know what you are doing."

We were ready to talk about this; we needed an opening and Mr. Jordan provided it. David and I knew each other so well that we could communicate as well with a glance as most people could with long discourse. In this case, a glance assured me that David also wanted to pursue this discussion to see where it would lead.

We knew where we hoped it would lead; a sell-leaseback arrangement with Mr. Jordan would solve our short-term problems, and working with Mr. Jordan seemed easy. Our conversations with Mr. Jordan became more and more impersonal, but still friendly. I felt a need to be more on guard than before, but I had no reason to distrust Mr. Jordan, and I didn't. The dollars involved were large for a company our size, and caution was natural on everyone's part.

Mr. Jordan said, "I'm not interested in just a real estate investment. I will buy the plant for 1.2 million and lease it back to you, but I need a sweetener in the deal."

"What do you have in mind?" I asked.

Mr. Jordan said, "As part of the deal, I want you to sell me 100,000 shares of stock in New Bros., Inc. for $20,000. And I have one more request. I want you to use Wendell Calhoun as your lawyer for day-to-day matters. I have confidence in Wendell, and with over a million dollars invested in the business, I think that asking this is reasonable."

David and I knew Wendell and considered him to be a competent attorney, so we had no problem with this. And if Mr. Jordan wanted somebody to look over our shoulders, that was okay, too. If this made Mr. Jordan feel more comfortable, we didn't have a problem with it. We didn't have anything to hide.

"Sure, Mr. Jordan. We have no problem with Wendell representing us."

Finding an Underwriter

We chose a large, well-respected law firm in Atlanta to represent the company in the stock sale. Only a few firms in the State had the knowledge to deal with The Securities and Exchange Commission in regards to IPO's (initial public offerings). Kilpatrick & Cody was one of these.

Barry Phillips, the senior partner at Kilpatrick & Cody, was our initial contact person. Mr. Phillips was a colorful, vintage man, with a generous supply of character. His extensive knowledge of equity offerings calmed us. We left the offices of Kilpatrick and Cody confident that, if we were determined to go through with this, and we were, then these were the people to guide us.

Chris Rouse, the CEO of our auditing firm, referred us to a small investment banker in Atlanta. "Hereth, Orr, and Jones might be interested in this," Chris said. "They are a small firm but they have a good reputation in the bond market. They have never done equity offerings, but have expressed an interest in expanding into equities. I think talking to them will be time well spent. Here is their number. Harry Lenz is the person you will need to talk to, if you decide you are interested."

This was all new to us and we really didn't know what we were interested in. Barry Phillips had mentioned the deal to Johnson Lane's investment banking division. New Bros., Inc. was not large enough to get much of a hearing from them.

David said, "It can't hurt anything to talk to Hereth, Orr, and Jones. They sure have a good reputation in the bond markets. Since this will be their first venture into equities, they will have a lot riding on its success." The next day we met with Harry Lenz in Atlanta.

Harry said, "With all the interest in the Vidalia Onion, and with New Bros. at the forefront of the industry, a public offering has a lot going for it. I'm sure you already know that our history at Hereth, Orr, & Jones does not include equity offerings, but we have the contacts and we can do it. Our background is in bonds, especially tax-free municipal bonds, but we have the expertise available in-house, and this is something we want to get into. The timing may be perfect for both of us. Investment banking is our only business, and you can be confident that we know what we're doing."

We left the offices of Hereth, Orr, and Jones eager to get started. Finding an enthusiastic investment banker is the first major hurdle for a small company aspiring to go public.

The Prospectus

We were vaguely aware of the complexity of going public, but actually doing it goes beyond description. The lengthy process of writing the prospectus made the offices of Kilpatrick and Cody very familiar landscape.

The Equitable Building, towering over downtown Atlanta, came to suggest that we were nearing the finish line of a race started long ago, or maybe the starting line of a new race. And it felt as though success had truly arrived.

The first challenge—for us, Kilpatrick & Cody, the underwriter, and the accountants—was the preparation of the prospectus. SEC rules prohibit any offer to sell securities to any member of the public without first providing the potential buyer with a prospectus that the SEC has approved. Every word in the prospectus has significance, and Kilpatrick & Cody dissected every sentence before issuing a badge of acceptance.

Mr. Phillips said, "The accountants, the lawyers, the underwriters, the printers, and everybody else connected with this deal will bend over backward to make sure that they don't make any mistakes. You will hear a lot about "due diligence." When a stock offering goes sour, regardless of whose fault it is, lawsuits fly from every direction. Everyone will be accused of doing less than he or she is supposed to do, regardless of how much anyone actually did. Therefore, we will take every precaution to assure that everything written in the prospectus is correct."

The rules and regulations set down by The Securities and Exchange Commission governing the sale of securities, either debt or equity, fill volumes. For six months, we spent a monumental amount of time working on this document, and other matters related to the IPO.

I said to David, "It feels like we're in the stock business instead of the onion business."

When the prospectus was ready to print, David Stockton, a lawyer with Kilpatrick & Cody, said, "I have a bid of $20,000 from Stein Printing for this job. The four color process with all the pictures runs the price up, but they do good work and they do it on time."

Body Under Siege

PRELIMINARY PROSPECTUS DATED NOVEMBER 23, 1983

1,000,000 Shares
Common Stock

NEW BROS., INC.

Prior to this offering, there has been no public market for the Common Stock. The initial public offering price has been determined by negotiations between the Company and Hereth, Orr & Jones, Inc., the Underwriter, and is not based on the present assets, earnings or book value of the Company. See "Underwriting."

This offering involves special risks and immediate substantial dilution from the offering price. See "Special Risk Considerations."

THESE SECURITIES HAVE NOT BEEN APPROVED OR DISAPPROVED BY THE SECURITIES AND EXCHANGE COMMISSION NOR HAS THE COMMISSION PASSED UPON THE ACCURACY OR ADEQUACY OF THIS PROSPECTUS. ANY REPRESENTATION TO THE CONTRARY IS A CRIMINAL OFFENSE.

	Price To Public	Fees and Commissions(1)	Net Proceeds to the Company(2)
Per Share	$5.00	$ .50	$4.50
Minimum Total (3)	$3,000,000	$ 300,000	$2,700,000
Maximum Total (3)	$5,000,000	$ 500,000	$4,500,000

(1) Does not include a nonaccountable expense allowance payable by the Company to the Underwriter equal to 3% of the Price to Public of the shares sold in this offering. In addition, subject to the sale of 600,000 shares, the Company will issue the Underwriter a warrant (the "Warrant") to purchase up to 100,000 shares of the Company's Common Stock at an exercise price of $6.00 per share. The Company has also agreed to indemnify the Underwriter against certain liabilities, including liabilities under the Securities Act of 1933, as amended. See "Underwriting."

(2) Before deducting Underwriter's nonaccountable expense allowance, in a minimum amount of $90,000 and a maximum amount of $150,000, and other offering expenses estimated at $140,000.

(3) The first 600,000 shares will be offered by the Underwriter on a "best efforts all or none" basis. After the receipt of the proceeds from the sale of 600,000 shares (the "Minimum Capital"), the offering may be continued on a "best efforts" basis until all the shares offered are sold or the offering terminates, whichever first occurs. All proceeds from the offering will be promptly deposited in an account with Bank South, N.A., Atlanta, Georgia, as escrow agent. If the Minimum Capital is not received prior to 5:00 P.M., Eastern Standard Time, on   , 1984 (subject to extension for up to 45 days by mutual consent of the Company and the Underwriter), all payments received will be promptly refunded with interest. See "Underwriting."

Hereth, Orr & Jones, Inc.
500 Northridge Road
Atlanta, Georgia 30338

The Date of this Prospectus is   , 1983.

We expected a smaller printing bill. The cost for the offering now exceeded $100,000 and continued to climb. The time and money invested exceeded our expectations.

But when we saw the printed prospectus, our enthusiasm returned.

The Underwriter Goes Belly-Up

"Danny, Barry Phillips is on line one," Donna said. I assumed that this concerned the red herring that we had recently distributed.

A red herring, in regards to securities offerings, is a preliminary prospectus distributed prior to SEC approval of the final prospectus. It is complete with legal disclaimers, and informs the potential investor that "this prospectus is not an offer to sale or a solicitation of an offer to buy." It is a less official opportunity to test the waters.

I picked up the phone and said, "Hello, Barry. We weren't supposed to be in Atlanta today, were we?"

Barry said, "No. But I do have some bad news. The SEC forced Hereth, Orr, and Jones to cease operations."

"Why!" I asked in disbelief.

"They failed to meet their liquidity requirements as required by the SEC," said Barry.

Any dealer offering securities to the public must maintain a certain percentage of its assets in a fluid state.

"Can they rectify the problem?" I asked.

Barry said, "I don't think so. We can assume that, for our purposes, they are out of business. If you and David can come to Atlanta we will all get together and consider the options, if any exist."

This was like being ahead thirty points in a big football game and losing it in the last quarter. I told David the news; we just sat and stared at the walls in an eerie silence.

In anticipation of funds being available, we had signed contracts for equipment and had made other commitments that we could not easily reverse. We had to do that or the new processing line could not be completed in time for the 1984 onion season, and we felt this was critical.

I said, "We can feel sorry for ourselves later. Right now, let's look for some options. We need to be in Atlanta tomorrow morning; maybe somebody will have a brainstorm."

Later in the day Harry Lenz called. He said, "I'm sure you've already heard what happened. I hope you don't hold any of this against me. I learned about it at the same time you did."

I knew there was no reason to start assigning blame. What happened, happened. Even if we could have identified a villain, it wouldn't have accomplished anything. I said, "No, Harry, we don't blame you. I do think, though, that someone with Hereth, Orr, and Jones should have been up-front with us about the financial condition of your company, but that's all water under the bridge, now."

Harry had put a lot of work into this deal himself, and he really wanted it to work. I think he really needed it to work. In any event, I liked Harry Lenz and I wasn't going to hold him accountable for this. He was a good man who, like us, got caught up in someone else's problems.

Harry said, "I think I might know a way out of this for all of us. Can we meet somewhere?"

I said, "We'll be in Atlanta at Kilpatrick and Cody's tomorrow. You can meet us there."

The next morning we all gathered in Atlanta. In the conference room were three attorneys from Kilpatrick and Cody, the senior partner from Mauldin & Jenkins, Harry Lenz, David, and me.

Barry said, "Everybody knows what happened, so let's look for a solution. Harry has indicated that he knows something that might work."

Harry said, "First of all, I would like to see this project brought to a successful conclusion, and I think we can. I regret what happened with Hereth, Orr, and Jones, but I met with someone yesterday who might have a way out for us. E. G. Frances & Co., Inc. is a small investment banker here in Atlanta. They have agreed to underwrite the issue on basically the same terms as Hereth, Orr, and Jones."

Barry asked David and me to walk out of the room with him. "I don't know that much about E. G. Frances & Co., Inc.," he said. "They're a small company, but right now you fellows don't have a lot of options."

We really had no options. We couldn't walk away now—too much had been invested. The prospectus needed the new underwriter's name, which meant another printing bill. But that expense looked small now. "Let's go for it," I said. "I don't think we have a choice."

Danny S. New

PRELIMINARY PROSPECTUS DATED JANUARY 19, 1984

1,000,000 Shares
Common Stock

NEW BROS., INC.

Prior to this offering, there has been no public market for the Common Stock. The initial public offering price has been determined by negotiations between the Company and E. G. Frances & Co., Inc., the Underwriter, and is not based on the present assets, earnings or book value of the Company. See "Underwriting."

This offering involves special risks and immediate substantial dilution from the offering price. See "Special Risk Considerations."

THESE SECURITIES HAVE NOT BEEN APPROVED OR DISAPPROVED BY THE SECURITIES AND EXCHANGE COMMISSION NOR HAS THE COMMISSION PASSED UPON THE ACCURACY OR ADEQUACY OF THIS PROSPECTUS. ANY REPRESENTATION TO THE CONTRARY IS A CRIMINAL OFFENSE.

	Price To Public	Fees and Commissions(1)	Net Proceeds to the Company(2)
Per Share	$5.00	$ .50	$4.50
Minimum Total (3)	$3,000,000	$ 300,000	$2,700,000
Maximum Total (3)	$5,000,000	$ 500,000	$4,500,000

(1) Does not include a nonaccountable expense allowance payable by the Company to the Underwriter equal to 2.5% of the Price to Public of the shares sold in this offering. In addition, subject to the sale of 600,000 shares, the Company will issue the Underwriter a warrant (the "Warrant") to purchase up to 100,000 shares of the Company's Common Stock at an exercise price of $6.75 per share. The Company has also agreed to indemnify the Underwriter against certain liabilities, including liabilities under the Securities Act of 1933, as amended. See "Underwriting."

(2) Before deducting Underwriter's nonaccountable expense allowance, in a minimum amount of $75,000 and a maximum amount of $125,000, and other offering expenses estimated at $140,000.

(3) The first 600,000 shares will be offered by the Underwriter on a "best efforts all or none" basis. After the receipt of the proceeds from the sale of 600,000 shares (the "Minimum Capital"), the offering may be continued on a "best efforts" basis until all the shares offered are sold or the offering terminates, whichever first occurs. All proceeds from the offering will be promptly deposited in an account with Bank South, N.A., Atlanta, Georgia, as escrow agent. If the Minimum Capital is not received prior to 5:00 P.M., Eastern Standard Time, on April   , 1984 (subject to extension for up to 45 days by mutual consent of the Company and the Underwriter), all payments received will be promptly refunded with interest. See "Underwriting."

E. G. Frances & Co., Inc.
3495 Cumberland Club Drive
Atlanta, Georgia 30339
(404) 436-0900

The Date of this Prospectus is January   , 1984.

Strike Two

For a few weeks, everything seemed to be on schedule. A constant barrage of phone calls and questions from brokerage houses, newspapers, and potential investors reminded us that the work had just begun. We spent more and more of our time on public relations rather than management of our business. Things David and I once did ourselves we now delegated.

David said, "I just got a call from Merrill Lynch. They have some clients interested in our company, but they wanted to ask a few questions not covered in the prospectus."

We longed for the day when only running the business occupied our time. We had a simpler life then. But if the stock sale enabled us to take the business where we wanted it to go, we knew it would be worth the effort.

When I walked into the office the next day, David met me and said, "I just got a call from David Stockton. I'm not sure whether to laugh or cry. E. G. Francis & Co., Inc. has just closed their doors. The unimaginable has happened—again."

All of our years developing The Onion, learning to farm, building the food processing business, and everything else we had done, was all a piece of cake compared to going public. This was shaping up to be the biggest mistake we had ever made.

"There is not enough time to even think about finding another underwriter," I said.

"Are there any options left?" David asked.

I didn't have an answer, but David already knew that.

The Homerun

This time we didn't expect a call from Harry Lenz, but soon one came.

Harry said, "If you decide to kill the deal, I certainly wouldn't blame you. At this point, I just want to help you get through it, if I can. As I see it, you have two options. You can hang it up and take your losses, or you can manage the stock sale yourself. The company can manage the sale; no law requires you to market the stock through an underwriter. It can still be listed on NASDAQ, and if interest develops, brokers will get involved. It's not an ideal situation, but it's the one you're in, and I will help in any way that I can. We have a substantial list of potential investors, and you couldn't get a more capable lawyer to guide you than Barry Phillips."

The stock offering had developed a life of its own. Something in us refused to let it die. We had spent too much money and had made too many commitments to stop now.

This meant the third printing of the prospectus. But this time we were not depending on somebody else; we controlled it now. A limited demand for the stock was already in place, and the lawyers at Kilpatrick and Cody were qualified to guide us.

We took Harry's advice. Not having an underwriter diminished our chances of success, but we couldn't turn back now.

Body Under Siege

600,000 Shares
Common Stock

NEW BROS., INC.

Prior to this offering, there has been no public market for the Common Stock. The initial public offering price has been determined by the Company and is not based on the present assets, earnings or book value of the Company. See "Plan of Distribution."

This offering involves special risks and immediate substantial dilution from the offering price. See "Special Risk Considerations."

THESE SECURITIES HAVE NOT BEEN APPROVED OR DISAPPROVED BY THE SECURITIES AND EXCHANGE COMMISSION NOR HAS THE COMMISSION PASSED UPON THE ACCURACY OR ADEQUACY OF THIS PROSPECTUS. ANY REPRESENTATION TO THE CONTRARY IS A CRIMINAL OFFENSE.

	Price To Public	Fees and Commissions(1)	Net Proceeds to the Company(2)
Per Share	$5.00	$ .50	$4.50
Minimum Total (3)	$1,500,000	$ 150,000	$1,350,000
Maximum Total (3)	$3,000,000	$ 300,000	$2,700,000

(1) The Company will pay a commission of up to $.50 per share for sales effected by selected members of the National Association of Securities Dealers, Inc. that may be engaged by the Company to act as selling agents ("Selling Agents") in connection with the offering. No commissions will be paid on sales of the Common Stock solicited by the Company. The figures in the table assume that all sales will be effected through Selling Agents. The Company will also agree to indemnify Selling Agents against certain liabilities, including liabilities under the Securities Act of 1933, as amended. See "Plan of Distribution."

(2) Before deducting offering expenses estimated at $150,000 and certain expenses, in a minimum amount of $10,000 and a maximum amount of $65,000, payable to E.G. Frances & Co., Inc., which has been engaged by the Company to act as a Selling Agent, in consideration of its assistance to and consultation with the Company in connection with the offering.

(3) After the receipt of the proceeds from the sale of 300,000 shares (the "Minimum Capital"), the offering may continue until all the shares offered are sold or the offering terminates, whichever first occurs. All proceeds from the offering will be promptly deposited in an account with Bank South, N.A., Atlanta, Georgia, as escrow agent. If the Minimum Capital is not received prior to 5:00 P.M., Eastern Standard Time, on April 30, 1984 (subject to extension for up to 45 days at the option of the Company), all payments received will be promptly refunded with interest. See "Plan of Distribution."

The Date of this Prospectus is April 11, 1984.

Wall Street at Last

In April of 1984, the offering closed, and New Bros., Inc. became a public company traded on NASDAQ, The National Security Dealer's Automatic Quotations.

We had hoped to raise three million dollars in the public offering. We structured the deal as a maximum-minimum stock offering. The SEC authorized the sale of $3,000,000 in common stock, with a minimum requirement of $1,500,000. If we failed to reach the minimum, the deal died and we had to return all the money raised.

The money stayed in an escrow account until we reached the minimum. The purchase by the last investor put us a little over $1,700,000. But that was enough.

Our stock went public at $5 a share. Looking in the Wall Street Journal each morning to see the close on New Bros., Inc. became a routine for the first couple of weeks. But soon we left the world of high finance and drifted back into the daily routine of running a business.

The offering closed too late to complete the expansion of the production line in time for the 1984 onion season. But we could handle that now. We had huge demand for the processed products. The demand for the new items, especially the refrigerated salad dressings, exceeded expectations. Eventually, our production capacity would match our sales capacity, and our enthusiasm returned in full force.

We developed the salad dressings so that they required refrigeration. This improved our chances of getting the dressings into the produce department and keeping them out of "the jungle." We competed in the South against Naturally Fresh and Marzetti's. They were in produce, and we felt we had to be.

We were a public company now and the future looked great, but we didn't get there without some setbacks. The bad luck with the offering resulted in a substantial amount of wasted advertising dollars. In support of a tie-in campaign with the fresh onion, we had promised the advertising. Our production capacity limited the orders we could fill. But the demand was there and the equipment would eventually be in place to fill it. Finishing the stock sale and once again controlling the day-to-day operation of the business dissipated all the built-up pressure.

THE WALL STREET JOURNAL, Friday, August 3, 1984

r-the-Counter M:

Continued From Next Page

Stock & Div.	Sales 100s	Bid	Asked	Net Chg.
Natl Paragon	9	2⅞	3	+ ⅛
NtlPennBs .96	1	23¼	25	...
Nat Western L	26	8	8¼	+ ⅜
Nationwd Pwr	23	2⅛	2¼	+ ⅛
Natural Orgnc	z50	1½	1⅞	...
NautilsFd .83d	15	26½	28	+ ½
NBSC Corp .76	5	12	15	...
NCB Fncl 2.60	4	44½	46	...
NewAmFd 1d	4	32	34	...
NewBros Inc	4	4¼	5	...
NewCentBnk 1	19	13¾	14½	...
NEngBsSv .48	201	28½	30	...
New Frontier	557	15-16	1	+ ¼
NH SvBk .51d	1	15⅜	15⅞	...
NJNtlCp 1.12	z64	16½	17	...
N F A Corp	30	7¼	7¾	+ ¼
NeworldB .05d	10	8¾	9	+ ½
NeworldBk ut	107	9⅜	9¾	+ ⅜
NYAirline ut	10	8	8¼	...
NYMarine Gn	15	12¼	13	+ ¼
NwYorkr .60a	4	135	139	+ 1
NICO Inc	94	7¾	8½	...
NobilityH .08	15	5⅛	5⅜	+ ¼
Noland Co .56	2	18½	19½	...
NorpacEx Svc	355	3½	3⅝	...
NorrisOil Co	64	4¾	5	...
NorskData B	316	36½	37	+ 2½
NoAmNtl .01f	17	7½	7¾	+ ¼
NC Fed SvLn	35	7¾	9¾	...
NCaroNG 1.68	17	18¼	18⅝	...
NrthFork .55d	3	25	25¾	...
NoHills Elec	19	5¾	6¼	...
NoestBc 2.40g	21	42	45	...
NorthnAir Frt	23	3	3½	...
Photo Contrl	1	6¼	6½	...
Photon Sourc	60	3¾	4	...
Photronics Cp	140	4½	5¼	+ ¼
Physcnln .04d	11	6½	8	...
Physio Technl	10	4	4½	...
PiedmntM .36	12	9⅜	9⅝	...
PioneerFd SL	25	6½	6⅞	...
PioneerGr .80	23	14	14½	+ ¼
PittsbrghBr 51	55	9	9½	+ ¼
Plains Resour	8	2 7-16	2½	+ 1-16
Planters .84	3	22	22¼	...
Plasma Thrm	7	1½	1⅝	...
Plen7mPbl .88	14	20¾	21½	− ¼
P N C F pfC	3	16½	19	...
Po Folks Inc	221	14⅞	15⅛	+ ⅜
Polycast Tech	8	8¾	9¼	...
Polymerc Res	35	3	3½	...
PonceFSL PR	128	7¼	7⅝	+ ⅝
PossisCorp .10	34	6¼	7	− ¼
Prab Robots	25	8	9	− ½
PfdRiskLf .74	27	22	23	...
PresdntlLf .12	3	29	31¾	...
Preston Cp .50	261	13½	14	+ ½
Primo Inc	186	2⅝	2¾	+ ⅛
PrimoInc ut	2	2⅞	3¼	+ ⅛
Prof Sys .40	x16	10½	11¼	+ ⅛
Program Syst	11	4¾	5	+ ⅛
Progroup Inc	239	6⅛	6¼	+ ⅝
Pro-Med .21d	9	4	4½	...
Prop Inv Colo	35	1¾	2⅛	...
ProtctvCp 1.20	33	28¾	29½	+ ¼
Provdnt Bcrp	z44	43½	45½	...
ProvLfAc 2.88	60	68½	69½	+ 2½
Prvnctn Bost	20	9¼	10	...

STOCK QUOTATIONS

Danny S. New

The Vidalia Advance/Sept. 27, 1984/Page 15a

New on Wall Street: Brothers of Vidalia

By Ray Tapley

When you're close to something, you're likely to take it for granted. A case in point is the New Brothers, Inc., operation in Vidalia.

The expanding magnitude of that company and its growing impact on the Vidalia area may not be fully recognized by many area residents. But that splashy feature story about the firm in the Savannah *Morning News* recently may have gone a long way toward correcting that condition.

Banner-headlined "Vidalia Onions Hit the Big Time" and written by Marcus Holland, a Reidsville native who for many years served as the paper's sports editor, the story probably was an eye-opener for a number of Vidalians.

Among other gems of information contained in the story were these:

--The company's recent public stock sale netted almost $2 million in new capital to finance further expansion into the field of processed foods.

--About 2,000 jars of onion relish currently are being produced at the company's facilities on the Lyons Highway each day, and the number will increase to 6,000 soon.

--The company's products now are being carried by every major food chain in the southeastern United States.

And what a coup it was for the firm to acquire the services of well-known food/industry executive Bill Beckworth, who will head up the firm's Food Service Division. Beckworth, a Wrens native and Mercer University graduate, is bound to make his presence felt in Vidalia.

From a simple family-owned onion/growing and distribution operation to a stock-company entry on the boards of Wall Street is quite a testimony to the imagination and business acumen of the Brothers New, Danny and David.

Body Under Siege

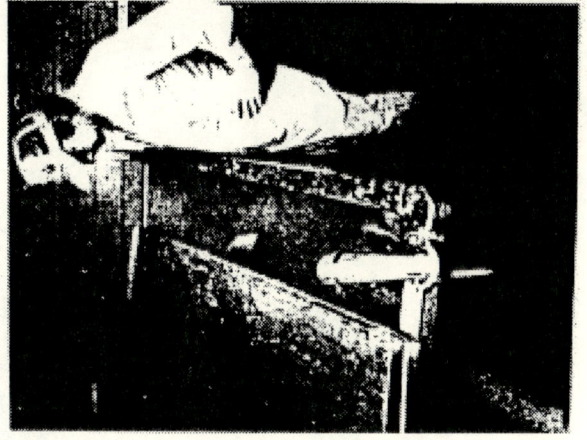

Vidalia Onions Hit the Big Time

By MARCUS HOLLAND
Agricultural Editor

VIDALIA — Something new is happening with the Vidalia onion.

It's the same mild, sweet Vidalia onion all right — but with a new marketing twist.

New Brothers Inc. of Vidalia, almost $2 million healthier as a result of a recent public stock sale, has gone into the processed food business in a big way, using the Vidalia onion as the prime ingredient in its products.

About 345 people bought shares of stock in the public sale that raised money to finance New Brothers' venture into the processed food business, Danny New, chairman of the board, said. Most of the stockholders are from Georgia.

Other moves have been made by the rapidly expanding company. One was hiring Bill Beckworth, formerly an executive with Morrison's Inc., to head the new food service division.

"I feel like Br'er Rabbit who has just been put back in the briar patch," Beckworth, who hails from Wrens, joked after accepting the food services assignment with New Brothers.

The 46-year-old executive also is a veteran of Savannah Foods and Industries and General Foods.

"I'm just a country boy," Beckworth said. "It feels great to be back in Georgia... in a small town. I must admit, however, I wasn't too excited about the job when Fletcher (Fletcher Jones, vice president of marketing for New Brothers) approached me. In fact, I had no interest at all in the job. Then the excitement of Fletcher and the other executives sort of rubbed off on me."

Beckworth, a graduate of Mercer University, expects to do a lot of ground and detail work in his first year on the job. "Hopefully," he said, "I can channel New Brothers toward avenues they haven't explored yet."

Jones and his associates at New Brothers are "tremendously excited" about landing Beckworth. "I dropped to my knees every time I saw him, begging him to take the job," Jones said.

"No," he added, "I didn't go that far, but we did keep after him for more than a month. We're just glad Bill decided to come with our company. He'll do a great job

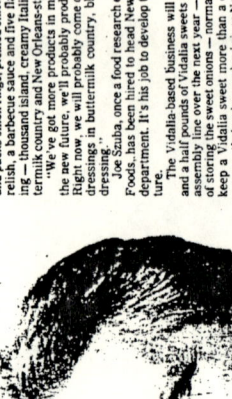

Bill Beckworth, Food Services Head

Danny New, Chairman of the Board

for us."

The idea of processed Vidalia onion food products first emerged about two years ago, New said.

"It was a gamble we felt we had to take," he said. "Customers keep calling, telling us how they love the Vidalia onion taste. They kept wanting the Vidalia onion taste in other products. We had to sit up and take notice.

"We sold stock in the company to raise revenue to get started. We're listed on the NASDAQ board on Wall Street every day. We're dedicated to the processed food business now," he said.

"Once a store gives us shelf space for our products Jones said, "it depends on us to fill that space yearround. That's one reason we have to be committed to the processed food business."

New Brothers will still sell freshly bagged Vidalia onions, but, in the future, the company's priority will be the processed food business, New said.

From the Vidalia sweets, New Brothers processes and packs onion rings, pickled onions, two types of onion relish, a barbecue sauce and five flavors of salad dressing — thousand island, creamy Italian, blue cheese, buttermilk country and New Orleans-style French.

"We've got more products in mind," New said. "In the new future, we'll probably produce 'light' products. Right now, we will probably come out with 'light' salad dressings in buttermilk country, blue cheese and slaw dressing."

Joe Szuba, once a food research expert with Rainbow Foods, has been hired to head New Brothers' research department. It's his job to develop the recipes of the future.

The Vidalia-based business will use about a million and a half pounds of Vidalia sweets in its processed food assembly line over the next year... or sooner. The tank of storing the sweet onions — normally it's impossible to keep a Vidalia sweet more than a couple of months — apparently has been solved since New Brothers will produce processed food year-round.

"We cut the onions and freeze them," New said. "That way, we don't have rotting problems. We're also able to use a lot of Vidalia sweets in our processed food products that we can't sell as fresh onions in bags, either because they are too small or have a blemish on them."

The company's assembly line now is canning 2,000 jars of relish or pickles a day. After a new capping system is installed (within the next couple of months), the capacity will jump to 6,000 jars a day.

After the public stock sale, New Brothers purchased about "three-quarters of a million dollars worth of equipment," New said.

And, he added, "We have almost outgrown our facilities already. Within the next 60 days, we'll probably be going around the clock to keep up with our orders."

The company has been running at full production for about 60 days and the products already are being carried by every major chain store in the southeastern United States, New said.

"We're even in convenience stores. We're doing a lot better than we figured to do at this point," he said. "We're not nationwide . . . we don't want to be, really. But we're heavy in about 28 states."

CHAPTER 5

The Beginning of the End

* MS Pushes On 94
* The Brined Onions 94
* The Fiasco—August 1984 94
* Our Reaction 96
* The Switch 98
* My Struggle with God Begins 98
* Relapse #6 100
* Relapse #7 101
* More Steroids 105
* Total Cognitive Failure 105
* Disclosure 107
* The Relapse Ends—But Not in Time 107
* The Death of a Dream 109

MS Pushes On

The constant strain associated with going public made me ultra aware that the macrophages, T-cells, and any other cells in the immune system that felt at liberty to be part of the attack, were still hard at work.

Nevertheless, I could still do whatever I wanted; it just took a little extra effort. But I also had an awareness of a problem remembering things. But it wasn't a major problem, and I didn't think MS caused it.

Preoccupation with the stock offering made me forget all about multiple sclerosis. Now the constant fatigue reminded me. Still, I was confident that my mental and physical stamina would be restored by a few weeks of routine.

The Brined Onions

During our mental absence, while the company went public, many management jobs normally handled by David or me were necessarily delegated to others. We had confidence in our management so this didn't concern us too much. Joe knew more about food processing than we did; therefore, he made the decisions in that area.

After the offering closed, David and I felt in control again. But we knew there wasn't room for mistakes.

Expanding the production line required a substantial investment, but it would provide little income until the 1985 onion season. The delay in installing the new line mandated that we place a substantial part of the crop in storage; we would need them when the equipment was finally in place.

Joe had been working on a procedure to store onions in a brine solution, much like the pickle industry used for cucumbers. In fact, we had tested the system with onions from the 1983 crop and were convinced that the low pH solution worked as a storage medium for onions.

In the early part of July, 1984, I said to Joe, "How 'bout bringing us up to speed on the brined onions."

He said, "Everything looks good. We worked overtime for the last six weeks brining onions. We'll have enough to process through the winter."

With this reassurance, David and I concentrated on getting the expansion completed.

The Fiasco—August 1984

David asked, "Have you looked at the onions they're using now? They're discolored, and the crew has hauled some to the dump. I asked Joe about it. He said there were some problems with that batch, but he didn't think it was anything to worry about. I'm worried about it."

Joe had experience with brining vegetables. The pickle industry had been doing it for years, and our tests on the onions from the '83 harvest went well. But we knew that our preoccupation with the stock offering had left us more out of touch than usual.

I said, "Let's pull some random bins from the storage and see how they look."

David said, "I'll get the forklift."

The onions in the first bin looked off-color, but usable. Otherwise, the quality seemed okay, and the yellow #5 covered up any discoloration.

"I'm going to pull out another bin," David said. We inspected this one and then another, and another, for a total of 20 bins. The onions in 16 of the 20 bins were completely ruined.

Obviously, Joe selected the good bins and discarded the bad ones, in the naive hope that we would not notice the inventories disappearing. This was Joe's project and he wanted to cover up its failure.

But why didn't the onions hold up, we wondered? Joe habitually painted a picture that was rosier than true, but we saw the results of the previous year's tests on storing onions in brine; the results were good. And Joe had many years of experience and a natural talent in the area of commercially processed foods. We had no reason to question Joe's ability, and we didn't.

"We have over a million dollars worth of onions in the storage," I said, almost in a whisper. After the problems with the stock offering, I think David and I figured that we had reached our quota of troubles for the decade. We were wrong.

We decided to dump the brined onions. Some of them were probably okay for processing, and we believed that no health risk existed, but we weren't going to take any chances.

Something made the '84 crop different from the '83 crop. In the winter before harvesting the '84 crop a severe freeze blasted the Deep South and killed many onions. We concluded, and investigation supported this, that the onions damaged by the freeze could not be stored. But this supposition, if correct, came too late.

Things were mixed up now. Before, the business played like a chess game, with everything making sense. Now the board was all jumbled up and nothing made sense.

Danny S. New

Our Reaction

The pressure of going public was intense; but the satisfaction at seeing it finished made it worthwhile—for a moment. But this loss was the epitome of the proverbial "anti-climax." Everything seemed out of control now. The stock sale raised $1,300,000 less than we planned for, and closed four months later than it should have. This resulted in $250,000 in advertising with limited impact, and over a million dollars in orders that we couldn't fill.

But all of this we could have survived; however, the loss of more than $1,000,000 in stored onions created an atmosphere of panic.

We couldn't just let the company go under; too many people depended on it and too many people had invested money in it. We had twelve long, hard years invested in developing the Vidalia Onion. I believed that everything would fall into place if we could survive until the next onion season.

We were a small company and I knew that a loss of this magnitude would scare a lot of people very important to the business. We might lose our lines of credit. It might even mean bankruptcy (a move that would have made sense, but was unimaginable to me at the time).

There must be a way, I told myself. We could leave the spoiled onions in place and try to fool the auditors about their condition, and, thus, their value. But that would not work. The onions had deteriorated beyond the point of usefulness. Nobody needed a food scientist to tell them that what those containers held had no value.

We needed to destroy the spoiled onions, but to do it in a way that preserved their value on the books. A plan began taking shape in my mind.

David had fundamental religious beliefs; something was either right or it was wrong—there was no in-between. I considered myself a Christian, but less rigid. I would compromise my principles if "situational ethics" showed a strong enough hand.

If I could figure out a way not to disclose the loss of the onions, I knew I would do it. Too many people depended on that business, too much work had gone into it, and MS made my future far too uncertain to lose the only financial security I had. If I lost the business, I would also lose my health insurance and my disability insurance. The world is a scary place for someone with multiple sclerosis and no insurance.

The mix of altruistic and selfish motives, in my mind, adequately justified any reasonable strategy that saved the business—I thought. I formulated a plan that inflated the value of our onion inventories, and thus offset the loss of the brined onions on our financial statement. It wasn't that difficult. And there was no one that could be hurt by this—no one that I could see.

I approached David about this. "We can't just let the business fail," I said.

I gave all my rationalizations. The backbone of my argument centered on the situational ethics theme. I knew that I would have to counter David's fundamental arguments about right and wrong, and I knew that for David no middle ground existed. At this point in my life, I saw nothing but middle ground.

I said, "We can't turn our backs on our employees, our families, the investors. What about Mr. Jordan? He invested a substantial amount of money in the company. What about our mother?"

Our mother's situation was the most compelling argument for me. She was sixty-five and depended completely on David and me for support, and the business had caused that. Our grandfather on our mother's side—Papa we called him—worked all of his life farming. The wealth he accumulated consisted almost entirely of land, much of it in timber. After his death, our mother inherited timberland with a value of around $85,000.

When she sold this land, she loaned the money to New Bros., Inc., secured by packing equipment. Then, it seemed like the best investment for her money, and the risk looked small.

But we made a mistake. If the business failed, the repayment of this debt would be in jeopardy. And I had an uncertain future under the best of circumstances.

I could not stand by and let the business fail. I described my plan to conceal the inventory loss. It would require a lot of effort and the participation of two of our key employees.

Soon we had everything in place. My mind camouflaged all other options and stayed irreversibly set on this path. I felt bad about the deception involved, but the consequences of doing nothing seemed horrendous.

I remembered reading a book on "situational ethics," and it made good sense to me. It said that we could only judge right and wrong in the context of a specific situation. From a very fundamental approach, it is wrong to lie—period. But for me, the complexity of the problem went beyond that. I rationalized my version of right and wrong, but it never felt right.

Late one night in early August of 1984 the emotional reservoirs burst. David yelled with intense crescendo, "The business is too important to you. This is wrong. It's against everything I believe."

David was a dedicated Christian, a deacon in the First Baptist Church of Vidalia, and generally a good person. But I was a strongly outspoken person, and defended my position to the end. With at least an equal degree of force, I yelled, "Maybe this is wrong. I agree that it is wrong. But the hurt we will cause to so many people if we allow the company to fail is even more wrong."

The shouting match soon ended in a stalemate. But nothing was ever the same between us after that night.

The Switch

Because we were a public company now, the SEC required audited financial statements each year. Our fiscal year ended on August 31, and, therefore, whatever we planned to do about the inventories had to be done right away.

To help relieve the guilt, an inevitable consequence of my plan, I decided, as though a mental proclamation of correctness justified the deception, that if I could find ONE person who would be damaged by this, then all bets were off and we wouldn't go through with it.

I found no one. If what I proposed saved the company, then everybody won—at least I rationalized it in that way.

David and I had talked about dehydrating Georgia onions. Dehydrating onions is common in the West, but the low solids in Georgia onions made commercial dehydration impractical. But the auditors probably didn't know that, I figured.

I said to David, "I think the simplest way to do this is to find a supplier of dehydrated onions in a bulk pack. We can then purchase a quantity of onions equal to what would be reasonably expected from the dehydration of the onions we had in brine. We will basically be changing the inventory from brined onions to dehydrated onions. We can create a paper trail to document the transaction. Some of our spice mixtures use dehydrated onions as one of the ingredients. It will take a long time to use all of them, but they will last for years."

From another world, David said, "Yeah, I guess that's what we need to do."

Fletcher and Ronnie joined the effort, but I'm not going to suggest motive. These were good men trapped in an awkward situation. They were employees, and had a job to protect. They were stockholders, and had an investment to protect. Fletcher was a family man, and had a family to protect. I should not have involved them. These were good men who were as unprepared for these problems as David and I were.

The first step required Ronnie to go to Colorado to set things up. He did, and the nightmare began. Within a few days, we located and purchased the dehydrated onions. We embarked on a journey that carried us to an unfamiliar world.

My Struggle with God Begins

We had few problems going forward with the plan. The auditors asked questions, but the answers and the documentation were convincing. But the business was not the same. Everything was different. The plan resulted in a high wall between David and me, and we could not reestablish the symmetry that had been the strength of our partnership.

We created a fictitious company in Colorado and purchased, on paper, the dehydrated onions from this company. We couldn't use the actual supplier. That would be too easy to trace. We chose the name Glacier Foods, and had stationery made.

I knew that the auditors would send confirmations to document large transactions like this. We needed a checking account in the name of Glacier Foods. We needed a mail service for an address. We needed an answering service for a phone number. One lie led to another. Soon my whole life seemed like a lie. What started as a misguided attempt to save our business grew into an ever-expanding scandal.

I never questioned the existence of God. I proclaimed myself, in loose conversation, a Christian. But my actions did not support that claim.

Now I had a very real sense that this God was not pleased with my decisions in this matter. More and more I questioned the doctrine of "situational ethics" which allowed, even demanded, compromise of fundamental Christian principles.

In the middle of the night on September 8, 1984, I awoke with a distinct feeling that I was not alone. God spoke to me. We were wrong when we overstated the inventories on our financial statements. My situational ethics argument was wrong. My priorities were wrong. We had to make a complete disclosure to the auditors.

For the first time in many weeks, I felt at peace.

I dressed and went immediately to the office. It was only 5:30 A.M. and I knew that nobody would arrive for at least an hour. I spent that hour retracing the ethereal events of the night. The consequence of changing our direction now might be the collapse of the business, but I was determined to end the internal debate on the matter.

All of the rationalizations for the deception tried to reclaim lost ground, but I refused to yield. I knew that if I failed to end this now that I risked being cast into a deeper darkness beyond—one from which an escape might not exist. I was anxious for David to get to the office. I needed support.

Soon David did arrive. I told him about my night and about my decision. I said, "We should tell the auditors before this goes any further." David agreed. I knew that he would. I had forced him into a circumstance that was unnatural to him.

I said, "We will have to talk to Ronnie and Fletcher."

They were an integral part of Glacier Foods and we thought it only fair that we involve them in any decisions connected with it. We saw this as a courtesy. I was the architect, but this effected them too. Vivian liked Ronnie and Fletcher. Swain liked Ronnie and Fletcher. I liked Ronnie and Fletcher.

We met that morning at my house. I said, "We can't do this. It is wrong. I made my situational ethics argument to you, but I was wrong. I know that now.

We have decided to tell the auditors the truth and let the cards fall where they will."

I expected a sigh of relief from them. I didn't get one.

Fletcher said, "But what about the business? This will probably mean bankruptcy. What about me? I borrowed money on my house and bought stock in the company. I will lose everything I've got."

The list of potential disasters went on and on. Ronnie and Fletcher knew that their risk was relatively limited. If anyone discovered the errors, Fletcher and Ronnie could take the innocent employee approach and point fingers at David and me. There was little or no downside for them.

My faith was weak. I yielded. The day ended with our plans unchanged and my self-image deflated. I liked myself very little now. I feared that I had lost any privilege that I had to call on God.

Relapse #6

Soon my energy level and my balance had deteriorated significantly. I felt out of control. My mind seemed unclear and without direction. I became extremely forgetful of even important things. I reasoned that this was the result of the tremendous stress, the lack of sleep, or the mountains of business concerns that relentlessly bombarded us.

The future seemed as uncertain as life itself. The fear of being permanently disabled haunted me. Until now, the business had always been fun. It provided a sense of security and it occupied my time. For the first time since the diagnosis, I feared the future.

By the middle of October, 1984, the pressure of the business was crippling. Or maybe I was just experiencing the natural progression of MS; regardless, things were changing too fast for comfort. Dr. Roberts warned me to keep a handle on stress. Glacier Foods had not exactly put me in a pressure free environment, and I didn't see one coming in the near future.

My balance was the most obvious casualty to an observer. I walked like a drunkard, but I wasn't emotionally prepared to use a wheelchair, or even a cane. I didn't think I needed them; I could get from one place to another, and it was a rare event to actually fall down—although I occasionally did that, too.

> **Ataxia**
>
> Ataxia is the inability to coordinate muscles in the execution of voluntary movements, typically caused by lesions in the cerebellum or brainstem (see page 164).
>
> Ataxia can result in loss of balance and can cause a swaying, "drunken" type of gait. In severe cases of "sensory ataxia," numbness in the feet may be so bad that the patient can't feel the floor or know where his/her feet are.

Relapse #7

In early January, 1985, my vision worsened dramatically. The most familiar face in my life was Vivian's, but unless I heard her voice I had difficulty recognizing her.

There was a blind-spot (scotoma) in my central field of vision.

I had a slight, upward repositioning of the left globe, and had diplopia (double vision) in the mid field of vision.

My eyes jerked back and forth (nystagmus), making the world appear as though I was in the middle of an earthquake.

I had my first problem with "cerebellar" movements in my hands. I was particularly clumsy with my left hand.

But my main concerns were not these problems. I had always remembered names easily, but lately it was not easy at all. When I forgot our plant manager's name, even though I talked to him several times a day, I knew that something was wrong.

As I walked into the office one morning, Donna said, "Danny, your ten o'clock appointment left about eleven. He said that he would call and make another one next week. I've never seen you miss an appointment before; is everything okay?"

Everything was not okay. That was the first appointment I had actually missed, but I had forgotten three appointments that week, and had to be reminded at the last minute. Twice in three days I had even forgotten my home phone number.

Scotoma

A scotoma is an isolated area within the visual field in which vision is absent or reduced, commonly referred to as a blind spot. Visual field defects, such as a scotoma or a generalized impairment of the whole field, are very common in MS. The defect is usually central but in about 5% of the cases it may be peripheral.

Nystagmus

Nystagmus is a rapid, involuntary, "jerking" movement of the eyes. This is a classical sign of MS, resulting from damage to the cerebellum or brainstem (see page 164).

Some forms of nystagmus with oscillopsia, an illusory sensation of swaying of the visual field, can sometimes be partly compensated for with converging prisms.

One study found nystagmus present in 56% of the cases (9).

This condition can sometimes be treated with clonazepam (Klonopin), a central nervous system depressant.

In severe cases, surgery is sometimes beneficial.

> ### Cerebellar Symptoms
>
> The cerebellum is the large, posterior portion of the brain lying above the pons and the medulla and beneath the posterior part of the cerebrum. The cerebellum plays an important role in the coordination of voluntary muscular movements. Many symptoms of multiple sclerosis are a result of lesions in the cerebellum (see page 164).
> Ataxia is usually the result of cerebellar disease (39, 40). MS lesions in the cerebellum can cause problems with speech (dysarthria), limb movements, eye movements, and gait. Severe gait ataxia can prevent ambulation, even in patients with no decrease in strength.
> Lack of coordination and imbalance are typically signs of cerebella dysfunction.
> It is clear that demyelination in the cerebellum is common, as was demonstrated in one study that found the prevalence of cerebella signs in MS patients to be as high as 70% (41). Early cerebella ataxia is suggestive of a bad prognosis.

"You need to see Dr. Roberts tomorrow," insisted Vivian. "You can't walk down the hall without bouncing off the walls. I don't think you even recognized me when I walked in."

As usual, the business had so much going on that I resisted being out of town except in an absolute emergency. I adapted to the blurred vision. My lack of coordination and balance were awkward, but they didn't stop me from doing anything. But the problem with my memory worried me. Dr. Roberts had told me that MS didn't cause problems with the mind. If not MS, then what was it?

I said to Vivian, "If you can get me an appointment, we'll go to Savannah tomorrow."

Cognitive Impairment - (cont. on page 122)

A great deal is known today about cognitive problems and MS. Even Charcot (31), the first physician to describe multiple sclerosis, in the 19th century, recognized that memory was often severely impaired and intellect damaged by the disease.

Most attempts to measure the impact of multiple sclerosis on the patient's life have concentrated on physical disabilities while ignoring or minimizing the effects of cognitive dysfunction on daily living or quality of life.

As early as 1929, Ombredane (32) found intellectual deterioration in 72% of the 50 patients in his study. He noted that "The changes were often not apparent in ordinary converse or on routine examination."

Van den Burg et al (33) in their study confirmed early cognitive impairment in patients with mild physical disability. Rao et al (34) found that there was no correlation of mental changes with duration of disease or severity of disability.

It is very unusual to find reports of no memory dysfunction in MS patients (35).

Grigsby et al (36) believed that "impaired working (short term) memory and impaired information processing systems would place MS patients at a significant disadvantage on complex and/or novel cognitive tests." They believed that the subsystems controlling the reasoning process itself would be more affected as the disease progressed. Patients often report that they can no longer keep track of two things at one time or that they often forget why they were doing a certain thing.

Speech dysfunction is not common, even in severely disabled patients (37). This substantially increases the chances that even severe dementia will pass unnoticed in casual conversation.

In a study by Grant et al (38), they concluded that "learning, short term memory, and reasoning may be impaired early in MS and are likely to be more disturbed during relapse."

Body Under Siege

More Steroids

Dr. Roberts didn't say much that encouraged me. I knew that the only treatments available for an acute attack of multiple sclerosis, in 1985, were oral steroids and ACTH, and I thought that these were only of marginal value.

Dr. Roberts agreed with my reservations and said, "We don't have anything better than oral steroids that you can take as an outpatient. I like ACTH, but the intravenous injections require hospitalization. I really don't think the long term results are much better than the Prednisone, but I will leave that decision to you."

I had no intention of wasting time in the hospital for a treatment with such iffy returns. "I think I'll pass on the ACTH," I said.

Finally, we talked about my main concern. I asked, "Why am I forgetting so much? You told me that MS did not cause any problems with the mind."

Dr. Roberts said, "I don't think MS is the culprit. You probably just have too much on your mind. I'm forgetful when I try to think about too many things at one time. Most people are. I really wouldn't worry about it too much. I am confident the problem will just disappear soon."

This didn't comfort me much. I had been under a lot of stress before without forgetting my phone number or our plant manager's name. And lately, I struggled to keep my thoughts organized. Nothing made any sense anymore. But I accepted the doctor's explanation and went about the business of New Bros., Inc.

Total Cognitive Failure

The financial pressures now were severe, but we were prepared for that. We expected cash flow problems until the next onion season, but if we could make it until then we knew we would be okay.

But we also knew that we could not handle much unexpected expense. Unfortunately, for the past year the unexpected seemed like the norm.

In early January of 1985, the unexpected did happen. Ronnie and Fletcher, for good or bad reasons, depending on perspective, chose to tell Wendell Calhoun about Glacier Foods and the errors in the financial statement. That should not have been a major problem—Wendell was our lawyer. But he was also Mr. Jordan's lawyer, and we should have seen a conflict of interest. We didn't. But I'm not going to fault Fletcher and Ronnie. They are good people. I was the architect of my own ruin and it's my job to live with that.

David and I went to Wendell's office that day for other reasons. Wendell said, "Ronnie and Fletcher left a short time ago. They told me about the errors in the financial statement. You know, this is very serious. You are a public company now and you have The Securities and Exchange Commission to deal with."

We were speechless. I think we both believed that something like this would eventually happen—that it had to happen. I had compromised my principles. I closed my eyes, hoping this would help me to focus. It didn't. I was confused, and my mind flew in fifty different directions. I knew that I had taken the wrong road, and I feared what I would find at the other end. But I could find no place to turn around.

In the past, David and I would have put our heads together and we would have reasoned through this. But this past was light-years away now, and I saw no way to travel back. We weren't together in this fight. By David's reckoning, when I insisted on overstating the inventories I lost my soul and no supernatural power could retrieve it. At a time when we needed to be together more than at any other time in our lives we were separated and isolated from each other. We had inadvertently created a vacuum, and neither of us operated well in it.

As we sat in Wendell's office his words became distant, meaningless, gibberish—as if spoken in a tongue unknown to me. The ceiling and the walls closed in and Wendell's words echoed from every angle. But all I could really hear was the deafening blast of David's silence. Words lost their meaning.

Wendell said, "Your only chance to stay out of jail is to try to appease the Jordans."

I wasn't concerned about appeasing the Jordans. I wanted to appease God. I made the wrong choice when I distributed a financial statement containing errors.

Wendell said, "I think I can solve the problem if we handle it right. The Jordans are the largest stockholders, besides you two. I spoke with Mac (Mr. Jordan's son) after Ronnie and Fletcher left. He wants both of you to transfer all of your stock to him. If you refuse, he says he will do everything he can to send you to jail."

But my concerns went much deeper than jail.

Wendell said, "And you need to call Brett Merrill and tell him not to file for bankruptcy protection; no judge will allow that now." We thought that we might need this protection to assure that we would make it to onion season.

I could not assimilate the facts and reach a logical conclusion. I sensed that there were other forces in play and that I needed help. I saw Wendell as the appointed guide. I trusted him. David had removed himself completely, and my mind rambled irrationally. Nothing made sense anymore.

When we left Wendell's office I felt as though I was in a trance. I knew we were no longer the same people. We would never be the same people again. We had metamorphosed into somebody else. Wendell knew that, too, and he knew how to take advantage of it. He had complete control of me, and I had no control of myself.

My life had reached a new low. FDR said, "I shall pursue my principles without calculating the consequences." I knew my mistake. I had calculated the consequences and compromised my principles. I betrayed God and my family.

But Mr. Jordan's son was a Christian, and he would do the right thing. He would see that we intended no harm to anyone and he would do the right thing. He would have access to all the books and he would understand. He would see the truth and he would understand and everything would be okay.

I tried to process the overload. I failed. Information poured in like a waterfall and my brain couldn't keep up. I told Wendell that we needed him to make any decisions. I delivered my stock certificates to him and David followed my lead. Within an hour, our lifetime's work ended and our lives changed forever.

Disclosure

The bond between David and me broke. The energy between us evaporated. The brother thing vanished. We were strangers. We were total strangers separated by a vast gulf of emptiness. But we still had things to do, and we had to do them together.

I couldn't think clear, and now Wendell did the driving.

"We owe an explanation to Chris Rouse," I said. Chris was a senior partner at Mauldin & Jenkins. The stock offering had depended on their work, and our failure to disclose the loss of the brined onions would cause problems for them.

I could not undo what happened, but I wanted the news to come from us. Mauldin & Jenkins operated with integrity. None of this was their fault, but I knew that they would be the deep-pocket for any lawsuits that surfaced.

David said, "I agree. Let's tell Wendell our plans and call Chris Rouse. I think we should do this in person."

I said, "We need to do the same thing with Barry Phillips."

Wendell went to Atlanta with us to see Barry Phillips. These disclosures were going to be hard, but it was the right thing to do. And it had to come from us.

The Relapse Ends—But Not in Time

In the break room, David and I embraced like brothers, and I said, "I caused this. I'm sorry. I'm so sorry." David agreed on who to blame, but I expected that. I made the plan. By now, Wendell knew that he could do whatever he wanted. No longer bound by a common goal, but rather joined by a common infamy, I knew that I had lost a brother. All direction had to come from me now, and I was navigating with a damaged compass.

Multiple sclerosis had made many changes that were obvious. Others were not so obvious. Optic neuritis had reduced my vision in one eye to 20/200 by early January, 1985. Nystagmus made it even worse. Ataxia made walking difficult.

But what MS had done to my mind dwarfed these other problems. I didn't handle problems in the same way that I once had. I didn't think through them in the same way. I made mistakes, and I accept responsibility for those mistakes. Still, MS did play a major part, and the story is incomplete if I leave that part out.

If I had known the impact that MS could have on the mind, then I could have prepared for it. Yielding to Wendell, Mr. Jordan, and his son Mac defied logic. It served nobody.

An unfortunate combination of sickness and circumstance altered many fortunes. Including, ironically, C. M. Jordan's.

A Warning About the Danger of Cognitive Impairment in MS

Dr. W. B. Matthews (45), one of the world's leading experts on multiple sclerosis and Professor Emeritus of Clinical Neurology at the University of Oxford, wrote about MS patients: "Particular care may be required when dementia occurs in otherwise relatively active patients. Difficulties at home and at work may arise from lack of emotional control or from thoughtless dispersion of the family assets."

Impaired Information Processing (See pg. 210 for More Details)

Findings of impaired information processing would likely indicate frontal lobe disturbance, which has been confirmed by several studies of MS patients (42,43,44).

Impact of Relapse on Cognitive Impairment

It has been observed by clinicians that cognitive function may worsen during a relapse and may improve during remission. This decline may occur over a short period of time and the impairment in intellectual ability may be dramatic. This is most apparent during an acute attack.

The Death of a Dream

In a few weeks, I felt normal again. But the world didn't look normal. My vision returned, the nystagmus disappeared, and I walked straight again; and I could think, reason, and remember. But I saw devastation in every direction.

Our business, our dreams, and a lifetime of work were gone. New Bros., Inc. had traded on NASDAQ at $4.50 a share. In one passing moment of disease produced cognitive dysfunction, I, and David followed, transferred nearly six million dollars worth of securities to Mr. Jordan. The financial statements would need to be corrected, but that had little to do with the intrinsic value of the company. In an instant, we went from multi-millionaires to paupers, and the business that was our dream and our life was gone.

So ended New Bros., Inc.; but not before The Vidalia Onion had become a household word. I knew that people would not remember the accomplishments. The difference between goat and hero, between loser and winner, can be no more than one decision; all the right choices are quickly forgotten. Right or wrong, the world judges everyone by his or her last act.

Regardless of what the future might bring, I knew that there would always be an emptiness—a vacuum where the dreams once lived. It was David and I who had dreamed the dreams and fought the fights. The Vidalia Onion was a vision, and it was our vision. But now it was all just a memory.

CHAPTER 6

Starting Over

* Struggling with Hate 111
* The Why Me Story 111
* Where to from Here? 112
* Back to School 113
* The First Quarter at UGA 115
* Adjusting to College Life 117

Struggling with Hate

I saw little purpose in life now. MS raced forward at a logarithmic rate. One relapse ended everything I had hoped for and had invested my life in. My mind was paralyzed. Over and over I said, "Oh, God, what have I done?" I begged for another chance, but I found none.

The depression crushed me. On a Sunday afternoon, in May of 1985, I walked outside with a pistol in my hand. I had no way to support my family. Multiple sclerosis would eventually cripple me, and I had no way to finance the treatment of a disease this costly. When I lost the business, my health and disability insurance went with it.

I knew that Vivian wanted more out of life than to be a nursemaid to a disabled person, and I wanted more for her; she deserved more. My material worth now consisted of a life insurance policy and a house I could no longer afford.

But I quickly learned that wanting to die and actually holding a gun to your head and pulling the trigger are two very different things. I remembered seemingly catastrophic events of the past that loomed like giants for a short time and then vanished. I felt that, if I could survive, the doomsday mentality would disappear eventually, and I would look back on this day and laugh at my mania. I knew that time might bring healing instead of more decay.

I was tired of fighting life, but I could not end it in this way. I laid the gun down and hysterically bludgeoned a pine tree until blood gushed from my knuckles.

I buried my head in the grass and wept. I cried for my wasted past. I cried for the lives broken by my poor judgment. I cried for the brother I had lost. And I cried because I was tired—tired of hating and tired of regretting. I saw uncertainty in every direction. In my mind, I said over and over to God, to myself, to Vivian, to David, to my mother—I'm sorry. I'm so sorry.

The Why Me Story

Now that the business was gone I quickly realized just how integrated my life had been with New Bros., Inc. Everything looked purposeless. Suddenly, I had plenty of time to feel sorry for myself, and I had little trouble finding fuel for the ovens of self-pity. I knew that others in the world had suffered major losses, and many had chronic, incurable diseases, but the knowledge of shared misery didn't help.

In addition to the business, I lost my livelihood, my identity, my self-esteem, and my emotional escape from the constant fears intrinsic to life with multiple sclerosis. I understood none of this. With only one in a thousand people getting multiple sclerosis, why did God choose me?

I sat for hours in troubled contemplation of a life gone awry. I asked, "Why me?"

But with deeper analysis, I realized that I was asking the wrong question. Why should I be exempt from tragedy? Then I asked, "Why not me?" And I began the search for a way out.

Where to from Here?

After the loss of New Bros., Inc., I had a huge vacuum in my life to fill. From age 19, I had known no other life. The business had occupied every day from early morning to late night, with exceptions that I could count on one hand. It had sustained my spirit. It made challenge a way of life. But now a vacuum existed where challenge once lived.

A rare relationship existed between my brother and me. I had lost that, too. But I was determined not to throw away the rest of my life mourning the loss.

David and I made the city of Vidalia known to the world, but those days for us were over. I knew that I had to let the past remain in the past and I had to concentrate on the future. I also knew that starting a new life in Vidalia would be difficult, if not impossible. There, too many memories held the power to cripple me emotionally.

The prospect of starting a new life in another world terrified me. But no future for Vivian and me existed in Vidalia anymore. I reminded myself that 32 was not old, and the possibilities for a new life were only limited by my willingness to try. I focused on the inspirational one-liners that almost everyone grew up on— "You can do anything and be anything if you try hard enough."

I believed the premise, but I knew that logical limitations fostered pragmatic restrictions. My brain quickly reminded me that I had MS, and I knew that this disease had played a very important part in the loss of the business. I didn't know what that part was, yet, but I intended to find out.

I knew now that multiple sclerosis was a much more formidable foe than I had at first imagined. Nevertheless, I didn't want to just sit on the sidelines while it destroyed me. I wanted to play on the offense—if I could not quit the game. I had other dreams before The Onion. The loss of New Bros., Inc. didn't have to be the end. Maybe it was never meant to be the end. Maybe it was meant to be a new beginning, and all I had to do was to believe it.

I backtracked to age 18 and started where I had left off. I said to Vivian, "I want to finish school now." After I graduated from high school, I went to Georgia Southern University for one year. Then we got married. I had always intended to go back to school, but after Daddy's second heart attack I got too deeply involved in the business to think about that anymore.

Besides, I fell in love with the business and had no desire to do anything else. Vivian always wanted me to go back to school. She never liked the business; she saw it as competition for my time, and the business usually won. Vivian said, "You know how I feel about it. I think a thirteen year break is long enough."

I had forgotten how much I liked school. The years had not dampened my appetite for knowledge. But the tragic loss of the business had redirected my interest. MS had turned my life upside down. I wanted to understand the disease. I wanted to be a real participant in the fight. I wanted to be a doctor, but at 32 I considered myself too old for that.

All of my friends and classmates from high school were set in their lives by now. A couple were doctors. One or two were lawyers. Most worked at the power plant, or had a job with the government or a large corporation.

But most of them were content with their position in life, just as I had been content with mine.

The hope of the future overcame the uncertainties; I became intoxicated with thoughts about Athens and the University of Georgia, and a medical school somewhere out there that I dreamed of attending one day. MS blackened the sky, but I refused to tarnish these images with fears of tragedies that might never be.

Still, I feared multiple sclerosis. I loosely clutched the eternal optimist philosophy, but I knew that the odds of the disease getting much worse were near 100%. Progression is its nature.

Nevertheless, I needed to carve out a new niche for my life. I had never been afraid of risk, and I didn't plan to pick-up the habit now. The tragic loss of New Bros., Inc. extinguished any flames that still flickered within me concerning business. My interest turned toward science. I wanted to learn all that I could about multiple sclerosis. I read books on immunology and neurological diseases. I asked questions.

I was soon addicted to the subject. I refused to voluntarily limit my future because of my age, or because I had MS. The thought of returning to college and the hope of medical school filled the future with promise again.

Back to School

I needed three more years of undergraduate school to finish my microbiology degree. I needed two more years before an application to medical school would be taken serious. I had everything against me. I was probably too old, I had multiple sclerosis, and we had no money. But I was determined to try.

The loss of New Bros., Inc., and the way it happened, had shaken my confidence. I knew that something beyond my control had been in play. The memory problems disappeared, just as Dr. Roberts had said they would, but I needed an academic challenge to convince me that I still had the ability to handle school. I enrolled in two classes at Georgia Southern University, fifty miles from Vidalia.

When the quarter ended, I still had my 4.0 GPA and felt ready to tackle any academic challenge thrown at me. However, I knew that we could not live in Vidalia. To succeed in another life, the break from Vidalia needed speed and completion; The Medical College of Georgia, in Augusta, looked like my best hope, and I had been told that MCG had a slight predisposition for graduates from The University of Georgia. Anyway, I wanted to major in microbiology, and, in 1986, Georgia Southern didn't offer a degree in microbiology.

But I needed some assurance that my new ambition was a real possibility, and not a fabrication of an irrational mind, or perhaps an inappropriate response to a mid-life crisis—or did 33 qualify for that designation? I decided to visit The Medical College of Georgia campus in Augusta. I attended a gross anatomy lecture with Vivian's cousin (now Dr. Stanley Morgan), a first year medical student, then, at MCG.

"I don't think your age is a factor," Stanley said. "There are others here in there thirties."

I met several students older than me. But I saw an obvious difference; most of the non-traditional medical students—anyone over 30, by my definition—came to MCG with a science background that went beyond undergraduate school. A few had completed other advanced degrees—some even with a Ph.D. But I had only one year of college, with no background in science.

Nevertheless, the academic challenge didn't scare me. Multiple sclerosis did. I lost a business because I had MS, but I refused to let the rest of my life be defined by that one failure.

At MCG, I spoke with Dr. Logan, the Assistant Director of Admissions. "Age might be a factor at some point," she said. "But you haven't reached that point yet."

I developed an almost cavalier certainty that I would complete a degree in science at the University of Georgia and that a medical school somewhere would accept me.

Now it all depended on Vivian. I had to know that she really wanted this, too. We both had grown up around Vidalia. We had built our home there, just as our parents had before us. Our lives were tied in every way to that community. Leaving it would not be easy. The final decision had to be Vivian's.

I asked, "Can you handle leaving your family and everything you're familiar with?" Vivian was a strong person, much stronger than she or I ever knew. If she was against the move, I failed to read it.

She said, "We have no future here anymore. If this is what you want, then it is what I want. Neither of us planned for life to turn out this way, but we have to play the cards we are dealt. Yes, I am ready to go."

The First Quarter at UGA

Soon we moved to Athens and began the business of starting a new life. It wasn't easy, and more than one ghost from Vidalia came along to make sure we didn't forget our past. The uncertainty about the future made the transition difficult. I was not as naive as many in my family thought; I knew that getting into medical school with all that I had going against me was a long shot.

The first day of class was like a journey through time. Students of non-traditional age were not rare at UGA, but I quickly discovered that they were very rare in the science department. Most of my classmates came straight out of high school. Still, I made friends quickly, but not close friends. Our differences went beyond age; no common ground existed in our experiences.

Nevertheless, I enjoyed the new life. I had returned to a younger day, but with the advantage of having all the experiences that life had so abundantly provided me.

David and I had averaged 100-hour weeks for most of our years in business, so our time spent building The Onion equaled thirty years of work for the average person. And the experiences fate gave us exceeded the number that, I think, comes from two or three average lifetimes. Anyway, I concluded that it was my lifestyle since age 19 that now made me feel much older than I actually was.

"What are you taking?" Vivian asked at the end of my first registration.

"Physics 127, biology 102, and math 254," I said. "I want a difficult load. If I can't handle it, now is the time to find out."

MS caused no specific limitations at first. An awkwardness in my movements bothered me, but had little effect on my academic performance. At first I tried to hide the fact that I had MS. My age made me self-conscious, and I resisted adding physical disability to the list of differences between me and the other students.

Although my vision had improved, it still stood as the most immediate threat to my success at UGA. I sat near the front in all my classes, but I still couldn't read what the instructor put on the board. Fortunately, taping the lectures usually sufficed, and soon a select few knew that I couldn't see well, and they usually knew when I needed help without me asking.

Refunds will be made at the end of a quarter. No refunds for reduction in course load after the drop/add period are allowed unless such reduction is the fault of the University.

The following are not entitled to any refund of fees paid: students who withdraw after a period of four weeks has elapsed from the scheduled registration date; students suspended for disciplinary reasons; students who leave the University when disciplinary action is pending, or students who do not formally withdraw.

Student Financial Aid

Students desiring information regarding student financial aid should write the Office of Student Financial Aid, 220 Academic Building, University of Georgia, Athens, GA 30602 or call (404) 542-6147 and ask for a general counselor.

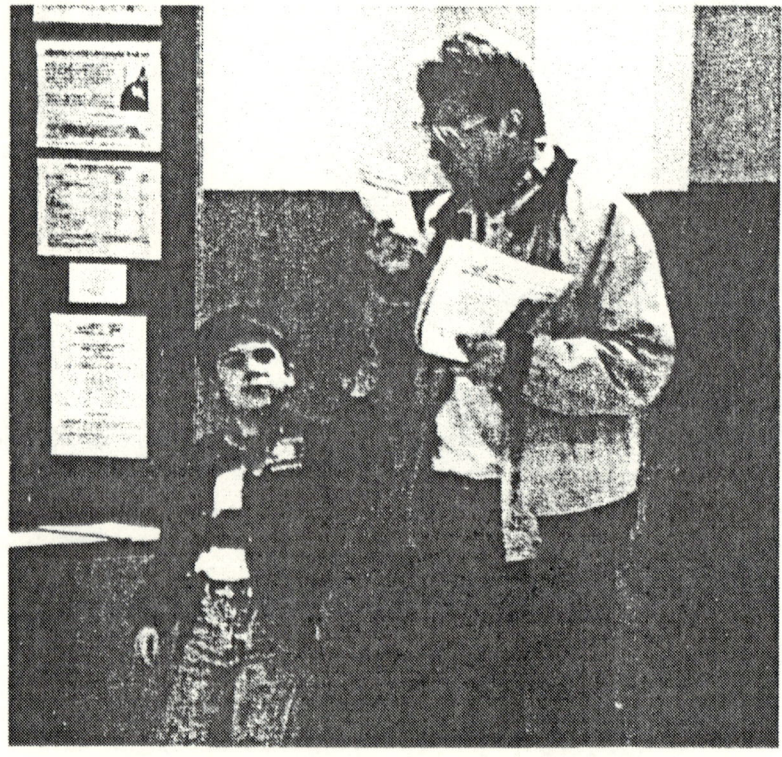

**First registration at UGA Danny and Swain
Article out of UGA catalog.**

The fingertips of my left hand had little feeling and this made me particularly clumsy in the labs—holding test tubes in chemistry lab was especially tricky. I also had trouble differentiating colors. Color is a common identifying characteristic in the chemistry lab; fortunately, the didactic was relatively easy, and we usually worked in pairs.

At the end of the first quarter, I still had a 4.0. I felt that the future held formidable problems, but I was finally confident that they would not be intellectual.

(When I reread the last paragraph, I realized that it made me come across as arrogant and perhaps a little conceited. That is not my intent, as I am confident that I am neither the former nor the latter. I hope the reader will not misinterpret my comments as too cavalier, but this information is needed to establish the setting for future events.)

Adjusting to College Life

It's human nature, I think, to want to be like the crowd that you're around—to conform, to be part of the group. I didn't want to be identified as one of the brothers who started the Vidalia Onion. But, likewise, I didn't want to be the pre-med with multiple sclerosis. I just wanted to be one of the many science majors struggling to get into medical school.

Eventually, I overcame my self-consciousness and concentrated on what I came to the University of Georgia for. Nothing really mattered except getting into medical school.

Jane Barrett, a freckled-faced coed right out of high school, sat next to me in chemistry. Her energy and love of life seemed boundless. Jane said, "Danny, you remind me of my big brother. He takes everything so-o-o-o serious. Loosen up. Let's go get a Coke after class."

Jane made the transition to college a little easier. She was easy to talk to, and soon we were both comfortable sharing each other's problems. I was like a big brother to her, and I wanted it that way. Time was critical to me, and being married at the University of Georgia had its advantages; and being married to Vivian made simple flirtations a one-sided matter.

By the beginning of my junior year, I felt good about my chances of being accepted at one of the medical schools. Age didn't seem to be the negative it once was. Ten years earlier, a thirty-five year old man didn't have much of a chance. MS worried me more than age. It takes a lot of money to educate a doctor and I feared that no medical school would take a chance on a person who had multiple sclerosis. But I felt my chances were better than average as long as I maintained a 4.0 GPA, and, thus far, that had been surprisingly easy to do.

Vivian started a new job at a local bank. Swain started pre-school at Athens Christian. I studied. A strange normalcy developed.

CHAPTER 7

The Battle Rages

* The Reading for the Blind Program 120
* MS Murders the Mind—Circumstantial Evidence Mounts 121
* The Application and the Interview 124
* The Letter of Acceptance 125
* The Guilty Verdict 127
* The Struggle to Graduate 130
* MCG Accepts Me as a Non-Degree Student 131
* Nystagmus 131
* Preparing for the Battle with Vision in Med-School 132

Danny S. New

The Reading for the Blind Program

My first two years at UGA went so smoothly that I almost forgot that I had MS. I didn't see very well. I was clumsy in my movements. I had a little trouble walking straight. And I had a numbness in my fingertips. But I had little trouble compensating for these problems. Generally, my condition hadn't deteriorated after coming to UGA. Then, early in my senior year this changed.

In the fall of 1988 my eyesight took a dive. Reading was difficult and slow. I couldn't see detail in a microscope. My balance worsened, and I could no longer hide the fact that I had a problem. But I still resisted putting a name to it; having MS didn't embarrass me, but everyone knew I was pre-med and I felt foolish saying I wanted to go to medical school and at the same time acknowledging that I had a serious disability. On the surface, the two seemed incompatible. I avoided the subject when I could, but that got harder to do.

John, a physics major and fellow pre-med student, became a good friend. We were lab partners in Physics 127 and Physics 128. John was one of the few people at UGA who knew I had MS. He knew that I could not see well, but now the problem had worsened. I couldn't read the lab manual. I struggled in the lab.

John said, "Danny, is there anything the doctors can do? Jane Barrett asked me that yesterday. She said you seemed unusually depressed."

I said, "I saw a neurologist here in Athens yesterday. He prescribed prednisone. I hope it works fast. I'm really getting behind. Studying with a magnifying glass is slow."

John said, "You know, UGA has a program called Reading for the Blind. They set it up to help visually impaired students. I know from working with you in the lab that some of these students can see better than you can. I know, because I do volunteer reading for the program. I wish you would go talk to them. It might make the difference in graduating or not graduating."

I wasn't blind, but MS had impaired my vision enough to qualify me for this program, and I realized that John was right—without help, I probably would not graduate; medical school appeared more and more iffy.

In the Reading for the Blind program, readers tape record the portions of the text covered in class. Students familiar with the terminology in a particular course did the reading.

Trying to learn by listening to a sequential tape was tough, but I figured out little aids to this new kind of studying. I rewrote key words and important remarks in large print in my notes. I knew about Visual aids, such as video-magnifiers, but I couldn't afford them.

MS Murders the Mind—Circumstantial Evidence Mounts

By Christmas, 1988, my vision had stabilized, but it had not improved. Time became invaluable.

To take some of the pressure off, I withdrew from Latin 101. This meant summer school in order to finish my language sequence if any of the medical schools I had applied to accepted me. But I didn't have a choice; there wasn't enough time.

Although my poor vision caused plenty of problems, another symptom overshadowed it. For the first time since leaving Vidalia, I recognized problems with my memory. I had trouble memorizing new information. Things I once learned by reading or hearing it in lecture, I now had to repeat many times—and even then I usually forgot it by the next day.

In Vidalia, I had accepted, though I never really believed it, that "too much on my mind" caused my memory problems. But that didn't cause it. Multiple sclerosis did. I lost a business in 1985 because of this. I feared what might be coming, now.

I had no information about MS causing cognitive problems, and no doctor had told me, but something deep down did. I had mentally changed into a different person again. For the second time, cognitive problems appeared concurrently with the worsening of other symptoms. The empirical evidence for indicting MS mounted.

Cognitive Impairment - Part 2

In a study of cognitive impairment in early-onset MS, Laura Bracco et al (46) found that MS patients with a mean duration of disease of only 1.58 years and low-level neurological disabilities showed defects in verbal memory and abstract reasoning compared to normal subjects. Their conclusion was that cognitive and neurological deficits do not develop in parallel. They also observed that, "the extent of intellectual decline...proved to be an important independent predictor of handicap in work and social activities..." Their findings highlight the role of cognitive deficits in MS on everyday life.

Cognitive changes in MS have sometimes been described as a presenting symptom (47, 48, 49). A decrease in word fluency has often been observed (50, 51, 52). Beatty et al (53) concluded that the cognitive outlook for an MS patient cannot be predicted by the course of the disease (primary or secondary progressive or relapsing/remitting) and duration of disease or from degree of disability. But it is predictable that a patient with severe damage to the spinal cord, and the expected severe motor dysfunction, might be spared severe cognitive problems, which would be expected from cerebral disease.

Today it is accepted that cognitive impairment is common in MS. Peyser et al (54) found evidence of intellectual deterioration in 55% of their patients. They too found that dementia was often hard to detect on routine neurological examination.

Rao et al (55) found that 40% of MS patients subjected to a battery of neuropsychological tests showed evidence of cognitive dysfunction and these deficits had an adverse effect on daily living (56). This is not related to disease duration (57) or to degree of physical disability (58) but has a strong correlation with lesion load as seen on MRI (59).

New lesions detected on MRI are not always correlated with new symptoms or changes in old ones. It has been suggested that these clinically "silent" lesions result in cognitive impairment (60). It is therefore predictable that treatments impacting total lesion load might also affect cognitive impairment.

Since spinal cord disease can only result in physical

manifestations and cannot result in cognitive changes, Rao has suggested that cognition may be a sensitive indicator of brain pathology.

More serial MRI studies to correlate clinically silent lesions as determined by MRI and increases in cognitive impairment are needed. It is very possible, and probably likely, that changes in brain lesion load can explain changes in cognitive function.

It has been reported that chronic progressive patients, because of demyelinating lesions in the prefrontal cortex, are likely to lose their capacity to actively control their information processing ability (61, 62). This may result in dramatic changes in behavior.

The Application and the Interview

Even with all the question marks, I went forward—clinging to the belief that I would be accepted to one of the three medical schools I had applied to. The Medical College of Georgia in Augusta topped the list, but I also applied to Bowman Gray in North Carolina and The University of Alabama in Birmingham.

After submitting the application, the next step, for the lucky few who have a next step, is the interview. The pre-med advisor at UGA used a bulletin board in the science library to display the names of students invited for interviews, and other announcements.

On a frigid morning in January of 1989, I walked toward the bulletin board—more out of habit than anticipation. Jane Barrett skipped toward me with a glow on her face that could only mean good news for her. "Danny, we've both been invited for interviews at MCG. It's scary to be this close."

It was especially scary for me. Decent MCAT scores, a 4.0 GPA, and good references from five of the faculty at UGA got me to this point. But I knew that I had changed. It was as though someone had transplanted another person's brain into my head, and this new brain was damaged.

I expected to do okay at the interviews, and now I even thought I would be accepted at MCG, but the substantial cognitive and visual problems made me question my ability to carry a heavy enough load to graduate by summer quarter.

On February 3, 1989, Vivian and I left for MCG and the all-important interviews. Because of its brief nature, I knew that this evaluation was a measure of first impressions. The applicants interviewed would have no opportunity for a second impression, and these first impressions could mean the difference in going to medical school and not going.

I had one major personal dilemma to resolve before the interview. If I told them that I had multiple sclerosis, I feared their reaction. I had no legal obligation to disclose it, but I felt I should. Besides, these were doctors, and they could see that I had a physical problem. They couldn't see my visual problems or know about the cognitive impairment, but they would see my awkwardness and unnatural gait. I decided that I wanted everything out in the open on this, regardless of what happened.

At MCG, two different people on the admissions committee conducted separate interviews. I had my first interview with Dr. Joplin, a MD/Ph.D. with a doctorate degree in physics and a medical degree. Dr. Joplin said, "Danny, why do you want to be a doctor?" I think they always asked a few stock questions that everyone expected; this was one of them.

Many, if not most, who make it to medical school claim some lifelong passion to be a doctor, as if they were conceived with the ambition in place. I could not make that claim. On the contrary, I was well established in life with many years behind me before this impression appeared.

I said, "I know I am supposed to say that from my childhood I always wanted to be a doctor, but that isn't true. I have no stories about doctor's kits at Christmas, or even an early interest in science. But in 1980, doctors told me that I had multiple sclerosis. It changed my life drastically. I wanted to know everything I could about the disease, and medical school was the place to learn. And now for my altruistic plug, I truly feel compassion for people with MS and other chronic diseases, and maybe my personal experience with it will give me insights other doctors might not have."

Dr. Joplin said, "We knew that you had MS when we invited you for the interview. With your academic record and your references, that will not keep you out of MCG. Some on the admissions committee might even look at it as a positive thing. We want a well-diversified student body. You have a tally of experiences, because of MS and because of your business background, that most of the applicant pool lacks. I can't say that you will be accepted, but if you're not, I can tell you that it won't be because you have MS."

The Letter of Acceptance

One by one, in early February, letters of acceptance started showing up for a lucky few in my class. By early March I started to worry. If I didn't receive a letter of acceptance within a couple of weeks I knew that I probably wouldn't be getting one.

On March 31, 1989, I met the postman at the mailbox. This had become a daily ritual, but now it held a new urgency. With each passing day, I knew that my chances declined. The loss of the business and everything we had in Vidalia, and the burden of having multiple sclerosis, and the pressure of moving my family to Athens, needed a reason. And it looked like there might not be one. But on this day a letter came from MCG; but I feared a letter of regret.

My heart pounded as I walked back to the house. Even if I opened it, I couldn't see good enough to read what it said. I gave the letter to Vivian and sat down. "It is my pleasure, upon the recommendation of the Admissions Committee of the School of Medicine, to offer you a place in the 1989 Entering Class of the School of Medicine," Vivian read.

Suddenly, all the problems the world had given us faded into insignificance. Vivian's face glowed. She was happy for me. I was happy for her. For the moment, the future showed nothing ugly.

Danny S. New

School of Medicine
Office of the Dean

March 30, 1989

Mr. Danny Swain New
190 Lakeover Drive
Athens, Georgia 30607

Dear Mr. New:

It is my pleasure, upon the recommendation of the Admissions Committee of the School of Medicine, to offer you a place in the 1989 Entering Class of the School of Medicine.

It is important that you carefully read the enclosed information. If you wish to accept this position in our 1989 Entering Class, you must sign the enclosed acceptance form and return this form in the self-addressed envelope. Failure to comply with the requirements stated in the acceptance form and the enclosed documents will result in reconsideration of your application and may result in the withdrawal of your acceptance.

All of us at the Medical College of Georgia congratulate you and look forward to having you join our student body.

Sincerely,

Charles H. Wray, M.D.
Interim Dean

CHW:ec
Enclosures

Augusta, Georgia 30912-4750 (404) 721-2231
An Affirmative Action/Equal Opportunity Educational Institution

The letter of Acceptance to Medical College of Georgia

The Guilty Verdict

My MCG acceptance rekindled dying flames, but it hadn't changed the facts any. MS had drastically diminished any intellectual abilities that I might have once had. When I needed directory assistance to get my own phone number, I knew the problem was substantial. I feared that I faced an omen of things to come.

My short-term memory disappeared. Learning new information became more difficult than I ever imagined possible. The load I took in the spring of '89 demanded less than any schedule since I had started back to school three years earlier, but I still had problems. I remembered things I learned in high school, 20 years earlier, easier than I could things I learned, or tried to learn, the week before.

MS affected my long-term memory, too, but not as much as my short-term memory. I didn't understand the changes. I needed more information to navigate in this new world. I knew that whatever happened four years earlier when I lost my business was happening again.

I started searching for the answer. Without a solution, my acceptance to medical school meant nothing. Dr. Roberts had told me that MS didn't affect the mind—and I had no reason to doubt him. But now I did doubt him.

I contacted The National Multiple Sclerosis Society in New York. "Yes, MS can cause cognitive problems. It isn't that rare."

> ## Short Term vs Long Term Memory
>
> Both short term and long term memory appear to be impacted in patients with MS. Litvan et al (93) found impairment of verbal short-term memory. In this study, MS patients presented with a list of 5 syllable words had greater difficulty than controls in recalling words. This impairment was more pronounced for words near the end of the list, suggesting that the recency effect was not as strong in the patients as it was in controls.
>
> In their study, Ruchkin et al (94, 95) found that, relative to controls, MS patients were significantly slower on tests which required rapid information processing. The patients had longer reaction times and made more errors than controls. The study also showed that the performance of MS patients on verbal short-term memory tasks was impaired. They showed that verbal-phonological short-term memory was more vulnerable to disruption by MS than Visuo-spatial short-term memory.
>
> Verbal short-term memory impairment may be explained by the fact that the language cortex is in the posterior part of the brain and the speech production cortex is in the anterior part of the brain (96, 97). The distance between the regions means that the fibers involved are relatively long and thus are particularly susceptible to MS plaques.

In fact, a Society grantee is doing research on that very subject. He recently published an article called Cognitive Problems and MS in *Inside MS*, a publication of the NMSS."

I received this periodical, but I hadn't read it lately. I could read with a strong magnifier, but the nystagmus made it extremely time consuming. But I found this article and read it twice. It described me perfectly.

Current information convinced me that medicine had overlooked, or ignored, cognitive dysfunction in multiple sclerosis for a long time. But now there were a lot of researchers studying the effects of MS on the mind. Dr. Rao et. al. (55) reported that 40% of MS patients subjected to a battery of neuropsychological tests showed evidence of cognitive dysfunction. Van den Burg et. al. (221) believed that the cognitive trouble in MS was in learning and in recall.

Learning that multiple sclerosis caused cognitive problems didn't surprise me. In fact, learning that it didn't would have. It is inconceivable to think that scar tissue and active plaques can be scattered through your brain with no cognitive consequences.

I went to one of the local MS Society meetings in search of others who had experienced this problem. If fifty percent of people with MS have some degree of cognitive impairment, I figured it would be easy to find someone. It was.

I struck up a conversation with Marie Jansen and her husband Robert. After a few minutes, I said to Marie, "Have you had any memory problems, or noticed any changes in your judgment?"

Robert answered for her. "She sure has. Marie can't make it through the day without a notepad."

Marie said, "Robert's right. When the doctors diagnosed me four years ago, the neurologist said to Robert, 'Don't worry. It doesn't affect the mind.' What an idiot. Robert thought I just didn't care enough to try anymore. We are both lawyers and work together in our private practice. Finally, we attended a workshop by more knowledgeable neuros. They told us that cognitive impairment is very common in MS. The cognitive and emotional problems never seem to end. I have to concentrate on one thing at a time. No more juggling ten crises at once."

I asked, "Have you found anything that helps?"

Marie said, "I take Cylert. That helps me focus a little better. I've also learned to slow down when I'm talking. I have to consciously think about the words."

Soon, Vail Kinsley, a man of 32 who had been listening to our conversation, joined us. Vail said, "I wouldn't even have known that I had any cognitive problems if it hadn't been for my assistant's girlfriend teasing me. I mean, I knew it, but I thought it was just my imagination. JoAnn's kidding about me losing my train of thought and substituting words that weren't even close to what I meant to say suggested that it might not be my imagination.

"When I finally went to the doctor, he noticed other problems too. I had poor balance for one thing. Six months later my doctor told me that I had multiple sclerosis. I still sound like an idiot sometimes, and I forget everything unless I write it down."

If I had not chosen this academic environment, where an intellectual measurement is almost a daily occurrence, I might have explained the problem away, or blamed it on preoccupation as Dr. Roberts did in 1985. But now I knew.

It was obvious, too, that this aspect of the disease followed the typical pattern of relapse and remission that is usually the case with MS. At least I still had the hope of a partial remission. But it also meant that there would probably be more relapses, with the problem getting progressively worse.

The Struggle to Graduate

I only had two quarters left to take the classes needed to graduate, and my acceptance to MCG was contingent on me receiving a Bachelor of Science degree from UGA. By the middle of spring quarter, I knew that I couldn't handle a full load, unless a remission started soon.

A true dilemma faced me; if I withdrew from any classes I would not have enough hours to graduate before medical school started. My grades could drop some without a major problem, but if they dropped much MCG could withdraw my acceptance. My inability to start in the fall would necessitate a reapplication, and I would relive the pressure of "hoping" to get accepted.

For now I had one priority—to be in the 1989 medical school class at MCG. I would worry later about staying there. Age and disease made waiting another year unimaginable. MS is progressive and would probably get worse, and right now I had a place in the 1989 class.

Nevertheless, I knew that starting with the 1989 class was not my only problem; the cognitive and visual problems had not gone away, and I knew they might even get worse. They probably would get worse. MS works that way.

Vision worried me less than the cognitive problems, but the combination might be insurmountable in med school. Nevertheless, I stayed optimistic and accepted my problems and concentrated on going forward. That was my deal with life when I left Vidalia.

The MS landscape changes unpredictably, making adjustment difficult. I heard about one medical school in the North that graduated a totally blind student. But he knew what he had to adjust to. With MS, you mentally have to be prepared for blindness this week, paralysis next week, and an assorted array of intellectual impairments the next; or they might all come at one time, and with one or more of dozens of accomplices.

To make matters worse, I would not have the benefit of The Reading for the Blind program at MCG. But on the lighter side, finding the money to buy visual aids would be easier in medical school than it was in undergraduate school.

But I needed to graduate before the other problems even came into play. To make it at MCG, I knew my memory had to improve; and I didn't know that it would. Nevertheless, I had come too far, and I wasn't about to stop then. Moreover, I sensed a remission starting. My vision had improved a little; maybe my memory would, too.

Through the midpoint of spring quarter, I struggled with 20 hours of classes. Soon, I knew that I couldn't carry that load in that condition. But dropping a class would necessitate taking 25 hours in the summer to graduate. I could only do that if a remission occurred, and occurred soon.

A make or break decision faced me. Nobody could solve this problem for me, but I needed a sounding board. Vivian listened and said, "It doesn't seem so complicated to me. If you keep all of your classes, and your grades drop, you will jeopardize your spot in this year's class and diminish your chances of being accepted next year, if you have to reapply. If you withdraw from a class now, there is always the hope that a remission will occur before summer quarter, and then you can take 25 hours of classes and still graduate."

I took Vivian's advice. The next day I withdrew from one of my classes—and prayed for a miracle.

MCG Accepts Me as a Non-Degree Student

No miracle came. Spring quarter was a total disaster. Even after withdrawing from physics, I still made a C in medical microbiology and a B in Latin. These were my first grades below an "A." Now the problem seemed insurmountable.

I would have to take 25 hours summer quarter to graduate. I could have done that a year earlier, but not now. I started taking a high dose of Prednisone, hoping that it would help. It didn't. I knew now that graduating before medical school started was impossible.

I reluctantly called Dr. Logan, the Associate Dean for Admissions at the Medical College of Georgia. I explained that medical problems would prevent me from graduating summer quarter. I knew that MCG could accept a non-degree student, and had on extremely rare occasions.

Somewhere between a plead and a question, I said, "Dr. Logan, I will only lack 10 hours finishing my degree. Every course that MCG requires will be completed. I spoke with Dr. Roth, the head of the microbiology department at UGA, and he said that UGA would give me my Bachelor of Science Degree in microbiology after I complete my first year at MCG. Will MCG accept me as a non-degree student and allow me to start this fall?"

After a moment, Dr. Logan said, "It is rare for us to allow anyone to begin classes before they complete their undergraduate work. There are provisions for doing that, but I will need to consult with other members of the admissions committee. Don't get your hopes up. It isn't done very often."

In a few days, I received a phone call. "Danny, this is Dr. Logan. MCG is accepting you as a non-degree student. Good luck with your classes this summer and we'll see you at orientation in August."

Nystagmus

While still reveling over MCG's decision, a second episode of nystagmus began. Now, in addition to blurred vision, everything jerked back and forth wildly.

Nystagmus is very common in multiple sclerosis. A lesion within the brainstem causes a constant jerking of the eye. Nystagmus magnified the adverse effects of optic neuritis. Now, reading was even more difficult.

Preparing for the Battle with Vision in Med-School

The summer ended without any remission of the cognitive problems. My vision was marginally better, but still impaired. I found nothing that would improve my memory, but I did find visual aids that might be invaluable in medical school.

At MCG, I would not have anyone to record the text, or the volumes of handouts, or the mass of class-notes we would need to learn. Besides, I quickly discovered that, even if the text were recorded, there would not be enough time to study from sequential tapes, where quick reference is virtually impossible. I decided to see a low vision expert in Atlanta before classes started.

Dr. Wesley had devoted his optometry career to the treatment of people with low vision. He took his specialty very seriously and had an extremely high level of competence in the field.

With the inquisitive style of an investigative reporter, Dr. Wesley said, "Tell me something about your lifestyle—your hobbies, your job, the things in life that interest you. Knowing this can tell me a lot about what visual aids might be appropriate. The needs of an astronomer are different from the needs of an accountant."

I immediately felt that I was in the presence of a person who could help with my visual problems. I said, "My interests are somewhat different from what you might imagine." I explained that I had multiple sclerosis, and my visual impairment resulted from this. Then I explained my present concern. "I start medical school at The Medical College of Georgia in about two weeks. I will not have the luxury of spending the extra time needed to read with a hand-held magnifier. But I worry more about the labs. I really don't know what to expect in gross anatomy, but I know that small structures, such as nerves, veins, and arteries, will be difficult for me to see. Histology requires the use of a microscope. Although I majored in microbiology, and I needed to use a microscope a lot, it amazed me how little it affected the grade. I got through most of the classes by knowing the didactic information alone. But medical school will not be that way. I will have to SEE what I'm looking at."

Dr. Wesley said, "I have equipment that will help."

He suggested a hand-held, prescription, monocular, telescopic lens to help in the anatomy lab. Binocular eyeglasses with telescopic lens would have been better, but I could not afford them.

For reading, he recommended a video magnifier. This system had two drawbacks. First, it would wreck my budget. But even more problematic, it was not portable. I needed something I could use in class, library, or lab. I needed to read an atlas of anatomy at the same time that I studied a cadaver.

Financial restraints still restricted me. I came away with hand held magnifiers and a monocular telescopic lens. But these did help, and now I was aware of available equipment, if my financial situation improved.

CHAPTER 8

Medical School—More Than a Dream

* Orientation 135
* Classes Begin 135

Orientation

Medical school started with orientation in late August, 1989. The tone of this assembly was somewhere between very slight intimidation and very strong inspiration. The 1989 freshman class at MCG had 180 students

"You represent the best of the best," stated the keynote speaker. "Still, you will not all graduate. Some of you will decide that you do not like medicine. Others will be unable to handle the academic pressure. A few will be compelled to quit for personal reasons. But for those of you who complete the program and become doctors, the emotional rewards from your chosen profession will be beyond compare."

Orientation at MCG occurred almost completely atop a pedestal. Some never came down, but most were violently thrown off within a few days. Before orientation was over, we all felt invincible. No one questioned on this day that from our ranks would be found the solution to every medical enigma that continued to perplex man. I almost forgot that I had MS, and even refused to consider that I might be one of the few that would be "compelled to quit for personal reasons."

Between speakers, Kevin, a fellow student from UGA, said, "We have about an hour before the next speaker. Let's go to the cafeteria and grab a sandwich." Kevin went to UGA with me, but he was not a microbiology major and we had had only a couple of classes together.

"Sure," I said. "Do you know where the cafeteria is?" We walked across the campus and sat at a table with several other "inductees." My balance was not as bad now as it had been a couple of months before, so I wasn't using a cane to walk. But I was wobbly and awkward, but still determined not to initiate a conversation with anyone about my condition. Not yet anyway.

During lunch, Julie Partin said, "I'm not sure if we're supposed to be intimidated or inspired by these speeches. One speaker puts us on top of a pedestal and the next one kicks us off."

If I was on a pedestal, I didn't have very good footing. I knew that finishing at MCG was going to be an uphill battle for me.

Classes Begin

The first week of classes made the "best of the best" syndrome disappear for almost everyone. The discovery of how little we all knew was a very humbling experience, and I don't think that anyone was spared this trauma.

The visual problems were both emotional and functional in this new setting. At UGA, I eventually arrived at a point where it really didn't bother me for others to know that I had MS. But at MCG I kept this within a pretty tight circle, at first.

My age made me a little different, but as much as possible I wanted to just fit into the crowd. That wasn't possible. Something as routine as walking down the hall was an unpleasant task. Not only did I have an unusual gait, but also I couldn't recognize anyone I walked by, and I couldn't read anything that was written on the board—and there was a lot written on the board. Fortunately, the freshman class had note-takers that took lecture notes and distributed these to the class. This relieved some of the pressure.

CHAPTER 9

Gross Anatomy

* Dissecting the Human Body 138
* My Dissecting Team 139
* Disclosing My Problem to the Team 139
* Removing the Brain and Spinal Cord 140
* The Cranial Nerves 143

Danny S. New

Dissecting the Human Body

The most awkward spot of all for me—the anatomy lab—took up most of my time. My hand-held, monocular lens was invaluable, but it had some serious drawbacks.

First of all, the focal length required to get the needed magnification was such that I had to hold the lens, and, therefore, my face, only a few inches from what I looked at. That was somewhat uncomfortable, since the target of my observations was a cadaver. I could handle the strong smell of the formaldehyde, but the whole routine made me uncomfortably conspicuous. Fortunately, we had 24-hour access to the anatomy lab, and from midnight to two A.M. the lab was not very crowded.

Initially, all 180 first year medical students at MCG take the same classes; electives are virtually non-existent the first year. The first quarter everyone takes gross anatomy, biochemistry, embryology, and histology. The gross anatomy lab is divided into groups of four, with each group assigned a cadaver.

On the second day of classes, our group met in the lab for dissection. I wasn't sure if actually taking a scalpel and cutting into the lifeless remains of a once living, breathing person would bother me. It didn't. I don't think that it really affected anyone beyond limit. This was not a special group of cold, unfeeling people, but everyone had prepared themselves in their own way.

Admittedly, it did take a certain amount of emotional preparation to walk into a room with 45 dead bodies and immediately be asked to violate their privacy and sovereignty with a scalpel. Everyone handled the experience differently. Some students probed the faces of the lifeless subjects of our intellectual pursuits and saw brothers, sisters, fathers, mothers, husbands, wives, lovers, and friends. Other students saw only inanimate objects for our study, little more than manufactured tools, much like the plastic skeletons that hung in the anatomy hall.

Sometimes it was easy to forget that the cadavers had not always been cadavers. They had all made a conscious decision to donate their bodies to science, in the hope that their last act would benefit mankind. Each one of them had a story that died to the world with their last breath.

Our group's cadaver was a middle-aged man with a strong facial expression. I wondered what his life had been like. Did he have a family? What was the cause of his death? I felt as though we owed him an apology for disturbing his sleep.

Within a few days, the cadavers lost any reflection of actual human life. They were simply inanimate tools that we used in our academic pursuit—no closer to life than our textbooks and our microscopes. A sense of humor, tempered with respect, was indispensable.

Body Under Siege

The hours in the anatomy lab were long, sometimes ending at two A.M. and starting again at six A.M. Alone in the middle of the night with 45 dead bodies was an eerie feeling that I never got comfortable with. I often surveyed the room and the body bags, and wondered if they were all volunteers, or if the "resurrection men" had disturbed some.

At one time, the number of bodies donated to the medical schools were far short of the number needed to train medical students. Sometimes the schools purchased bodies from grave robbers. These perpetrators came to be known as "resurrection men." This is actually a very old profession. Charles Dickens, in *A Tale of Two Cities*, spoke of these less than honorable characters.

Soon my mind returned to the huge accumulation of didactic facts that my brain needed to store permanently—and permanent storage had not been a Herculean capability of my brain lately. Besides, the resurrection men were ghosts from long past. Cadavers were no longer recruited in this crooked tradition—or were they?

My Dissecting Team

At 36, I felt like the grandfather figure in our group. In reality, there were many medical students in there thirties, and a few in there forties. But these were the exceptions and I still felt like an old man.

To add to my self-consciousness, the other three members of my group all finished high school and went straight to college. They were all a very traditional age for the setting.

Jason was from Atlanta and seemed more comfortable with medical school than the rest of us. His baby-face and his lighthearted approach were made invisible by his uncanny ability to grasp the most serious concepts thrown at us.

Marie was the encyclopedia. She didn't forget anything. We could ask Marie what Dr. Colburn said about the mediastium in lecture today and she would recite it almost verbatim. I thought photographic memories were fabrications. They're not. Marie had one.

Danise was the team leader in performance. Like the rest of us, she had never used a bone saw or a scalpel, but on the first day she used them as though they were a natural appendage to her petite frame.

Disclosing My Problem to the Team

It only took minutes, not days, to realize that the actual mechanics of gross anatomy was going to be a problem for me. Between the slight diplopia, the nystagmus, the numbness in my fingers, and the substantial blurred vision (optic neuritis), it was apparent that dissecting was going to be a major challenge.

Our first dissection involved the skin and muscles of the back. Everyone seemed glad that we were working on the dorsal region first; this was easier to adjust to than dissecting the ventral region, with the cadaver looking at us.

Marie said, "Who wants to try out a scalpel first?" Nobody was particularly anxious to be first, even though we had all seen the tapes on the day's procedure, and had practically memorized the section of the dissecting manual on the skin and muscles of the back. Danise, with her scalpel in hand, said, "If one of you will mark the incision lines, I'll start the dissection." Everyone gave a sigh of relief. We all had a sense of what to do, but nobody wanted to be the first to do it.

"Sure, Danise. I'll do that," I said. I had the procedure well memorized. I marked a line on the skin of the cadaver from the external occipital protuberance, down the mid-line of the back to the tip of the coccyx.

I marked several more important lines. Danise then incised the skin and reflected it laterally, exposing the superficial fascia.

We took turns reflecting the skin with our scalpels and forceps. From the beginning, my problems were significant and apparent to everyone. When dissecting, it is important not to cut too deeply or the underlying structures could be damaged. Between the double vision, the nystagmus, and the blurred vision, my depth perception was gone. Something as simple as reflecting the skin was almost impossible. To see anything, I had to hold my face a few inches from the cadaver.

I knew that I had to give an explanation to the others. They knew something was wrong, but they didn't know what. Before the first day of dissecting ended, Jason asked, "Danny, are you okay?" I wanted to keep my problems to myself. I couldn't. I told Jason, Marie, and Danise that I had multiple sclerosis.

I explained that my vision was limited and the numbness in my left fingers made handling tools difficult, and palpating structures on the cadaver was of only marginal value. Each one of us on the dissecting team was supposed to carry his or her weight, so I made my disclosure apologetically. I knew I would not be able to contribute as much as they would.

"Don't worry about it," Marie said. "You let us know what you can do and what you can't do. Everything will fall into place."

Removing the Brain and Spinal Cord

The opportunity to dissect and study the human body is one of the greatest intellectual privileges that any person can ever have. It is difficult not to be intimidated by the genius behind a creation as marvelous as the human body.

When the time came to remove the brain and spinal cord, some felt that the very essence of mortal life confronted us.

Since coming to MCG I had quietly dug around the halls of medicine in search of any morsel or feast of information that I could find about MS. Gross anatomy, particularly the removal of the brain and spinal cord, filled in a lot of the gaps. Anything dealing with the central nervous system (CNS) did, since MS is a CNS disease. As the direction my life had taken was so directly tied to disease of the CNS, it seems appropriate to include a brief overview of this biological system in my autobiography.

Scientist divide the nervous system into two major parts: the central nervous system and the peripheral nervous system. The central nervous system includes the brain, the optic nerve, and the spinal cord. The peripheral nervous system includes all the nerves that branch out from the central nervous system to the head, trunk, legs, and arms. These carry sensory information to the brain and motor information from the brain to the voluntary muscles. The CNS includes the autonomic nervous system, which controls involuntary functions such as heartbeat and respiration.

The brain is divided into two basic parts: the brainstem and the cerebral cortex. The brainstem connects the brain to the spinal cord, and, thus, to the rest of the nervous system. The brainstem carries out many management functions, including control of the autonomic nervous system. Memory, emotion, thinking, vision, and voluntary movement are all associated with the cortex.

The brain is divided into four lobes: the frontal, parietal, occipital, and temporal. The visual cortex is located in the occipital lobe. The language center is in the temporal and parietal lobes. Mood, personality, and emotion are associated with the frontal lobe. The frontal lobe is unique to man. It is the least understood portion of the brain. Through a hole in the base of the skull, called the foramen magnum, the brain is attached to the rest of the body by the spinal cord.

The autonomic nervous system consists of two parts—the sympathetic nervous system and the parasympathetic nervous system. The sympathetic system stimulates the adrenal glands and sweat glands, increases heart rate, and generally extends energy. If a mugger attacks you, it is your sympathetic system that takes over. The parasympathetic system does the opposite.

Designation of certain localities in the brain as repositories of many intangible human traits is not a modern concept. As early as the fifth century BC, Anaxagoras of Athens hypothesized that the brain was the seat of the soul and intelligence.

In four hundred BC, Hippocrates proposed his belief that, "The brain is the interpreter of consciousness. Men ought to know that from the brain and from the brain only, arise our pleasures, joys, laughter and jests, as well as our sorrows, pains, griefs, and tears. Through it, in particular, we think, see, hear, and distinguish the ugly from the beautiful, the bad from the good, the pleasant from the unpleasant. It is the same thing which makes us mad and delirious, inspires us with dread and fear, whether by night or by day, brings sleeplessness, inopportune mistakes, aimless anxieties, absent-mindedness, and acts that are contrary to habit. These things that we suffer all come from the brain..."

This enigmatic mass of neural tissue that has been the inspiration and object of countless pages of philosophy through the ages is the very same object that breeds insurmountable dread when it goes awry. Multiple sclerosis is a direct attack on this most exalted organ.

I related as much of what we studied as I could to multiple sclerosis. Sometimes this made the brute memorization required in medical school a little more digestible. In gross anatomy, the removal of the brain and spinal cord was a dissection that fit right into this strategy.

Marie approached the table with a bone saw in hand. Unlike the first day, everyone was finally comfortable with the situation and actually competed for the opportunity to get hands on experience dissecting. By now, we all knew that actually working with the cadaver was the easiest way to remember the huge amount of information that they expected us to know.

Marie said, "I found a bone saw not being used. Isn't the next step to remove the calvarium? How 'bout one of you reading the manual out loud and I'll take the first shift with the bone saw."

Jason started reading: "Saw through the outer lamina of bone all the way around the skull. In the places where the saw cut is incomplete, use the bone chisel and mallet carefully to break through the bone. Pry up the skull cap on one side with the chisel to expose the endosteal layer of the dura mater." Within a few minutes, we had removed the calvarium, or skullcap, and exposed the underlying meninges and brain.

Next, we removed the brain with the spinal cord attached. A continuous membrane, called the arachnoid, covers the brain and spinal cord. Cerebrospinal fluid (CSF) fills the subarachnoid space. Diagnosis of many diseases, including MS, involves analysis of this fluid.

Doctors collect the fluid by inserting a needle into the spinal canal, usually at the juncture between the fourth and fifth lumbar vertebrae—a procedure commonly referred to as a spinal tap, or lumbar puncture. Since the spinal cord extends only to the first lumbar vertebrae there is no danger of injuring the cord with the needle. This is basically the same procedure that's used to inject anesthetic agents into the spinal canal—a technique often used in childbirth, and referred to as a spinal block.

The CSF provides a mechanical cushion to protect the brain from impact with surrounding bone when the head moves. The buoyant force, resulting from the brain literally floating in the CSF, reduces the brain's weight from 1400 grams in air to less than 50 grams afloat in the CSF.

Many diseases alter the makeup of the CSF, making analysis of this fluid of diagnostic importance. Multiple sclerosis often increases the gamma globulin content of the CSF to more than 13% of total protein. This increase may occur without a corresponding increase in blood gamma globulin content, and, therefore, can be attributed to production of gamma globulins in the brain.

Jason continued, "Carefully elevate the occipital lobe of the cerebrum to expose the tentorium cerebelli."

The MRI scan done when I was at UGA showed plaques in the occipital lobe. This is the posterior lobe of the cerebral hemisphere and is associated with vision. I wasn't sure that these plaques had anything to do with my visual problems, but I thought that they could.

After cutting the 12 pairs of cranial nerves, the 31 pairs of spinal nerves, and the appropriate arteries and veins, we removed the brain and spinal cord from the spinal canal and the cranial cavity.

The Cranial Nerves

In the next dissection, we identified each of the twelve cranial nerves. Lesions in these pathways cause many of the problems in MS.

Jason asked, "Danny, have any of the cranial nerves or pathways been affected in you?"

I said, "The second, third, fourth, sixth, and eighth nerves, that I know of."

The second cranial nerve is the optic nerve—the only cranial nerve that can be viewed without an invasive procedure. An ophthalmoscope, an instrument in almost every doctor's office, is all that is needed to visually inspect this nerve.

Most doctors, and patients, agree that vision is the most important of the special senses. Visual information is transformed into electrical signals in the retina. The optic nerve carries these signals to the visual centers of the brain where they are interpreted. Optic neuritis, inflammation of the optic nerve, results in a loss of sight, which worsens with heat.

Jason asked, "Since the optic nerve leaves the brain, why isn't it considered part of the peripheral nervous system?"

I said, "By the strictest sense of the word, the optic nerve is not really a nerve at all. It is composed of secondary sensory axons rather than primary sensory axons, and, thus, forms a central nervous system tract, rather than a nerve. But the name, nerve, has traditionally been accepted. Since the optic nerve is actually a central nervous system tract, its axons are subject to central nervous system diseases, such as multiple sclerosis."

Jason said, "What problems did the eighth nerve cause? I assume it affected either your hearing or your balance."

I said, "A loss of hearing in my left ear was my first symptom. Eventually, my hearing returned to normal."

The eighth cranial nerve is called the vestibulocochlear nerve. This nerve has two components; the cochlear component brings auditory information (hearing) from the cochlea, and the vestibular component brings information having to do with balance from the semicircular canals.

Jason asked, "Why did they lump two groups of sensory fibers carrying completely different information into one named nerve? Wouldn't it have made more sense to have a vestibular nerve and a cochlear nerve?"

I said, "I wondered that, too. One reason is that they run together for most of their length, they enter the skull through the same opening, and they join the brainstem at about the same point. Some anatomists think they should be renamed as separate nerves."

Jason asked, "What caused the diplopia?"

Since I had been reading some on the subject, I knew the answer. I said, "The third and sixth cranial nerves are responsible for the diplopia and the nystagmus. Both problems are caused by an internuclear ophthalmoplegia (INO). An INO is always due to a lesion within the brainstem, either the pons or the midbrain. In my case, demyelination of the medial longitudinal fasiculus (MLF) caused the INO lesion. This type of lesion is common in multiple sclerosis. The MLF connects the nucleus of the sixth nerve, in the pons, to the nucleus of the third nerve, in the midbrain."

The third nerve is the oculomotor nerve. This nerve, along with the fourth (the trochlear nerve) and the sixth (the abducens nerve), controls the six extraocular muscles that produce movement of the eyes. Involvement of the brainstem, which controls these nerves, is common in MS.

CHAPTER 10

Multiple Sclerosis—The Basics

* Explaining what Multiple Sclerosis Is...146
* Differentiating MS, ALS, and MD..151
* Diagnosing MS – A First Year Medical Students Perspective..........152
* Attack of the Macrophages..153

Explaining what Multiple Sclerosis Is

I avoided the subject of multiple sclerosis for awhile, but I soon gave up on that. Word spread quickly, and ultimately I was glad. Now I no longer wondered what my classmates thought when they saw my awkward gait, or my clumsiness in the labs, or my monocular magnifying lens that I used in anatomy. Occasionally I used a cane, too. Now everyone knew why.

"Danny," said Carl Miles late one day in the anatomy lab, "What exactly is multiple sclerosis? I know that it's neurological, and I think it's autoimmune, but that's about all I know."

The first year of medical school concentrates heavily on basic science. We had clinical correlations once a week to help the class relate the basic science to the real world of clinical medicine, but the emphasis the first year is clearly basic science. Most of the first year instructors are Ph.D's—not MD's.

I said, "Most doctors believe, as you said, that MS is an autoimmune disease. But the literature is full of other theories.

"MS is the most common neurological disorder, next to stroke. It usually begins in the early to middle twenties, but frequently begins at any age between 12 and 50, and rarely presents at much younger or much older ages. It is a chronic, progressive, inflammatory, demyelinating disorder of the central nervous system."

Carl asked, "Is there much epidemiological information on MS?"

I said, "Probably more than you want to hear."

Carl said, "I'd like to hear. I'm ready to take a break from the formaldehyde."

Epidemiology is the study of the prevalence and spread of disease with regard to geographic, demographic, socioeconomic, genetic, and infectious variables.

I said, "Several factors probably play a role in multiple sclerosis, including environmental, genetic, viral, and immune system elements. Studies show that MS occurs more frequently in temperate climates than in tropical areas. Studies indicate that the risk of developing multiple sclerosis is related in some way to the area the person lived in for the first fifteen years of his or her life. This supports the belief by some experts that the disease is caused by early exposure to a virus. MS is more common among Caucasians than other races, and is twice as common among women. Clusters of MS also suggest that exposure to an environmental agent is involved."

Carl asked, "Is MS genetic?"

I said, "There seems to be a genetic predisposition for the disease, but, no, MS is not inherited. There are several factors involved and the genetic question has not been fully answered yet. The genetic component probably has more to do with an individual's susceptibility to whatever the triggering factor is that leads to the development of the disease. The risk of an offspring of a person with the disease developing MS is greater than the general population. Statistically, there is a greater chance that a sibling will contract the disease than an offspring."

Free time is non-existent in medical school. This was especially true for me because it took me longer to do things. Still, when I could squeeze an occasional break I spent it at the MCG library researching the latest in MS.

Epidemiology of Multiple Sclerosis

Epidemiologists are concerned with who gets a disease, what the geographic variations are, and when the disease occurs. Two measures of special importance to the epidemiologist are incidence of disease (the ratio of the number of new cases in a given period of time, usually one year, and the total number of people at risk for developing the disease), and the prevalence of disease (the ratio of the total number of cases alive in the given population and the total size of the population)

A summary of several studies before 1977 show the prevalence of MS in women to be 1.4 times greater than that for men (165). More recent studies indicate a much higher prevalence among women, with ratios ranging from 1.9 to 3.1, (166, 167, 168, 169) with an average around 2.

In the United States, the prevalence of multiple sclerosis above the 37th parallel of latitude is reported by one survey to be 68 per 100,000 population, and areas south of this line show a prevalence of 36 per 100,000 population (170, 171). Studies in Europe show comparable numbers for the same latitudes.

It is clear that location is a major risk factor for multiple sclerosis, with variations in prevalence ranging from 250 per 100,000 population in the Orkneys (172), to only 4 per 100,000 in Malta (174), and 5 per 100,000 in Japan (173). Surveys indicate that moving, before the age of 15, results in the individual assuming the risk factor of the area to which they migrated (175, 176).

The risk to black Americans is significantly less than in the white population. Multiple sclerosis is almost unknown in the black population of South Africa. The higher rate in the U.S. is probably the result of interbreeding—this supports the argument for a genetic predisposition for the disease.

Multiple sclerosis tends to be more common in higher socio-economic groups (177). This is the opposite of what would generally be expected. Incidence of multiple sclerosis is not related to poverty or other factors associated with lower socio-economic status, although the disease does usually result in a downward shift in social class, as with any chronic disease, because of the effect of disability on occupation.

Body Under Siege

In an effort to show an interest, sometimes sincere and sometimes not, classmates constantly asked me questions. Medical students, like most scientists, are naturally inquisitive. This gave me an additional incentive to learn all that I could.

Most people know very little about MS. Even where it exists in the family, ignorance abounds. Most people picture a wheelchair somewhere in the background. Others know only that it is a serious disease. An acquaintance asked me how long MS lasts. I said, "MS is a chronic, incurable disease. It lasts until you die, always changing faces. The faces get uglier with time, always more terrible than the one before.

But on a more positive note, sometimes the disease runs a benign course. There are less severe cases with only mild symptoms—and they do occur.

Multiple Sclerosis effects a half million Americans. It is thought to be an autoimmune response—the persons immune system mistakes the insulating material, myelin, surrounding the nerves in the central nervous system for a foreign material. It then proceeds to destroy the "invader."

After the immune system destroys the myelin, the nerve is left without its insulating protection. Then the body's natural repair mechanisms take over and scar tissue is left. This results in slowed transmission of impulses across the nerves. In some cases, the nerve can't transmit the impulse.

The symptoms vary, depending on where the lesions occur; lesions inside the brain may cause difficulties including visual problems, cognitive manifestations, deafness, loss of coordination and balance, fatigue, and speech disturbances. The most common visual problems resulting from brain lesions in MS include double

---

Demyelination

Myelin, the insulating material that surrounds the axons of nerve fibers, is critical to the conduction of impulses in the nervous system. The gray matter of the brain is composed primarily of nerve cell bodies and does not typically contain myelin. The white matter is composed of axons, which are surrounded with myelin, giving this part of the brain its white appearance. Myelin also surrounds axons in the spinal cord and optic nerves within the central nervous system.

Axons in the peripheral nervous system are also surrounded by myelin, but peripheral myelin is produced by Schwann cells instead of oligodendrocytes and is not effected by MS—at least not in a substantial way. Multiple sclerosis is a white matter

> **disease of destruction of myelin in the brain, optic nerves, or spinal cord. When myelin is destroyed, conduction of nerve impulses along the axons is slowed or stopped.**
>
> **Conduction along the axons is known to normally be saltatory—jumping from node to node as a result of segmental myelination. The internodal part of the axon is normally myelinated and the axon of the node is normally unmyelinated. When the demyelination is incomplete, but a thinner myelin sheath results, saltatory conduction is still possible, but is slowed and can be blocked completely. Complete blockage results in loss of function.**

vision and nystagmus (rapid, involuntary eye movements), sometimes with oscillopsia (an illusory sensation of swaying of the visual field).

Lesions on the optic nerves result in optic neuritis (inflammation of the optic nerve) which can result in visual problems including blurred vision, loss of part of the field of vision, or complete blindness.

Defects in color vision are common. Bladder and bowel problems are very common. Judgment is often impaired. Personality changes are not uncommon.

Lesions in the spinal cord can cause pain, spasms, weakness in the muscle, and temporary or permanent paralysis.

Multiple sclerosis may follow a relapsing-remitting course marked by periods of worsening followed by periods of improvement, usually incomplete. Or it may follow a chronic-progressive course of continued worsening with no remission. The chronic-progressive course can be primary progressive (progressive from the onset), or it can be secondary progressive (initially following a relapsing-remitting course that later becomes progressive).

Chronic-Progressive vs Relapsing-Remitting Disease

Originally, it was believed that the progressive and remitting forms of MS were distinct. Birley and Dudgeon (123) showed that they were not.

Primary progression refers to disease that is progressive from the onset. Initial relapsing and remitting disease can develop into the progressive form—secondary progression. In a study by Muller (124), 25% of cases became progressive within two years of the onset and 50% within ten years. In this study age of onset had an important bearing. Eighty percent of the patients with onset after the age of 35 became progressive within five years. Weinshenker et al found (125) that 41% of patients with remitting disease had become progressive from 6 to 10 years from onset, and between 11 and 15 years the percentage had risen to 58%.

But progression is not inevitable. Weinshenker et al showed that 11% of those surviving for 26 years or more from the onset had not developed progressive disease.

Muller (126) found that 13% in a clinic review were primary progressive. Four other studies varied from 9% to 26% (127, 128, 129, 130). There is a clear relationship between primary progression and age of onset. A study of patients with onset after age 40 reported 57% were primary progressive (119). Another study found primary progression in 49% of patients over age 40, and only 17% in patients below this age (131).

It has been generally accepted that the disease process in a majority of cases was remittent, but there is mounting evidence that this is not the case and the actual disease process is continuous (132).

Differentiating MS, ALS, and MD

Mark asked, "Danny, what is the difference in ALS and MS? ALS was mentioned in class today."

I said, "Amyotrophic lateral sclerosis (Lou Gerig's Disease) is characterized mainly by wasting and loss of muscle mass and by hyperreflexia. Many times there is spasticity in the lower extremities. Sometimes there is fasciculation, or twitching, in the muscles. In ALS, sensation is not affected. In contrast, MS involves the white matter of the CNS. MS does involve sensory disturbances and does not involve muscle wasting, except as would be expected if a muscle is not used due to paralysis. ALS is usually fatal."

Mark asked, "How does muscular dystrophy differ?"

I said, "Muscular dystrophy is a classic genetic disorder. The most common form, the one that most people are familiar with, is Duchenne muscular dystrophy. This is a sex-linked, recessive disorder. It usually presents in boys aged three to seven. All of the muscular dystrophies are characterized by progressive weakness and degeneration of muscle fibers, without any evidence of neural degeneration like you have in MS. To me, it's worse than MS because it usually affects children. MS can affect kids, but typically it's an adult disease. I was 26 when MS hit. I was 31 before it caused a major change in my lifestyle. That's not a tragedy, just a misfortune. A child crippled by muscular dystrophy is a tragedy. Most people with MS have at least had a normal childhood—not so for kids with muscular dystrophy. If I had a magic wand and could zap up a cure for one of those two diseases, it would be muscular dystrophy, not multiple sclerosis."

Diagnosing MS – A First Year Medical Students Perspective

Most medical students are inquisitive by nature, but God gave Carl an extra dose. In other settings people would have accused him of being nosy. But in medical school, people describe this kind of person as "investigative." Regardless of the adjective chosen to describe him, Carl liked asking questions. But I didn't mind. If it was a subject I knew something about, I liked to give answers.

Late one night in the anatomy lab, Carl asked, "How do they diagnose MS?"

I said, "It's a problem sometimes. It took three months for the doctors to diagnose me. Since 1983, when MRI became widely available, it has been easier, but it's still hard to make a definitive diagnoses, sometimes."

Carl asked, "But what diagnostic tools do they have?"

I said, "An MRI is standard now. They also analyze the cerebrospinal fluid proteins, with particular interest in oligoclonal bands and IgG. Evoked potentials can help."

Carl asked, "What kind of evoked potentials?"

I said, "Visual evoked potentials (VEP), auditory evoked potentials (AEP), and somatosensory evoked potentials (SEP) are all I know about."

Our first exposure to x-rays, MRI's, and other imaging techniques came in gross anatomy. MRI's (Magnetic Resonance Imaging) has been routine since the early '80s as a diagnostic tool for MS and many other conditions.

Carl asked, "How does the MRI work in diagnosing MS?"

I said, "The way they explained it to me is this. Basically, the lesions will show up as bright spots. These are areas of tissue with an increase in the free water content (water not bound to protein). Myelin is very high in fat and very low in water content. When myelin is damaged in MS, scar tissue replaces it. The scar tissue has less fat content, and, therefore, more water. Thus, the bright spots."

Attack of the Macrophages

Studying immunology at MCG answered many of my questions about the role of the immune system in MS. Many more were not. Every new fact suggested a new question. Fortunately, medical school was the perfect resource center for the answers—if they existed.

Mark asked, "If MS is an autoimmune disease, and the target is myelin, why is it specific to the CNS? Axons of peripheral nerves are also covered with myelin."

I said, "They are, but there is a fundamental difference. Oligodendrocytes produce CNS myelin; Schwann cells produce peripheral myelin. Maybe the CNS myelin has an antigenic determinant that is immunocompetent and the peripheral myelin doesn't have it."

Mark asked, "How do the immune cells damage the myelin?"

I said, "Strong evidence now suggests that macrophages are the immune cells responsible for stripping myelin from the axons in multiple sclerosis (87, 88). Electron micrographs have actually recorded the attacks; they have shown macrophages touching the degenerating myelin. It is possible that a receptor on the surface of the macrophage interacts with something on the surface of the myelin, such as an antibody.

"One of the activators of macrophages is interferon gamma, which is produced in response to viral infections and stimulates the release of tumor necrosis factors (89), among other things. TNF has been shown to damage oligodendrocytes. In addition, macrophage produce other molecules, such as prostaglandins, which suppress the immune system—a positive effect in this autoimmune disease. Interferon gamma decreases the production of these molecules. And leukotrienes and oxygen radicals, also produced by macrophage, have been shown to damage myelin in vitro (90, 91).

"Of course, it is possible that the macrophage are only acting as scavengers of tissue already injured by other means."

Evidence that Axons are Also Damaged in MS

Until recently, all the evidence indicated that only myelin was affected by the immune system in MS. But a recent report published in the New England Journal of Medicine (199) indicates that this is not correct. It now appears that the nerve fibers (axons) are also affected, and in many cases are actually severed from the nerve cell body.

The study, led by Dr. Trapp at the Cleveland Clinic Foundation in Cleveland, Ohio, did not suggest that the axons were targeted by the immune system, but were probably injured as a result of their close proximity to the attack on myelin, the primary target.

Undoubtedly, new research in treatment and basic science will result from this new information.

CHAPTER 11

The MS Story Continues

* The Cognitive Problems Progress 156
* Depression 156
* Color Changes 157
* The Lab Practicals 157
* MS-Related Fatigue and Pain 157
* Magnetic Resonance Imaging 160

The Cognitive Problems Progress

I never lost hope that some miraculous remission would reverse the cognitive impairment. But I knew that time was against me now; the longer MS symptoms persist without remission, the greater the likelihood that the problem will be permanent.

Unlike when they diagnosed me in 1980, it was common knowledge in medical circles by 1990 that memory, reasoning, and judgment may all be affected by MS. I felt its effect on me. The physical disability didn't scare me. I could use a cane if needed. They have some fairly high tech wheelchairs on the market, if things got that bad. I knew the field of medicine was wide enough to find a niche for almost any student, but no niche exists for a student whose intellect has been severely damaged by disease.

I could not reverse the damage done by the plaques scattered throughout my brain. I was aware of the impact on my mind. I could feel the decline and sense the decay. Each day my desire to be a physician increased, and my ability to be one decreased.

The severity of cognitive impairment in MS runs the gamut from mild "tip of the tongue" word recall problems to impairment so severe that the patient can't be cared for at home. Doctors can evaluate cognitive dysfunction with a battery of neuropsychological tests. I had these tests done at UGA before I started medical school. I wanted to establish a baseline for future comparison.

After being at MCG a few months, my doctor did more tests. The results were dramatic, but not unexpected. Cognitive impairment is a common symptom of multiple sclerosis, but nobody told me in time to save my business. Now my dream of being a doctor was in serious jeopardy, too.

Depression

Soon the monster that had invaded my turf recruited a now familiar fiend—as though MS needed any reinforcements to deliver its poison. Depression once again became my most immediate adversary.

I knew the progressive nature of MS, but, being an eternal optimist, I never gave up hope that the disease would eventually find a comfortable level of homeostasis and call off the attack. I was a strong person, by my measure, and I felt confident that I could adjust to most physical disabilities—if they would just sit still and let me know what I needed to adjust to.

But MS doesn't sit still. It will not surrender and it will not ease off on the attack. It changes. Each day's battle always seems new and more fierce than the last. Each fight diminishes your battle armor a little. Surely, depression in such a state is "normal."

I hesitated in taking anti-depressants for fear that they would cloud my mind even more. And I hadn't given up yet—I needed my mind more than ever. The fight stayed alive. I knew that exercise was a natural way to increase production of the neurotransmitter serotonin; investigators have demonstrated that increasing serotonin can decrease depression.

Researchers reported that chocolate helped too. I swallowed that pill easily; I loved chocolate. I assumed that The Association of Chocolate Manufacturers funded this study, but I figured, "What the heck."

Maybe it was just the positive impact of "doing something," but a temporary reprieve came, and the depression shifted from severe to moderate.

Color Changes

Discriminating colors became more and more difficult. I saw this most notably with yellow/blue colors, but all colors had an abnormal dullness. The problem was bilateral, but much worse in my right eye. Everyday things, like matching my clothes, could no longer be taken for granted.

This is a common visual problem in MS, caused by damage to the cones in the retina. Fortunately, this was not a major problem to deal with. It was more of a nuisance than a limitation.

The Lab Practicals

A more serious problem, but one I expected, was the actual mechanics of taking the practicals (lab tests).

In histology, the class passed slides around the room at regular intervals, usually 30 seconds to a minute. But time didn't kill me. Seeing did.

Gross Anatomy devastated me. We took these tests in a lab containing approximately 45 cadavers. The instructors affixed tags to anatomical structures on the cadavers. A pin and string held each tag in place. To my eyes, the nerves, arteries, veins, and strings holding the tags all looked the same.

Everything was a blur. The monocular, prescription, magnifier that I used to study in the lab, could not be used on the exams.

MS-Related Fatigue and Pain

Fatigue was not a new problem for me. But I was still uncomfortable discussing it with anyone—I knew it could be misinterpreted as laziness, and, for a lot of people with MS, it often was. I preferred to just avoid the subject.

Each medical student at MCG is assigned a small work area. These small cubicles became our home away from home, complete with bookshelf and work area, a small closet for dissecting tools, microscopes, and all the incidentals needed to survive in med-school. The rooms housing these miniature studies were sometimes noisy, necessitating a retreat to the library. Eventually, the short walk became a major challenge.

Andrew, another first year medical student, had a close friend with MS. Sometimes Charles came to the campus with Andrew. One day, Charles said, "I can't believe you have the energy to handle medical school."

I said, "Sometimes, I don't. Sometimes, just walking downstairs to the anatomy lab is a major effort. Standing for hours after I get there is torture."

Charles asked, "Then why do you do it?"

I said, "I want to be a doctor."

Going back to the subject of fatigue, Charles said, "Isn't there a difference in this and regular fatigue?"

I said, "MS fatigue IS different. Researchers are doing work to understand more about the difference. For one thing, heat is more likely to affect MS-related fatigue. It also happens sometimes with little or no exertion and is usually more severe."

Charles said, "Sometimes I'm fatigued right after I get up in the mornings. I sleep good, so I feel like my wife thinks I'm making it up."

I said, "It's not uncommon for somebody with MS to have fatigue early in the morning, even though they haven't done anything. The etiology of fatigue in MS is unknown, but about 80% of patients have it."

Charles said, "Sometimes I have a piercing pain on the left side of my face. Can MS cause that?"

I said, "Yes. That sounds like trigeminal neuralgia. You should see your doctor. It is treatable."

Pain

According to the NMSS, "55% of the patients in one study had `clinically significant pain' at some time during the course of the disease." Pain in MS can be acute or chronic, but chronic pain is much more common.

Acute pain often occurs as trigeminal neuralgia, Lhermite's sign, pain in optic neuritis, or burning in the extremities. Paroxysmal pain has been reported (198)

Trigeminal neuralgia, or Tic Douloureux, occurs in about 1% of MS patients (194, 195). It often manifests itself as sharp pain in the face. It is often treated with carbamazepine (Tegretol). However, this drug may aggravate many symptoms of MS, such as weakness of the legs, and therefore cannot be tolerated in high doses (19). It can also be treated with antidepressant medications, such as amitryptaline. There are other drugs that can help, and severe cases that do not respond to any of these medications may be treated by a surgical procedure called percutaneous rhizotomy.

Pain is common in optic neuritis, usually preceding visual symptoms but can be at the same time or after they appear. It varies in intensity and sometimes is only felt when the eye is moved. The pain may be caused by stretching of the meninges around the swollen optic nerve, according to Perkin and Rose (22).

Lhermite's sign is a neurological symptom of a pain that is often described as a sudden electric shock passing down the back to the legs when the neck is flexed. Sometimes the sensation is described as tingling or pins and needles. The sensation is always brief, lasting only a few seconds (196). MS is the most common cause of this symptom. At least one third of MS patients have experienced this at some time. Spontaneous firing of an irritative lesion in the cervical spinal cord is one explanation for this symptom. It is rarely found to be sufficiently unpleasant so as to require treatment. However, one researcher found that it could be abolished with carbamazepine (197)

Pain can also result from spasticity, which can be treated with antispasticity drugs.

Magnetic Resonance Imaging

Dr. Hess was a member of the neurology faculty at MCG and was now my physician and friend. He ordered a MRI scan—my third in three years. The MRI showed that the lesion load in my brain continued to increase.

A MRI, magnetic resonance image, is the latest and most advanced technology for studying white matter diseases, such as MS. Often it is a critical tool in the diagnosis of MS. I knew that soon I would have to make a decision about school and I wanted to understand what the MRI said. I already knew what my body was saying. I went to the MCG library and checked out all the books I could find on MRI.

As I sat at my cubicle looking through the MRI books, Jason walked in. Picking up a couple of the books, he said, "Now that's what I call dedication. All we need to know is the very basics about MRI right now. Why all the digging?"

I said, "I just had another MRI done and I want to understand it."

Jason said, "Things are getting worse. Right?"

I said, "Yeah. But right now I'm just trying to understand my MRI's."

Jason said, "What have you learned? How does MRI work?"

I said, "The water and lipid components of the human body contain a huge number of hydrogen atoms. The proton at the center of each of these atoms has a magnetic spin. Manipulation of these spins by an applied magnetic field results in signals that can be detected outside the body. This is the basis of MR imaging."

Jason asked, "How does it compare with CT scans?"

I said, "It is far superior to computed tomography (CT) in investigating intracerebral white matter diseases. Extracerebral lesions on the optic nerve and in the spinal cord can be detected on MRI, but rarely on CT."

Jason asked, "So it's the water content that differentiates the gray matter from the white matter on MRI's?"

I said, "Yeah. Myelinated white matter contains 12% less water than gray matter."

Jason said, "Now that they have MRI, diagnosing MS isn't so hard anymore. Right?"

I said, "MRI helps, but it's not definitive. It's a valuable aid, but alone it may still miss diagnosis in up to 25% of clinically proven cases (15). MRI is not specific for the diagnosis of MS. Many white matter lesions that mimic MS may be detected in normal people, as well as those with other pathologic conditions."

Jason asked, "Do the lesions develop randomly throughout the white matter?"

I said, "They don't know why, but there is a propensity for MS plaques to develop in certain regions of the white matter: the periventricular region, the brainstem, the optic nerve and the spinal cord. About 50% of MS plaques are periventricular (around the ventricles)."

Where the Plaques Are

On autopsy of well-developed Charcot type multiple sclerosis, it is common to find scattered lesions in both cerebral hemispheres, usually with a degree of symmetry. Predominance in either hemisphere is unusual.

In a study of the cerebrum by Brownell and Hughes (112), they found 74% of plaques in the white matter, 17% at the junction of gray and white matter, 5% were cortical, and 4% were completely in the central gray matter.

22% of the plaques in the cerebrum were in the frontal lobe, 15% in the parietal lobe, 12% in the temporal lobe, and only 1% in the occipital lobe.

Sometimes the cerebrum contains relatively few plaques while involvement of the optic nerve, brainstem, and spinal cord is usually widespread. In a study of 18 patients (113), 35 of the 36 optic nerves showed demyelination.

Cranial nerves are sometimes involved at their junction with central nervous tissue in the brainstem.

Plaques within the cerebellum are common.

A study by Oppenheimer (114) found that involvement of the cervical spinal cord was much more common than lower parts of the cord.

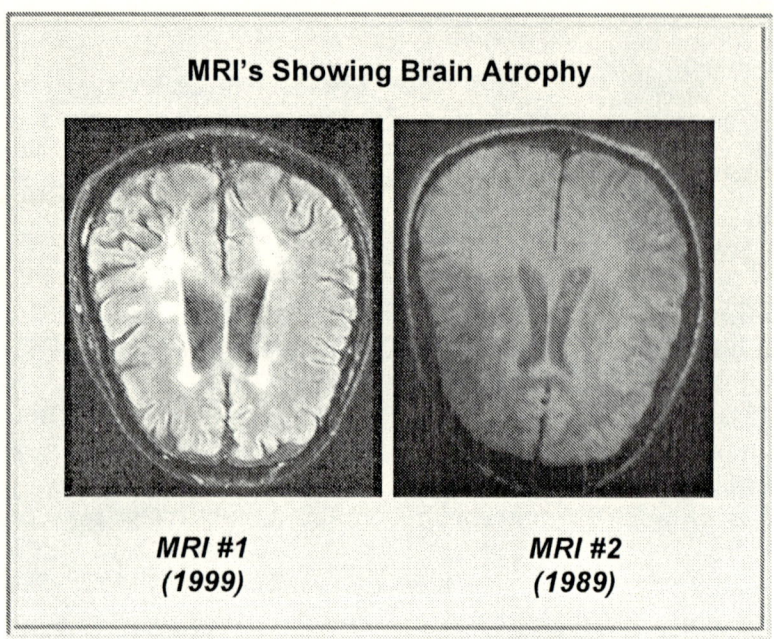

MRI's Showing Brain Atrophy

MRI #1 (1999)

MRI #2 (1989)

Multiple sclerosis is most commonly described as a demyelinating disorder, which it is. But current knowledge goes beyond that. MS involves damage to myelin that surrounds and insulates axons (nerve fibers), damage to the axons themselves, and brain atrophy (wasting away of brain tissue due to loss of myelin, damage to axons, or loss of axons). Brain atrophy becomes more pronounced over time. As brain tissue is destroyed by the disease process, the ventricles enlarge and cerebrospinal fluid fills the enlarged cavity. The loss of brain tissue and subsequent enlargement of ventricles is obvious in MRI's 1 and 2—two MRI scans of Danny New's brain, taken eight years apart. Brain atrophy measures are important markers of MS disease progression because they likely reflect destructive and irreversible pathologic processes.

Although it is difficult to perfectly correlate MS lesions as seen on MRI's, many symptoms are very predictable according to location of lesions, and many correlations can be made. Many studies have advanced our ability to correlate location of brain and spinal cord lesions with clinical symptoms. With the MRI's of Danny New's brain are relevant comments on the medical significance of each and, more generally, of the significance of MS lesions in these parts of the brain.

Body Under Siege

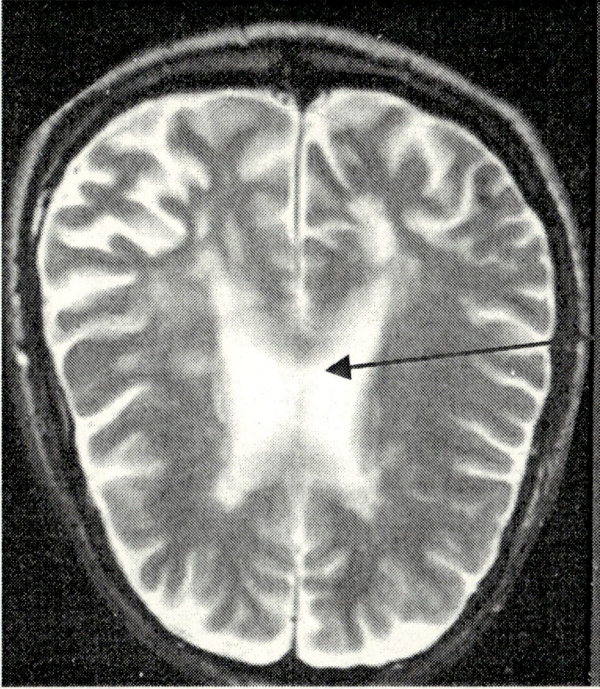

MRI With Large Lesion Load

Ventricles

T2 weighted MRI scan of brain showing high signal lesions around the lateral ventricles (perventicular plaques).

MRI #3

Ventricles

The ventricles are large CSF filled spaces in the brain. Measurement of ventricular enlargement is a reliable measure of atrophy. In a study by Dr. Stephen M. Rao, an NINDS grantee at the Medical College of Wisconsin in Milwaukee, ventricular enlargement correlated with cognitive impairment (specifically, performance on tests of memory and verbal intelligence). Brain atrophy can result in cognitive deficits in memory, judgment, information storage and manipulation, attention, orientation, and problem-solving.

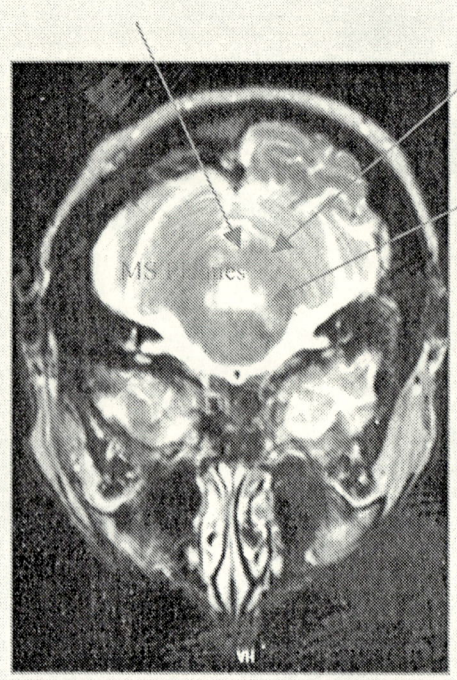

T2 weighted MRI showing high signal lesions in the brainstem and cerebellum. The plaques are gathered around the fourth ventricle.

MRI #4

Brainstem

The brainstem extends from the base of the brain to the spinal cord. Problems with eye movement (diplopia or nystagmus, for example), emotional lability (also known as the laughing/weeping syndrome), facial twitching, some speech disorders (dysarthrias), vertigo, loss of balance, rarely hearing loss, and some urinary problems can be the result of brainstem lesions. Facial expression and emotions are controlled by the brainstem.

Cerebellum

The cerebellum, situated above the brainstem, controls balance and coordination of movement. Lesions here can cause ataxia and tremor. The *patient may experience vertigo, dizziness, gait (walking) problems, dysmetria (failure to stop a motion at the intended point—the finger to nose test, for example). Cerebellar damage can result in fatigued muscles on the same side as the damage. The contraction and relaxation time for these muscles is slower than normal, resulting in slowed movements.*

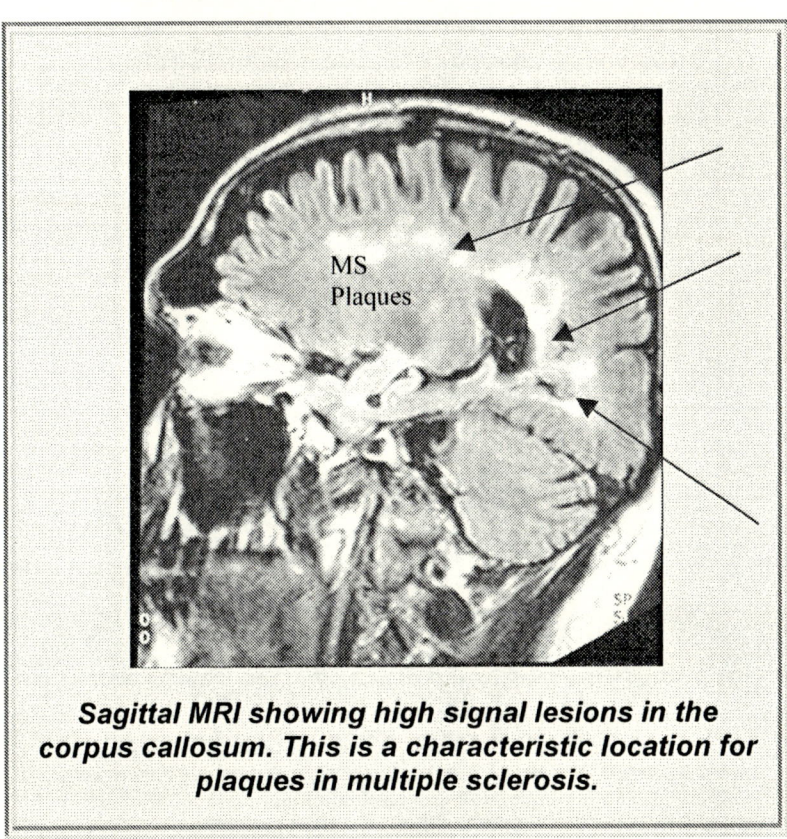

Sagittal MRI showing high signal lesions in the corpus callosum. This is a characteristic location for plaques in multiple sclerosis.

MRI #5

Corpus Callosum

The corpus callosum is the broad band of nerve fibers that connect the two cerebral hemispheres of the brain. Data indicates that damage to this structure can explain some of the cognitive dysfunction associated with MS. This may be due to interhemispheric communications being disrupted by demyelination.

CHAPTER 12

The Search Continues

* Leave of Absence 167
* The University of Chicago 168
* Carbamazepine 170

Leave of Absence

By the middle of winter quarter, I knew that I couldn't continue—not in my present condition anyway. Things didn't improve after leaving UGA. My physical condition constantly deteriorated. The cognitive impairment worsened. My vision continued to be a problem. My balance was embarrassingly conspicuous. My energy level almost incapacitated me. And the numbness in my fingers made simple tasks, like holding the dissecting tools, awkward. The nystagmus made the whole world appear to be in the middle of an earthquake.

"I think I am going to ask for a medical leave of absence," I said to Dr. Hess. "Do you think a remission is likely—or possible?"

Dr. Hess said, "I think if there was going to be any substantial improvement it would have already happened. But there may be some experimental trials going on somewhere that we could get you involved in if you're interested."

Normally I would have been interested, but I was in a race against time now—and time had MS on its side. I needed a solution before August, only seven months away.

The protocols of almost all experimental trials involve a double-blind format and a control group that receive a placebo. Double-blind means that neither the patient nor the doctor knows who is getting the placebo and who is getting the experimental drug. That only gave me a 50/50 chance of getting the actual drug in any trial that I got accepted to, and even then, the statistical chances of the drug being affective were not very great.

I said, "I don't think I have time for any trials; school starts back in August. But I would like to see one of the nations leading experts in this field, if you can recommend someone."

MS is much more common in the North than in the South, and therefore, it didn't surprise me when the trail led in that direction. Dr. Hess said, "One of the leading researchers in multiple sclerosis is at The University of Chicago. I can make an appointment for you if you want to make the trip."

My future in medical school depended on finding help with the cognitive problems. Maybe my future anywhere did. I said, "I think I would like to go."

The next day, MCG granted me a medical leave of absence and I made arrangements to go to Chicago. Dr. Arnason's reputation in MS was impressive. The doctors at MCG were as good as any in the world, but they had not seen as many cases of MS as Dr. Arnason had, or most neurologists in the North. I really didn't think that any solution existed for my problem, but for the next seven months I knew I would not give up the search. I clung to the hope of finding some magic elixir or pill that would return me to my previous state.

Danny S. New

The University of Chicago

Within a week, I flew to Chicago. I was a little uncomfortable making the trip alone, but we couldn't afford two plane tickets.

I arrived a day ahead of my appointment. I'm not sure why, but I wanted time to explore the medical school. I wondered in what ways it differed from MCG, but I knew that just walking around the campus wouldn't tell me that. Still, the leave of absence, even if temporary, was a festering wound, and I was drawn to the campus in search of an answer—although I really didn't know what the question was.

Medical schools, based on what their leaders perceive as their mission, have personalities of their own. Some are basically educators of primary care physicians. Others are notably research institutions. Most, including MCG and The University of Chicago, are involved in both areas.

As I strolled the campus, the first and second year medical students sluggishly emerged from the lecture halls. They had the same weary appearance that our class had at the end of the day. Only one week had passed since my leave of absence started, but I felt like my best friend was gone, and I knew that it might be forever.

After a short walk, I saw the Student Center and decided to get a cup of coffee. Chicago is a frigid place in the winter, and, for me, habit demands caffeine when the temperature drops. Besides, the walk had left me struggling to maintain an appearance of sobriety. Fortunately, I had my cane and, to an observer, my unusual gait obviously resulted from a physical problem and not a drinking problem.

Behind me in line were two medical students still in their lab coats. A young, tall, bearded guy said to a tired-looking girl, "Were you able to identify all six of the extraocular muscles in the dissection today?"

She said, "We didn't get completely finished. We're all meeting early tomorrow morning to finish."

I knew the feeling. Their words told me that they were first year students. I could feel a lump forming in my throat. In Vidalia, I lived a life that was everything I wanted, and more. I lost that life, but MCG, I thought, represented a rebirth. Now my life seemed like a huge question mark. Seeing these kids living the life that I wanted so much almost brought tears to my eyes.

But I knew that I had to let the past go—again. I knew that if any worthwhile future for me existed I had to start living in the present. My thoughts now seemed to mirror an earlier life—one that I thought I had escaped from.

I walked into the doctor's office the next morning and said, "I have an appointment with Dr. Arnason. I think I'm a little early."

A young, attractive woman with a hypnotic smile said, "Guessing from your accent, I bet you're the medical student from Georgia. Right?" The Northern hospitality, in that small part of Chicago at least, rivaled anything that the South could offer. "I'm Stacey," she said.

A nurse took me to an exam room and soon Dr. Arnason came in. He said, "We don't get very many patients from Georgia. Did you have a good trip?" After a few minutes of purely social exchange, Dr. Arnason went straight to my reason for being in Chicago. "Dr. Hess told me all about your case, and I've studied your records. Now I want you to tell me."

I related everything that had happened with me since 1980. I stressed that my main concern was the cognitive problems. I said, "I think I can handle almost anything that MS throws at me, if it will just leave my mind alone."

Dr. Arnason said, "I'd like to run some tests, but, as you know by now, mental impairment is a common symptom of MS. I have patients with no cognitive problems and I have patients with severe mental impairment and I have patients everywhere in-between. First I'm going to do an EEG. I don't think you had one done in Georgia. We need to know for sure that your cognitive problems are not a result of seizures. I've had more than one MS patient who had positive EEG's, and their cognitive problems improved with carbamazepine. I don't think that is your problem, but an EEG might tell us."

Doctors use carbamazepine, widely marketed under the brand name Tegretol, to control epileptic type seizures. This seemed like a long shot, but if this was the problem, then it was treatable. Fits or seizures are not common in MS, but they aren't unheard of either.

Dr. Arnason said, "Danny, it will be after lunch before we can run the EEG and some other tests. Why don't you grab a bite and come back around two?"

As I walked toward the cafeteria, I passed Stacey. She said, "Danny, I'm on my way to get a slice of pizza. Would you like to join me?"

"Sure," I said. For the next hour we talked about Chicago, about medical school, about Dr. Arnason, but mostly we talked about MS. Stacey said, "My best friend has MS. She's only 26, and just found out a few months ago. She's not handling it at all like you are. She was once so active, but now she has withdrawn from almost everything. I wonder why people handle things like MS so differently?"

I said, "I think the reason people handle it differently is simply because people are very different. My perception of what I lost when I got MS is different from what your friend perceives as her loss. And everyone's system for coping is different. Everyone's threshold for physical or emotional pain is different. For some people, the fear of disability is as damaging as the actual thing. I coped by staying busy and staying motivated. I didn't look at MS as an unbeatable foe. MS will lose the war one day, and I wanted to be part of the fight, if I could. If not a major battle, maybe I could at least be involved in a skirmish or two. Having a goal provides hope and hope builds endurance. Tell your friend not to concern herself with what she can't do. She has to concentrate on what she CAN do."

I saw a slight amount of hypocrisy creeping into my conversations; I wasn't as strong anymore as I sounded. I fought depression constantly. If this trip failed in its purpose, and if MS prevented me from finishing medical school, then I feared that my strength would vanish. I was becoming less and less optimistic about the future.

The next day, the results of all the tests were in. Dr. Arnason said, "Your EEG was negative. A lot of research is going on, but if an answer for this problem comes it will be in the future. But I would like to do one thing. EEG's are not foolproof. Sometimes they will fail to pick up tiny problems that can be significant. Carbamazepine is a drug with few side effects; I would like for you to try it for a few months."

Carbamazepine

I left Chicago discouraged. I didn't take the carbamazepine very seriously. But my desperation primed me to try anything. Any hope beat no hope, and Dr. Arnason knew as much about MS as any doctor in the world.

When I got back to Georgia, I made arrangements with Dr. Hess to have the neuropsychological tests repeated. I wanted to document any change that might occur after taking carbamazepine for a few months. I was skeptical, but I still wanted a measure of any effect that the drug might have. However, I realized that even if my condition improved I would not know for sure if carbamazepine caused it. Spontaneous remissions are common in MS, but I also knew that time probably ruled that out.

Doctors use carbamazepine in MS to relieve pain due to trigeminal neuralgia (tic douloureux). It has also showed good results in treating most paroxysmal symptoms such as paroxysmal dysarthria, ataxia, tonic seizures, and akinesia. It has few side effects, but I knew it could aggravate other symptoms of MS, especially weakness in the legs, and therefore should not be given in high doses to patients experiencing these problems. But I wasn't having these problems, and even if I had been, I was prepared to try anything if it improved my chances of finishing medical school.

Epilepsy

Fits or seizures are not common in MS, but they aren't unheard of either. Epilepsy is more common in young adults than is multiple sclerosis, and therefore coincidental association would be expected. However it is not likely that this is the whole explanation.

Drake and Macrae (98) estimated that fits occurred in 4.1% of cases of multiple sclerosis. In a large review, Elian & Dean (99) found that 1.1% of the patients in their study had multiple sclerosis and epilepsy—a figure higher than the statistical expectation of .5%. In six other reports higher figures were found, ranging from 2.4% to 8% (98, 100, 101, 102, 103, and 104).

CHAPTER 13

Second Time Around

* The Decision to Return to MCG 173
* First Year Medical Student—Again 173
* The Six-Year Plan 174
* Conceding Defeat 176

The Decision to Return to MCG

After a few months, Vivian and I did notice a change. Medical school started back in August and I had to make a decision about returning.

I needed more than my subjective opinion; I needed an objective measure to confirm that my mental condition had improved. In May of 1990, I had the neuropsychological tests repeated. If my problem had anything to do with "micro-seizures," then it made sense that carbamazepine might have an effect on it.

The tests revealed significant improvement in both verbal and non-verbal memory domains. On the Halstead-Reitan Category Tests, I made only six errors—a sharp contrast to the 41 errors I made prior to starting treatment with carbamazepine. Potential brain dysfunction is arbitrarily set at 50 errors.

The neuropsychological consultation report from MCG said, "Mr. New presents with significant improvements in memory and attention/concentration compared to his previous assessment."

My mental status had improved dramatically, but it was still a long distance from my pre-morbid state. But at least it was going in the right direction. I still lacked confidence, but I saw a flicker of light. And it only took a flicker to convince me that returning to medical school was a chance I had to take.

First Year Medical Student—Again

Taking the leave of absence meant starting completely over; I was a beginning freshman once again. But I didn't mind. I thanked God for the second chance, and prayed that MS would fail this time around.

But I knew that MS was already ahead in the game—if this was a game. I wasn't very optimistic. I also wasn't the only person in my original class repeating the first year—but I repeated it because of a problem that, in all likelihood, would recur. I tried to be optimistic, but I couldn't escape the thought of what I and everybody knew—MS is a progressive, not regressive, disease; it would only get worse, never better.

Everything went okay for a couple of months. Unfortunately, the improvements were short-lived. By Christmas, 1990, my memory and general cognitive functions reached a completely new level of impairment. Repetition helped, but time limited how much of that I could do. Immediate recall of large amounts of information was not an ability I had anymore.

Multiple sclerosis had slowed down the mental processes, just as it had slowed the transmission of nerve impulses involved with the skeletal motor system. I could retrieve most information, eventually, but I couldn't do it quickly enough. Sometimes, all the facts appeared jumbled together, and whatever the sorting mechanism in the brain is, mine was non-functional at all but the very laziest of speeds.

Sometimes, I would say something and later ask myself why I said that. I couldn't pull the word or the fact out quick enough and, in desperation, my mind would choose a totally inappropriate substitution. And the muscles controlling my speech seemed to work at a different speed than that part of the brain generating the thoughts. Carrying on a conversation was not easy anymore.

The Six-Year Plan

Jamie was on my dissecting team and had the study cubicle next to mine. Two months of studying a common cadaver, sharing a coffee pot through the night, and generally giving each other moral support through the trauma of the first year of medical school, established a friendship that lightened a load growing heavier by the minute.

Late one night, after days of emotional torment, I said, "I think I'm going to withdraw from school, Jamie." Although by now I had convinced myself that this was inevitable, actually saying the words gave a life to the gloomy image, and the words lingered like a dark cloud tethered to my bosom and raining drops of tears.

Jamie said, "Danny, you can't do that. There must be another way. Have you talked to Dr. DeVore?"

Dr. DeVore was in charge of student affairs. If compassion is a true measure of a good doctor, then Dr. DeVore was one of the best. I made an appointment for the next morning.

I knew that MCG could, and had, tailored programs for students with special problems. MS definitely fell into this category. Once MCG accepts a student, the school makes every reasonable effort to see that he or she graduates.

The next morning I went to see Dr. DeVore. I said, "Dr. DeVore, last night I decided to withdraw from school, but I'm not sure I can. I worked too hard to get here. But I can't complete medical school under the standard program. Nothing is going right. A member of the faculty told me that there might be options, like spreading the program out over six years instead of four."

Dr. DeVore said, "That can be done, but it will require the vote of the Phase I Subcommittee. I will make the arrangements to bring it before the committee, if you wish. I would like to see you complete the program; a lot of people would."

In a few days, a meeting of the full subcommittee met to consider my problem. Dr. Hess accompanied me and supported my request. The committee voted to modify my workload so that I would graduate in six years instead of four.

Body Under Siege

School of Medicine
Associate Dean for Students

October 31, 1990

Danny New
MCG BOX 1152

Dear Mr. New:

This is to inform you that the Phase I Subcommittee will meet on **November 7, 1990 at 5:00 P.M.** to consider your request to extend your curriculum.

Dr. Jack Ginsburg, Chairman, suggested that you be available at that time, and you may bring your physicians with you. The meeting will be held in room 1101 of the R & E Building.

If you have any questions please contact me.

Sincerely,

Margaret DeVore

Margaret B. DeVore, M.D.
Associate dean for Students

mr

c: Gregory Eastwood, M.D.
   Jack Ginsburg, M.D.

Augusta, Georgia 30912-4770 (404) 721-3817
An Affirmative Action/Equal Opportunity Educational Institution

Letter from Dr. DeVore

Conceding Defeat

MCG honored me with their support, but deep down I knew that this would not solve my problem. So far I had managed to get over each new hurdle. But the hurdles kept getting higher and higher. I hoped the six-year program would work, but I had my doubts. I didn't feel like the same person anymore. I sensed the problems with my mind. The physical complications progressed. The disease even changed my personality.

It is likely, or at least possible, that carbamazepine did have an impact on the cognitive problems, but it didn't eliminate them. I could find no scientific basis for any effect on the mind. Eventually, I knew that the problem was irreversible and progressing. No amount of desire could counter the destruction that multiple sclerosis had caused, and was causing. My intellect slowly dwindled away, and I had no power to stop it.

I think I had believed that I would be an exception and would somehow be spared the devastation that typically accompanies MS. I was wrong. Even beyond the physical limitations and the intellectual decay, now I felt the disease with every movement I made.

I finally considered, and believed, that even if I could continue in school I would not be able to finish. Six years is a long time with the disease progressing at this accelerated speed. I had exhausted all hope of finishing medical school. After two years of struggle I conceded to the defeat I knew was inevitable. I withdrew from the Medical College of Georgia in February of 1991.

CHAPTER 14

Adrift in Self-Pity

* What Now?..178
* The Guilt Trip..179
* Coming Within Inches of Your Dream and Never Touching It........180

What Now?

I didn't know what direction my life was supposed to take now. I didn't know if anything meaningful was still possible. Maybe the remainder of my life was doomed to a state of drift, awaiting the final close that would only come with the grave.

I endured the uncertainty, but fear ate like a scavenger in my heart. I had become like a ghost to everything I was most familiar. The steady drip, drip, drip of time was an incessant reminder of how my life was wasting, but I was powerless to stop the decay, and everything I was or ever hoped to be shrank away until it was only a dim flicker of light in the distant heavens, too remote to ever be retrieved. I chased the dream among the stars, but now I knew that I would never catch it. The horrible memory of a reality that nearly was, but now could never be, of a self-defining labor that now must be left undone, of the wasted years that could never be recovered, I lay stricken with this sorcery both day and night. I longed for some goal or harbor, but now I could find no purpose and no point of refuge. I wanted to understand why the losses had come so bitterly and so suddenly, but I doubted now that I would ever understand that. I wondered if the hard knowledge that life had taught me was common.

I felt like an observer, removed from any direct contact, watching all that happened in Danny New's world, but I wasn't part of it. I was a stranger to myself, traveling strange highways. All of the road signs were written in a language that I didn't understand. I didn't know where I was or how to get back; or even if I could get back.

The past twelve years had not been kind to me. A superstition of doom that I couldn't transcend controlled me. My ambitions were not compatible with a disease like MS. An overwhelming sense of loss permeated my soul. I looked in the mirror, into my eyes, and I knew that something inside of me was dying—or had died.

I lay awake many nights after leaving MCG, staring into a deep, blackness-filled emotional abyss, so thick with darkness that distant glimmers of light immediately dissipated into nothingness. These nights seemed as utterly void of life and as cold as any imaginings of empty space.

In the blackness, my mind wandered back in time. Maybe all hope was erased from my future on that dreary day in 1980 at Mass General Hospital when they told me about the malady I would have to endure for the rest of my days in this life. The words were meaningless to me then; I wasn't to know for years the hardships MS held in waiting. I remembered my carefree, almost cavalier, acceptance of the diagnosis.

The years spent developing the Vidalia Onion were a TOTAL investment of that part of my life. From 1973 to 1985 was like a trip to another world—a world where everything except The Onion held no importance, where time had no purpose except to serve New Bros., Inc. and The Onion.

It was 1985 and NBI was part of the past before I knew who Bruce Springstein was, or realized that Steven Spielberg didn't work the night shift at New Bros. Disco and Donna Sumners came and went without my notice. For several years, the business, or more specifically, The Onion, had all of my attention. I was not a part of the rest of the world for those years.

When Vivian, Swain, and I left Vidalia in 1986, I was convinced that we were on the road to a whole new beginning—that I was being given a second chance. I was going to do it right this time—the way I should have the first time around. I had to. Second chances—maybe. But third chances—no. I'm sure they don't exist.

When I started on this "second chance," I accepted MS as part of the enemy fleet, right up there on the front lines with age and poverty. But I believed that I would ultimately prevail and would not become one of the trophies on infirmity's wall. As I left the Medical College of Georgia campus for the last time, it appeared that I was wrong; MS had won again. In the end, no amount of effort worked. "If you try hard enough, you can do anything," was nothing more than a cruel joke.

The wound cut deep. I saw my life crumbling around me. I saw the hurt in Vivian's eyes, and my dreams for Swain faded. Vivian played the loyal friend that she was, but I felt more and more like a failure. My role was no longer well defined. And I knew that Vivian's role would change, too. My first memory of Vivian was her brown and clear and deep eyes. They withheld something unknown, or unknowable. Now, I knew that I would soon see what mystery they had withheld—from me and from her.

The Guilt Trip

As a teenager, with all the problems that growing up brings, escape came easy for me. I just sent all of my problems to a bottle of Jack Daniels.

By age 16, I was a teenage alcoholic. Alcohol was the only solution that I cared to apply to most problems.

Fortunately, it didn't take too many years to figure out the fallacy of that approach. Liquor was no escape; it only magnified the problems. When I decided, at an early age, that Jack was no friend of mine, I quit drinking, and for 20 years I never even thought about it.

Now I sort of wanted to again. I even bought a bottle and poured a glass. But I couldn't. Deep down, I knew liquor was no solution—I had been there before. I had to face my problems and I had to find a way out.

As terrible as alcohol is it never diminished my aspirations. I was a kid with big dreams and the passion to pursue them. I knew that if I had any chance of turning my life around I had to find a way to terminate the guilt trip I had sent myself on. I saw no way to atone for what MS had done to the people I loved the most. It was my disease and I was responsible for its actions. My family's financial problems were a direct result of me developing MS. It was my fault that others were able to take my mother's inheritance and her retirement. It was all my fault. I wanted so badly to be the person I once was, but I finally knew that MS never leaves you where it found you, and it will never let you go back there again.

Coming Within Inches of Your Dream and Never Touching It

The uncommon success that David and I nearly achieved with the Vidalia Onion stood as my first dream. In Vidalia, I very nearly made it through the doors that I struggled for 12 years to find. I could see across the threshold as with 3-D glasses and gaze at what I reached for; but I couldn't quite touch it. And then at the last moment it disappeared like a vapor.

I struggled to accept this as a divine conception—truly believing that medical school was part of a greater plan for me. I held to the belief that everything happened for a reason. So I invested five more years of my life into this second great quest. My acceptance to medical school at a very non-traditional age seemed like a new window to the future. I was a regenerated man with all thought of malady forgotten.

Withdrawing from medical school was one of the low points of my life. I struggled with emptiness. Like losing anything that is really important to you, I doubted that I could ever fill the void. Part of me died when I lost the business in Vidalia; another part died at MCG. These pieces of my life were buried, and I knew they could never be resurrected.

For the first time in my life, I was losing the drive to win. I was burned out, depressed, pessimistic about the future, down on myself, and down on the world. Finally, eleven years after the diagnosis of MS, I felt like a victim.

I felt sorry for myself, but even more, I felt sorry for Vivian. I could handle MS messing up my life, but it devastated me to watch it mess up hers. "For better or for worse, in sickness or in health," had assumed a new and frightening reality. I felt guilty for ever asking her to enter into such a vow.

Now all my days ran together. Saturday was no different from Monday or Thursday or any other day in this prison I had locked myself in. My heart ached with remorse. I blamed myself for having MS and for all the damage it was doing to my family.

CHAPTER 15

Searching for Peace

* On Hate and Forgiveness 182
* Reviving Hope 183
* What to Expect 184
* The Father/Son Thing 185
* Hope, and the Victim Mentality 185
* The Four C's 189

On Hate and Forgiveness

I saw myself slipping emotionally. All of the hate that had been simmering in deep cavities of my mind started erupting. I felt helpless and hopeless. But some small part of me said to hold on.

In desperation, I decided to talk to a psychiatrist. I had little confidence in the healing power of any words he might offer, but perhaps he would have a magic pill to help me survive. I knew that this chronic hate I harbored could kill me, and I was ready to try anything.

Dr. Jacobs was a pleasant man in his early sixties. He said, "Danny, tell me about yourself." It was not easy to give an abridged account of my past. I knew my immediate problem was the bottled up anger that had been simmering now for more than ten years. I wasn't just angry with the people that defrauded me of my business and my life, I was also mad at myself. And I was mad at life. I was mad at God too.

I knew that by hanging on to the past I died a little each day. But I couldn't turn loose; I had tried for years.

After I told a shortened version of my life, Dr. Jacobs said, "Some people have a horrible past, tragic to the point that they can't bear to think about it. You didn't. Most of your past was good. You had some tough breaks, but most people do somewhere along the way. You have to let the past go, anchor in the present, and start building for the future."

I said, "I've discovered that building for the future can be a little difficult when you have multiple sclerosis."

Dr. Jacobs asked, "Is MS the problem, or is hate the problem?"

I said, "Indirectly it's hate, but MS set up the situation that planted the seeds of hate. I want to ask YOU a question, if you don't mind. I didn't just pick your name out of the yellow pages. A friend told me that you are a devoted Christian. Are you?"

Dr. Jacobs said, "Yes, very much so."

I said, "I too am a Christian. That part of my life I'm sure about. Everything else gets a little fuzzy sometimes. But I feel guilty for having these problems coping. My faith should be sufficient to solve them."

Dr. Jacobs asked and answered, "Where does it say that Christians don't have problems? Not in the Bible. But because you're a Christian, the prognosis for your recovery is very positive. I'd say it's almost certain. You already know what the medicine is. All you have to do is learn to use the powers that are available to you.

"A Christian should not be burdened with anger and hate. You must learn to not question the "why" behind the position you now occupy in life. You cannot see the future, and therefore you have no basis for concluding that the plan was misguided or unfair.

"Whether your situation be by design or mischance, the final outcome is yet to be revealed. In the end, you might be glad that everything happened in the way that it did. How do you know what the world would be like if events had happened in any other way?

"You're a Christian. Ask God to use you where you are. Maybe you're right where he wants you. You have to start by being friends with yourself, again. You have to forgive yourself for having MS. It wasn't your fault. Then you have to forgive anybody else that you think wronged you in any way. It's not your place to judge other people. Let God take care of that."

Reviving Hope

Dr. Jacobs inspired me, but mostly he reminded me of things that deep down I already knew, but refused to accept. I still awake most nights with a sick, hollow feeling. More than once my mind placed me in danger of "quitting" life. Fortunately, the thought always withered and died before it could take root.

Life kept telling me "no," but I wouldn't take no for an answer. If I quit I would die, and I knew that. I had to overcome the habit of defining my life by where I had been instead of where I was going. By what I had been instead of what I would be. By what I had not accomplished instead of what I had accomplished, and what I hoped to accomplish still.

I searched desperately for some meaning to explain why all of this had happened. Why did I spend most of my life building a business, only to lose it? Why did I get MS? Why was I accepted to medical school if God had no plan for me to serve in that field? I didn't know the answer, but I was confident that somewhere there was one.

The depression almost crushed me. The Nortriptyline that Dr. Jacobs gave me only helped a little. I knew that in the end I would not find the answer to this problem in a pill. I knew that to survive I had to develop a positive belief in the future. I had to stop looking at life as the adversary. I had to quit second-guessing my past. I had to start asking "what now?" in a positive way, instead of "why me?" in a negative way.

I saw myself slowly losing the ability to wage the war, and I knew that just the ability to wage the war gave me a reason for living. It provided hope. I knew if I could stay in the fight until the last round, then I had won. Blindness or a wheelchair might make the struggle more difficult, but it wasn't the end. The only sure way for me to lose was for me to quit the fight. I had to believe that.

I became convinced that happiness had more to do with attitude than circumstance. I saw this in my own life. How I looked at life each morning determined the kind of day I would have. Maybe I had little control over my circumstances, but I might be able to control my attitude about them. My first mistake was to believe that the circumstance gives the joy. But it is us that gives joy to the circumstance. I had to concentrate on changing the sail—not the wind.

I remembered what one MS patient told another at a recent meeting. He said, "You have to want to survive. You have to decide to survive. No matter how hard it gets, and no matter how much it hurts, you can't let defeat even be part of your vocabulary. You can't let anything make you quit. Not now. Not ever."

Recently, I received a graduation invitation from a friend who went through the University of Georgia with me, and started medical school at the same time. My emotions were in a tug of war. I was very glad to see Nicole graduate, but the reminder that I was not graduating saddened me. I saw this as an opportunity to practice control over my emotions. I could choose to be happy because a friend had completed medical school, or I could be sad because I had not. I chose the former.

What to Expect

More than other things about MS, I did wonder how bad the cognitive problems would get. Years ago, the fund-raisers referred to MS as "the great crippler of young adults." That designation, fortunately, died an early death. MS does not always cause severe disability. Some people have MS and never know it. Sometimes an autopsy reveals MS plaques in an asymptomatic person. It is the huge range of potential symptoms that makes the disease so unpredictable.

At first I thought that MS would be like my mind trapped in somebody else's body, and theirs was a poor excuse for a body. But at least it would be my mind. I had reconciled myself to the loss of a lot of physical function. But it was much worse than that. It wasn't just my body under attack. It was my mind, too.

I knew I wasn't the first person—and would not be the last person—to walk this road. In the recent past, time was a very limited resource for me. Now it seemed as though I had an endless supply of it. I decided to invest some of this in talking to others that had traveled this road. Many of the things I wondered about somebody else had already been through. I wanted to find them. I had to get rid of the depression, and I knew that talking did help.

Joe Bailey was a middle-aged man with MS. I said, "Joe, you told me that you had to quit teaching. Why?"

Joe said, "I kept saying stupid things. I kept forgetting what I had told the students and what I hadn't. I repeated myself a lot. College kids aren't shy. They let you know. I was embarrassing myself."

I asked, "Did it get worse with time?"

Joe said, "It sure did. I've had MS for 20 years. From the beginning, I had problems with my mind. First, I had trouble remembering students' names. It kept getting worse. I could only teach things that I had known for a long time. I had a really hard time learning anything new. I understood it as I read it, but I couldn't remember it. I sure couldn't teach it."

Undoubtedly, the mind problems were progressive, too. I was determined to be as upbeat as I could, but I knew the ride would get rougher.

The Father/Son Thing

Most people who are diagnosed with MS, and many other serious conditions, go through a denial stage. I did. In this stage you don't want to talk about it. You want to ignore it and act like it's not there. Eventually, you go through an acceptance phase, where talking about it probably helps.

I think it is easier to be depressed in the acceptance phase though. If you can deny that anything is wrong, and believe it, then you remove a lot of the reason to be depressed.

Steve had only had MS for three years. Like me, he battled the Father/Son thing. He had the primary-progressive form of the disease and already used a wheelchair, although he had been diagnosed less than three years. We saw each other at MS meetings occasionally. Steve was in the acceptance phase, but he was having a hard time. He said, "It's hard to be a father with MS. I have an image of what I am supposed to do, but I can't do a lot of those things anymore. My son is twelve. I wanted to do all the Father/Son things, so I gave him a shotgun for his birthday. That was three months ago. It has never been fired. I can't take my wheelchair through the woods, so I can't teach him how to hunt. The gun just sits in the closet as a monument to MS."

I said, "You're being pretty hard on yourself, Steve. Maybe we should just be thankful that we have our kids, and let it go at that."

I was being a hypocrite again, but I wasn't going to make Steve more depressed than he already was. I've learned to keep my thoughts to myself when I start slipping into one of my self-pity moods. In reality, I knew exactly what Steve was saying. I had my own image of what fatherhood should be like. Baseball, Frisbee, hunting, fishing—they were all part of it, and I couldn't do any of those things anymore. It's easy to be depressed when you're a father with MS.

Hope, and the Victim Mentality

I realized that in me had evolved an unhealthy attitude that painted me as a victim. If I wanted a future, I needed a new mind-set; I had to get rid of all self-defeating thoughts that had taken up residence in my mind. I had to guard against feeling like a victim and acting like a victim. The problem with the "victim" approach is the ease with which blame is shifted to someone else, or to a circumstance, thus camouflaging your own shortcomings. MS makes the struggle altogether different and more difficult, but the battle isn't automatically lost. Man is the officer of his own happiness, and of his own mistakes. If I complain of the disposition of my circumstances, then it is my own disposition that I blame; we have to play the cards we are dealt.

Opportunities are the natural fallout of experience gained. I wrote this book inspired by misfortune. The race isn't over.

I observed others with similar or worse circumstances than mine, and saw a wide spectrum of reactions to their plight. I noticed that the presence or absence of one element—hope—could foretell the outlook of each of these people. The close tie of hope to happiness, and the independence of both to degree of disability, impressed me even more.

Without hope, the diagnosis of MS can be devastating, regardless of the level of impairment. With hope, almost any degree of impairment is manageable. When you have hope, you have life. I knew that hope was a child of faith in God, and that I would find the solution to my problems in the spiritual realm, although thus far it had eluded me.

Sharon was an attractive lady in her mid-thirties. We met at an educational forum sponsored by the MS Society. The disease had hit Sharon with more vengeance than most of the others in the room. MS had confined her to a wheelchair two years earlier. Yet, there was something about her demeanor that implied control. She seemed to be happy with life, even if disappointed with her circumstance.

"How do you keep a perpetual smile under these conditions?" I asked.

"Well, I didn't at first," she said. "When they gave me the bad news, I responded with deep despair. I didn't understand why God chose me to play this part. I questioned God, and even questioned the existence of God. I loathed life, and hoped for an early end to what I perceived as certain misery. I had extinguished all simmering coals of hope from my life."

I said, "But your attitude now seems to be the very opposite of what you describe; what caused the change?"

Sharon said, "I noticed that my outlook changed frequently, that I had moments of peace embedded in the long stretches of misery. I wondered why this was. My condition didn't change at these times; only my mental approach changed. Still, the periods of depression and apparent hopelessness were too much for me. I was ready to give up. I wanted to give up. I had lost the energy and the will to fight anymore.

"Then I met Barbara. Barbara was a classy, sophisticated lady in her seventies now. She was radiant, optimistic, and exhilarating. These traits didn't seem to coalesce with her condition. Barbara had multiple sclerosis, too, and had had it for over fifty years.

"She will be here later tonight. Would you like to meet her? I think you will enjoy talking to her, even if you don't find the answers you're looking for."

I said, "Yeah. Sure. I'm looking forward to it."

I really did look forward to it. Sharon had something that escaped most people—people with or without a physical disability. I didn't think that this Barbara had any answers for me, but I wanted to hear her story. Her effect on Sharon intrigued me.

In a few minutes, a lady with a commanding presence rolled into the room. I knew without an introduction that this was Barbara. She operated her hi-tech wheelchair by the slightest movement of her fingertips—because those were the only appendages that she could depend on. From her waist down, MS had completely paralyzed Barbara, and she had only limited use of her upper limbs. But that was all this powerful lady needed.

Soon, Sharon approached me and said, "I told Barbara that I wanted her to meet a friend. Give her a few minutes and she will be over to talk to us."

I had never spoken a word to Barbara, but I sensed that a real honor would soon be granted to me. Barbara's face so glowed with happiness that the radiance almost hid the wheelchair from view. Barbara and her wheelchair did not evoke pity in me. On the contrary, I think I envied her.

Sharon said, "Barbara, this is Danny. I've told Danny how you changed my outlook on life. I'm going to leave you two to chat."

Barbara asked, "When did you find out that you had multiple sclerosis, Danny?"

I said, "It was in 1980. What about you?" I was a little uncomfortable talking to Barbara. Her physical condition was much worse than mine was, but oddly, her emotional condition was much better. At some time over the years, Barbara had learned something revolutionary about life. I wanted to find out what it was.

Barbara said, "More than fifty years have passed since I learned that I had multiple sclerosis. I didn't even know what it was then."

I said, "You seem happy."

She said, "Sure I'm happy. I have no reason to be unhappy. Multiple sclerosis has altered the way that I live, but it hasn't stopped me from living. I see the same sun rise every morning that other people see. I breathe the same air. I have always thought of life as an adventure. MS is part of the adventure. Like mosquitoes on a safari, it is unwelcome—but not unwelcome enough to make me cancel the trip."

I asked, "How do you fight depression with nothing to look forward to but life in a wheelchair?"

Barbara said, "I have a lot more to look forward to than that. Besides, my wheelchair is not a curse; it is a blessing. I get around just fine with it. And I don't have to fight depression. It's not a part of my life. It shouldn't be a part of anyone's life."

I said, "But a huge number of people with MS do have a problem with depression. Suicide is a major cause of death for people with MS. What makes you different?"

Barbara said, "You have a very narrow approach to life. You see life as here and now; I see life as a continuum that started when I was conceived. Our physical life on Earth is a very small part of the overall picture. I have anchored myself in the spiritual world, and I draw strength from that dimension—a dimension untouched by the vast majority of people that have passed through this life."

I said, "I have no fear of what comes after death. I have no fear of death. I am confident that my place in eternity has already been reserved. My faith in my God does sustain me, but not at the same high level that you operate at. I do get depressed. Sometimes, for brief times, I even question God—and then I hate myself for it."

Barbara said, "You are on the right track, but now you have to make the quantum leap from materiality to spirituality; you still have one foot on each side. You are engaged in a tug of war with this world. This world is trying to bind you. You're trying, but you lack the resources to make that quantum leap and to free yourself of the ropes this world has bound you with. You will never make it without an advocate on the other side to help you."

I said to myself, "Wait a minute. This sounds like the teaching of some kind of cult." I asked, "Who is your advocate?"

I expected some weird answer like Beelzebub or some other dark analogy, but Barbara said, "Mine is Jesus Christ. There are other spirits, other contacts with the spiritual world, but not any others that can help us across. Jesus healed me. Obviously, not physically, but physical pain is easy to handle, compared to emotional pain. I have no emotional pain. I am at peace with myself and the rest of the world. That is true healing. The surest way to misery is to waste today fearing what might happen tomorrow. Fear and self-pity can paralyze us emotionally, just as MS can paralyze us physically. And they can cause you to lose what quality time you have left. All of our experiences are valuable, and I would not change any of mine. God gave me my experiences for a reason and together they make me who I am."

Barbara was right; I WAS on the right road. I had not traveled the distance, or learned the signs, or memorized the maps as Barbara had done, but I was on the right road. I had not learned to tap the huge reservoir of support that God had made available to me. After witnessing the victory that Barbara had achieved, with the help of Jesus, multiple sclerosis didn't look so big anymore. I didn't choose this road; it was chosen for me. But there is a reason, and I am not a victim.

The Four C's

Barbara taught me that the ability to handle adversity was, in some regards, independent of the magnitude of the problem. She also taught me that this ability is not something we can learn. It is a gift—a gift from God.

I started thinking that the world must be full of people with insights to share. I felt that I had missed a lot by not seeking out these people. At first, I thought that they must be very rare. Eventually, I realized that they weren't rare at all, and most people had a story to tell that I could learn from. But I had not listened; I decided to start listening.

Paul was an inspiring personality that seemed to always have an encouraging word for anyone who needed it. In a room full of people with multiple sclerosis, it wasn't hard to find someone who needed it. At one meeting, I overheard Paul and a few others talking. Paul was 65 years old and he had a firm foundation of experience to support his substantial wisdom.

A brunette lady said to Paul, "Why do you think some people accept hardship as a challenge, and others commit suicide?"

Paul said, "I think we all have basically the same goal—contentment, to be happy. Some of us find it easier than others, and some of us never find it."

The brunette lady asked, "How do we find it?"

Paul said, "When they told me I had MS, I was everything but a strong person. I withdrew. I hid from life. I still breathed, but really I had died. When I looked up and saw what was happening to me, I didn't like it. I wanted to do more than just subsist among the animate. I wanted to actually be alive again. Achieving contentment became a major goal."

She asked, "How did you do it?"

Paul said, "I read books, I talked to people, I meditated, and I prayed. I looked for the common elements in the lives of people who had found contentment. These common elements I call the four C's—confidence, competence, compassion, and Christ. I guess a person of a religion other than Christianity wouldn't have exactly this same list, but this is what I believe, and it has worked for me."

I thought about what Paul had said, and it made sense. The Latin derivation of the word "compassion" is compassio— "to suffer with." At first this seemed contrary to the notion of contentment. But experience shows the opposite. Compassion drove me into medical school. Empathy for others in desperate situations became a source of strength and moved me a step closer to contentment. Not because others had misfortunes, but because I had found a higher goal for my existence. Hospitals are filled with people who need help. This is a place where compassion from many sources converge into a great river of humanity. Yet, it is relatively no more than a trickle. The need is overwhelming.

Paul said, "To apply compassion in any useful way requires confidence—confidence in your knowledge, ability to use that knowledge, and the ability to relate this confidence to others without apprehension."

The next element Paul listed in his quest for contentment was competence. Paul said, "Without this, contentment will remain an illusory state. Like most things, competence is a relative concept."

I said, "But MS restricts the areas in which competence can be achieved."

Paul said, "But this does not mean that it can't be found in other areas, or that it will be any less rewarding once it is found. But competence in some area of living is a prerequisite for contentment. Trying to find this in an area no longer open to you is a certain formula for misery."

Paul was right. I knew that medicine was off limits to me now. That was hard. But it was not the end of the line. Everybody can be good at something, even if it's just being a friend to somebody. It takes a lot of effort to be good at being a friend.

CHAPTER 16

Questions from MS Patients—A Sprinkling of What I Missed

* The Questions 192
* Emotional Lability 192
* Stress 193
* Dysphagia 193
* Ignorance is not Bliss 195

The Questions

After others with MS learned that I had been in medical school, although I didn't finish, they often assumed that I knew more than I did. Actually, only experience perfects the craft of medicine. Knowledge harvested from books is critical, but without experience the knowledge is useless. I didn't have any experience at being a doctor; but I did have experience at having multiple sclerosis, and I knew enough basic science to talk intelligently about the subject. And I did pick up a few things in med-school, too.

Still, I wasn't a doctor, and I didn't pretend to know what a doctor knows, and I always gave that preamble before I made any comments. But I did try to stay informed and not give any wrong information. If I had any doubts about my answer, I quickly said that I didn't know. But I enjoyed the questions. I figured it was as close as I would ever come to being a doctor.

Emotional Lability

Doctors diagnosed Glen with MS in 1982. He always seemed cheerful, but withdrawn. He was reading an article and said, "Hey, this has happened to me several times. Sometimes I laugh when something really sad happens. I'm not laughing on the inside, but I can't control my emotions."

I asked, "What does the article say about it?"

Glen said, "It talks here about inappropriate responses to different things. I thought it was just me, but according to this it's not that unusual for people with MS. It says here that some people might have a seemingly cheerful response to what is really a sad situation. My best friend's wife was in a really bad auto accident not long ago and was seriously hurt. I hurt deeply for him and her, but my facial expression was the opposite of what it should have been—on the inside I cried, but on the outside I smiled. I knew it, but I couldn't stop it. I wonder what causes that."

I said, "That is called emotional lability. I heard the term used in medical school. Sometimes it is seen as a symptom in several neurological diseases, including MS. The patient will sometimes have exaggerated emotional expressions that do not fit the situation—laughing when the situation is not funny, or crying when inappropriate for the circumstance."

Glen asked, "Do they know what causes it?"

I said, "Damage to nerve fibers in the central nervous system that regulate the expression of emotions can cause it. As with other symptoms of MS, some factors—heat, exercise, and emotional stress—make it worse. This is a symptom of the disease and does not mean that you have become emotionally insensitive. If it's really bothering you, why don't you ask your doctor? Sometimes they treat emotional lability with some of the same drugs that are used for depression."

Stress

Glen asked, "Did you say that stress can make the symptoms worse?"

> **Stress**
>
> The influence of emotional stress on the course of multiple sclerosis is difficult to ascertain with objectivity, but several studies have been published. Systems to measure and quantify levels of stress have been developed, but inevitably a great deal of estimation is involved.
>
> One variable that presents difficulty is the accepted fact that disasters are borne by different people in different ways. Devastation for one person is simply "life" to another.
>
> Franklin et al (163) found a significant increase in risk of relapse in patients experiencing severe stress. Sibley (164) found a significant increase in relapse during the risk period, which he defined as the duration of the stress plus an additional three months. From the records, it appears probable that stress does have an adverse effect on MS, but there are studies that contradict this and it has not been proven.

I said, "I'm convinced that it can. Several published reports have demonstrated an increase in relapse during periods of significant stress."

Glen said, "You seem to put a lot of stock in scientific studies."

I said, "It depends on who publishes them. If it's not a well-respected journal, then I don't carry the information too far. And if I've had some personal experience with the topic, then I at least have a feel for what the researcher is saying; and there is no shortage of clinical reports."

Dysphagia

A not uncommon symptom of MS is difficulty in swallowing. I had noticed several times that Jerry often got choked while drinking. I had that problem sometimes, too.

Jerry asked, "Danny, MS can't cause me to get choked as much as I do, can it?"

I said, "It's a fairly common thing in advanced MS. I have some problems swallowing, too, but not as bad as you do. It's called dysphagia."

Jerry said, "I've had MS for 14 years, but this swallowing thing just started a few months ago."

I said, "It's usually people in more advanced stages. I haven't had that problem very long either."

Jerry asked, "What causes it?"

Dysphagia

Dysphagia, trouble swallowing, involves a large number of muscles and nerves, and thus there is ample opportunity for lesions, usually in the brainstem or cranial nerve pathways that affect the swallowing process. This is not a problem for most people with MS, but is not uncommon either.

A speech/language pathologist can determine specifics about a person's swallowing problems.

Liquids are more of a problem than solids.

Treatment can involve various exercises of the muscles involved. In severe cases the patient may be aspirating food or liquids into the lungs. If other strategies fail, it may be necessary to have feeding tubes inserted. This may be necessary to decrease the risk of pneumonia, malnutrition, or dehydration. This can be done with a nasogastric tube if only needed for a short period, such as following a surgery. If needed for a longer period of time, a percutaneous endoscopic gastrostomy (PEG) may be needed.

I said, "Instead of going down the esophagus, the food or drink is inhaled into the trachea. Sometimes this happens without the person even realizing it; then it's called silent aspiration."

Jerry asked, "Is it dangerous?"

I said, "If it's real bad it can cause malnutrition, dehydration, or pneumonia. In the most severe cases, the doctor might have to insert feeding tubes into the stomach. But those are the extreme cases; see your doctor."

Ignorance is not Bliss

The early days with MS didn't cloud my path; I knew where I wanted to go and I knew how to get there. But I didn't have anyone to teach me the fine points about the hateful disease I had to battle or the rare hateful people that will sometime take advantage of your misfortune. The one thing I have now, but needed then, is information. You can't have too much of it. My lack of knowledge about MS was costly.

I learned that ignorance about the malady is widespread—even among health-care providers. Most neurologists are well informed about MS, but many family medicine physicians and other specialists are not. That is not a mark against the medical profession—or, indeed, a mark against anyone. It is simply an observation of reality; there is too much information out there for the family doctor to be an expert on every subject. When one respected doctor, with a fine-tuned sense of humor, was asked to explain the difference in a "specialist" and a "general practitioner," he said, "A specialist is a doctor who knows more and more about less and less until eventually he knows everything about nothing. And a general practitioner is a doctor who knows less and less about more and more until eventually he knows nothing about everything."

The point is that a certain amount of responsibility falls on the patient. Unquestionably, the United States has the best health-care system in the world, mainly because it has the best doctors in the world. But the patient needs to be informed, too.

Jonathan rarely asked questions with answers that swam near the surface. He said, "I try to walk as much as I can, but that isn't very much anymore. Falling was never a problem, until lately. Several times over the last couple of weeks, while walking normally, I would suddenly start to stagger and then fall. For a few seconds, I couldn't get up, but in just a short period of time everything would be back to normal. This happened four times in one afternoon, and it happened a few times at home. It's really strange. Have you ever heard of that happening to anybody?"

I said, "It sounds like paroxysmal ataxia. These attacks are usually short and frequent. Ask your doctor. There are a couple of drugs that might help."

Jonathan asked, "How often do relapses usually occur, and what are the chances of a complete remission?"

I said, "The length of time that you have had the disease affects the rate of relapse, and there are other variables. The relapse rate is generally higher in the first five years. But like everything about MS, the chance of relapse in any particular case is highly unpredictable. The same is true about the degree of remission that can be expected."

Paroxysmal Symptoms

These are symptoms appearing suddenly with recurrent manifestations and brief episodes occurring frequently, often triggered by movement or sensory stimuli.

Trigeminal neuralgia was the first symptom of this kind to be identified in MS, although it occurs much more frequently in people without MS (19).

Dysarthria is occasionally paroxysmal. Generally these symptoms remit completely. Paroxysmal dysarthria is usually accompanied by other symptoms, the most common being ataxia. Andermann et al (105) described this in 1959. This symptom is highly characteristic of MS. More recent descriptions are on record (106, 107). The attacks are sudden and if the patient is talking at the time, the speech is slurred.

Paroxysmal ataxia is usually localized to the limbs on one side, but can be bilateral. There may be considerable clumsiness in the arm and a staggering walk may result in the patient falling. The attacks are short, usually less than 20 seconds, and they are usually frequent, maybe every 30 minutes or less.

With paroxysmal ataxia and dysarthria, remission is usually complete within a few weeks or months.

Paraesthesia is sometimes a paroxysmal symptom.

Paroxysmal pain has been reported (61).

Some other symptoms that can be paroxysmal are itching, diplopia, and loss of use of one or more limbs.

Many paroxysmal symptoms have been successfully treated with carbamazepine. Because this is poorly tolerated in some MS patients with motor disabilities, Acetozolamide (108) is an alternative for some of these patients.

Relapse Rate

A discussion of relapse rate first requires a clear understanding of what is meant by relapse. Other words, such as exacerbation, bout, episode, and attack are often used. The word "relapse" is slightly confusing without specifically excluding the first attack of the disease. In this book, I will use the very logical definition of one prominent researcher (152) who defined a relapse as "the appearance of a new symptom or the reappearance of a previous symptom at any time after the initial attack." No definition offers complete clarity. Often, it is necessarily a judgment call by the neurologist as to whether a temporary symptom is truly a relapse or the result of fatigue, temperature change, or some other factor that is independent of the disease process.

In a large study by Muller (124), an annual relapse rate of 0.5 was found. Thygesen (153) found a much higher annual relapse rate of 1.15. Averaging the rates in 4 studies (124, 153, 154, & 155). I calculated the average annual relapse rate to be .64.

The annual relapse rate is effected by duration of disease and other factors. Muller (124) found relapse to be much more common in the first five years of the disease, particularly in the first year. Broman et al (156) also found a sharp decline in relapse rate after the first five years.

The time from onset to the first relapse is usually longer than the time between the first relapse and the second relapse (157).

Prospect of Remission

In a study by Thygesen (153), almost complete remission was found in approximately one half of observed relapses, twenty five percent had partial remission, and the remaining twenty five percent showed no improvement. Thygesen found in this study that the degree of recovery was more strongly related to the rapidity of onset than to the severity or nature of the symptoms. Other studies have supported these findings (154,158,159).

Muller (124) described a relationship between duration of relapse and chance of remission. He found that in a relapse lasting two months, 85% of the symptoms remitted completely, at three months only 30% remitted, and at six months only 10%. After a year the remission rate dropped to 6%, and remission never occurred after eight years. Kurtzke (142) found no remission of symptoms lasting more than two years.

A relationship between the severity of the symptoms and the prospect for improvement has also been found. Kurtzke et al (159) found that the chance of improvement was greater for severe symptoms than for mild ones.

Complete remission occurs more often after the initial attack than after subsequent relapses.

Remission is less likely for patients already severely disabled (160).

A long first attack decreases the chances of recovery from the first relapse (126).

Significant recovery from a relapse improves the expectation of recovery from the next relapse (161) according to one study. Kurtzke (162) was unable to confirm this.

Symptoms that are usually attributed to small lesions—optic neuritis, diplopia, nystagmus, or cranial nerve lesions in general—have a better prognosis for substantial recovery (160) than do symptoms attributable to large lesions.

CHAPTER 17

Introspection

* The Fear of a Nursing Home 200
* More on Business and MS 201
* Losing Independence 203

The Fear of a Nursing Home

I put all my effort into extinguishing all negative thoughts and cultivating all the positive ones. This wasn't always easy. I pushed many negative imaginings into my subconscious, but occasionally a thought, or a fear, took root. Such was the case with nursing homes. I knew that most people with MS would never have to call a nursing home, home. But I also knew that a lot of people with MS would.

Steve Malcolm had to. Usually, when an MS patient needs nursing home care it is because of physical limitations. Steve had his share of these, but he also had serious cognitive problems. I avoided the nursing home environment as much as possible, but I did make exceptions to visit Steve occasionally.

My personal experience with cognitive problems provided a reservoir of empathy for Steve. He had little trouble talking, but he had considerable trouble making the words flow in any kind of orderly way. By the time he reached the end of a mental paragraph, he often forgot what he was trying to say. I asked, "Does it bother you to talk about the cognitive problems?"

Steve said, "No. I don't mind."

I knew that Steve was ultra aware of the intellectual changes that had occurred, because I was ultra aware of the changes that had occurred in me. He was aware of his forgetfulness. He knew that his reasoning ability was greatly diminished. He was aware of his difficulty in carrying on a fluent conversation. I knew from my own experience that this awareness of the problem could nourish a deep depression. Steve didn't admit to being depressed, but I knew that he was.

Fortunately, my problems only cost me a business and a medical degree; I could still carry on with an abridged version of life. Steve could no longer function on his own. His wife died and he had no family close by. He had no option but a nursing home.

I asked, "Did you notice problems with your memory first or was it someone in your family?"

Steve said, "Mary would get mad with me for not doing things she asked me to do. I knew something was wrong, but I didn't know what it was. Eventually, we realized it was the multiple sclerosis. It got worse real fast. After Mary died, I had to have someone to take care of me. There was no one."

I didn't want to wind up like Steve, but I knew it could happen. His daughter lived a thousand miles away and he saw her at Christmas. I was already more dependent on Vivian than I ever expected to be. I could no longer drive, and I couldn't leave the house without Vivian. Solidarity was quickly becoming my lifestyle. An acute awareness of the external losses and inner subsidence, of fresh limitations and flagging energies, continued to remove me from the independence that had been my lifeblood.

I still dreamed of walks through the woods, but not alone. The fantasy of ending my isolation was constant. The thoughts of poverty, and necessity, and living alone, and to ask nothing and to expect nothing but to match the solitude that I find with the solitude that I bring, carried my mind to places I never wanted to go. But I made certain that these mental journeys were nothing more than fly-bys. My stay in these dungeons never lasted long.

My most repetitive prayer is that I will not outlive Vivian. I am confident of my salvation, so I have no fear of death. But I have a very real fear of being left alone with MS, or of living and dying among strangers in a nursing home. I never did find the strength that Barbara had.

More on Business and MS

I saw that carving a niche in life, with multiple sclerosis as the backdrop, would not be easy. The cognitive impairment eliminated most intellectual pursuits from the possibility mix—at least any that I had interest in. Physical problems put a damper on most other ideas. Still, I resisted the temptation to quit.

The business had sustained my spirit and lifted me up and shielded me from unwelcome thoughts about MS. The Onion had made challenge a way of life for me, and for many years challenge was the backdrop in every direction. And now a vacuum existed where challenge once lived.

Business is by nature a risky intent. But most of my life had been spent in business, and if I had a future, I knew that I would probably find it there. It was my ignorance of what MS could do that caused the loss of New Bros., Inc. Now I knew, and maybe that awareness would be sufficient to safeguard me, if other opportunities arose.

Andrew Wallace and Gary Jansen were both ex-businessmen who now had MS. Gary had been half owner of a farm in South Carolina, and Andrew had been half owner of an auto repair shop in Charlotte. Andrew could not walk, but did okay in a wheelchair. Gary could still walk with a cane, but not well.

One day we were having a conversation about our business past. I asked Andrew how multiple sclerosis affected his business. He said, "It affected me, but it really didn't have much impact on our business. My partner took up all the slack. Within a few months of the diagnosis, he knew more about MS than I did. He protected both of us and understood my limitations. I couldn't have asked for a better partner. We were best of friends before MS and we were even closer after it started."

I asked, "Why did you leave the business?"

Andy said, "I couldn't do my part any longer, and I felt like a burden on Nick. I still own half the business, but I don't draw a salary. Nick sends me a check every month, but I don't cash them. My energy level was low. My mind functioned like it was in cold storage. My physical condition deteriorated to the point that I needed a wheelchair. It was obvious then that I was more of a burden than a help. My expertise was imported sports cars. I loved the business. I would like to return to the shop one day, and I have that option, but I will have to improve a lot. We all know that isn't likely."

I turned and asked, "Gary, why did you quit farming?"

Gary said, "I wasn't as lucky in my choice of partners as Andy. My partner, Derrick Osborne, never accepted that I had MS. I don't think he even knew what MS was, or what it could do."

I said, "It sounds like you're hanging on to some grudges."

Gary said, "I didn't hold it against him because he didn't understand MS. I held it against him because he didn't try to understand it. And I held it against him because he turned his back on me at a time when I couldn't defend myself. And when I looked up, there was nothing left.

"A few years after the diagnosis I made some disastrous mistakes in judgment. It was like I had become somebody else. My mind didn't function right anymore. Derrick didn't help. He blamed me when I was wrong, but he took no responsibility for his own actions. He would not accept that I had a disease that affected my mind and my body. When disaster struck, he took the 'I told you so' approach. And he couldn't understand that MS was the culprit, not me.

"We had a really special relationship before MS, but Derrick couldn't handle the changes or the added pressure that MS brought. Ultimately, we lost the business. It was almost as if he wanted us to lose it to get revenge on me for having MS. He owned half the business, so I know he didn't really want us to lose it, but it sure seemed that way at the time. We haven't talked much since then. After I got MS, the person I thought was the best friend I ever had turned out to be no friend at all."

I said, "Gary, maybe you need to put yourself in your ex-partner's shoes. Maybe he viewed the partnership as strictly a business arrangement, and personal matters went beyond the scope of his responsibility. I've talked to other MS patients who were damaged when they confused the real nature of a relationship—when they injected friendship into a formula that was completely financial in nature. That is not to say that your partner was of poor character; he simply was not prepared to handle the baggage that came with multiple sclerosis."

Gary said, "I know, but I could have still done so much. I wasn't dead yet. Derrick walked away and left me stranded with a disease that was slowly destroying me. I would never have walked away from him, if fate had switched our roles."

The talk of business was hypnotic. I had a burning desire to reestablish myself in some aspect of business, but I doubted that I could. I had experience in my favor, but that might not be enough to overcome the physical limitations and the mental impairment. Besides, it takes money to start a business, and Vivian and I didn't have a lot of that lying around. And I have learned that MS and banks make lousy friends, so debt financing of a new venture is almost impossible for a person with multiple sclerosis, regardless of the experience.

Losing Independence

It has been my history that I fight my own battles, and generally I had confidence that I could handle them. Even MS was simply another battle that I had to fight. Things got more difficult to do, and there were more and more things I couldn't do, but I always felt in control—even if what I controlled had declined.

Slowly, this all changed. The first casualty was my ability to leave town alone. Next went my ability to drive. Walking became a major challenge. Just the ability to see had shifted to the iffy column.

I am by nature an overly ambitious person, almost hyper-zealous about life. Now most of my plans never find a physical life, but stay bottled up in some faraway storage that the mind maintains. I had lost my independence.

But fortunately, Vivian was finding hers. Our family seemed destined to be involved with health-care—but not with me in the capacity of doctor. It was Vivian's turn now. Augusta State University accepted Vivian into their nursing program in 1999. Vivian had discovered her calling. The passion that was once missing in her life surfaced. The challenge provided her with lost hope. In 2001 Vivian became an RN.

CHAPTER 18

The Attack Continues

* Gait Problems 205
* The Rebellion Gains Strength 205
* Blindness 205

Gait Problems

Trouble walking was not new to me, but the severity of the problem increased dramatically by 1993. Gait problems are one of the most common symptoms of multiple sclerosis.

They are usually associated with muscle weakness in one leg (monoparesis), both legs (paraparesis), spasticity, loss of balance, or sensory deficits. A drunken type of gait, known as ataxia, is common.

My cane became a permanent appendage. I grew accustomed to it and eventually felt comfortable using it. In fact, I felt naked without it.

On vacation in Washington D. C., I had my first experience with a wheelchair. As with most MS symptoms, the problems of balance worsened with heat. We started out early at the Washington Monument. It was cool in the morning, and I was confident that my cane would sustain me on the walk to the Smithsonian. I was wrong. Using a wheelchair, for the first time, was an absolute necessity. The cane really didn't make me feel "disabled." The wheelchair did.

The Rebellion Gains Strength

The level of physical exertion required to incapacitate me became less and less. Compensating with my cane became more and more difficult. By early 1995, a wheelchair seemed like more than a possibility. Its status had been upgraded to almost inevitable.

It is, I contend, the ultimate betrayal when I tell my legs to hold me up, and they refuse. Or I tell them to walk in one direction and they take off in another. Or I tell my eyes that I want to read for awhile, and all they let me see is a blur.

After my legs entered into this mutiny with my eyes, and my brain continued with its work slowdown, the future didn't look any too rosy on the surface. But I didn't argue anymore. I knew now that I didn't have to have my legs or my eyes to be happy. It would be nice if my mind could still operate at one hundred percent, but I knew I would survive that, too.

Blindness

In November of 1996, the walls came tumbling down again. An acute relapse of optic neuritis left me legally blind.

Reading, without high magnification on a video magnifier, was now impossible. Any thought of driving was only a distant memory. Carrying a State ID Card rather than a Driver's License was an unpleasant reminder of the out-of-control direction my life had taken. I had lost my independence.

MS can cause total blindness, but, fortunately, this relapse didn't. Legal blindness and complete blindness are very different. I could still see light. I could tell the difference in a house and a car. I could even read with the help of a video magnifier. But I could not drive, and I could not recognize people. The world had become a strange and uncertain place.

Nevertheless, I had to believe that the man who trims his sail to the current breeze is dead already, and I wasn't dead already. The world defines disability, but that did not mean that I had to accept the world's definition.

I saw a ghost of old griefs in Vivian's eyes. I thought of my life as something that happened long ago. Medical school and business were both gateways, but the gates had been closed. I was not leaving or entering the gates. Vivian accompanied me on my trip to nowhere. I was bound in a vacuum with impermeable membranes at every edge. I had to find a gate that led out.

CHAPTER 19

Putting It All Together

* The Cognitive Story–An Overview 208
* Absolutes 209
* In Closing 211

Danny S. New

The Cognitive Story–An Overview

My story is incomplete without a final summation of the cognitive effects of MS. In, "*On Multiple Sclerosis*," I have included much of what I have learned about MS and the mind, other common symptoms of this disease, and a list of terms that crop up in the literature frequently (terms used in this book are included in the glossary on page 230). But my personal story is so tightly connected to the impact multiple sclerosis can have on the mind that I am compelled to include an overview of how this aspect of MS affected me.

The horrors that the disease held in waiting for me in 1980 were not at all what I had expected. I knew that at some point in my future a wheelchair would probably show up. And I knew that I might be blind one day. But seven years passed after the diagnosis before I heard anything about what MS could do to my mind. By then, MS had robbed me of a dream life. By the time I figured out the mind connection my life was in shambles.

Perhaps I had expected too much out of life. The Vidalia Onion and New Bros., Inc. were my legacy, and it should have taken more than an untimely relapse of MS to end that life. Each time I hear of a recent IPO, or have a new brainstorm about marketing The Onion, or consider the many dreams that losing the business shattered, or think of my son and David's son and the business we will never share with them, or consider the likely MS battles yet to come, then the loss cuts too deep to comprehend.

But somewhere, something positive has to come from the losses. In part, what I did not know about MS changed the course of my life forever.

Hopefully, my story will benefit others. What happened to my family and me should never happen to anyone.

Some of the information I needed in 1985 doctors had in 1985, but they didn't tell me, even when I asked the right questions. They didn't tell me what Rao knew—that MS usually results in some degree of cognitive impairment. Even if I had thought about it, I'm sure I would have assumed that cognitive problems only occurred in advanced disease, and on January 8, 1985, I had not reached my fifth year with MS. I still tried to deny that I had a problem, and, to a substantial degree, I had convinced myself of that.

In reality, doctors knew, albeit in much less detail, in the late nineteenth century that MS did affect the mind (34). And it wasn't limited to advanced disease. Rao et al (34) found that there was no correlation between mental changes and duration of disease or severity of disability.

I knew in 1985, when I transferred my life and my future, that a relapse had started. But I didn't know what Grant et al knew (38) and most neurologists know today—that cognitive impairment may worsen dramatically during a relapse.

In 1985, I didn't "feel" disabled, and I had not seen Van den Bury et al's study (33) that confirmed early cognitive impairment in patients with mild physical disability. I could still walk without a cane and I wasn't blind—yet.

Moreover, in 1985 the clinical use of MRI was only a couple of years old and studies relating total lesion area to defects in reasoning, language function, and recent memory (59) were just showing up in the medical literature.

I had not read the writings of Dr. W. B. Matthew's (45) warning of the potential need to protect MS patients from "the thoughtless dispersion of the family assets."

And as Ombredane and others have reported (32), "The changes (intellectual) were often not apparent in ordinary conversation or on routine examination." This greatly increased the chance that this serious problem would go unrecognized by friends and family. And speech dysfunction is not common, even in severely disabled patients (37). This substantially increases the chances that even severe cognitive impairment will pass unnoticed in casual conversation.

One aspect of the cognitive story deals with impairment of the brain's ability to efficiently process information. The relative slowness in processing and reacting to new information became more and more obvious to me, and more and more of a problem. Now I often question the appropriateness of my response when the volume of information is high, or unique, or the time to consider the new information is short. (For a discussion of the special case of cognitive problems during a relapse see page 109.)

Absolutes

The internal debate on "situational ethics" resurfaced often. Right and wrong were not simple for me in 1984. But now I have a guidebook, the Bible.

Every good man harbors convictions about right and wrong. They glue together the fragments in his life. When a man's conduct is at variance with

> **Impaired Information Processing (Cont. From Page 108)**
>
> The reduced speed of information processing and the reduced volume of information that the brain can handle are at least part of the cognitive story relative to MS. When bombarded with too much information in a short period of time, judgment may be impaired. This can result from unique, unexpected situations that require the brain to process new information at a rapid rate.
>
> Processing of visual information (188) and auditory information (189) has been demonstrated to be slowed in MS.
>
> Feinstein et al (60) found that, as a group, MS patients made more errors or performed slower on all psychometric task than a group of matched controls. Patients that showed an increase in lesion load either showed a worsening in performance on some psychometric tasks or a reduced ability to improve with practice on some tests having to do with attention and information-processing speed.
>
> In their study, Ruchkin et al (94) found that, relative to controls, MS patients were significantly slower on tests which required rapid information processing. The patients had longer reaction times and made more errors than controls.
>
> Attention deficits including short-term memory and information processing capacity appear to occur relatively early in the disease for many patients (190).
>
> It has been reported that chronic progressive patients, because of demyelinating lesions in the prefrontal cortex, are likely to lose their capacity to actively control their information processing ability (61, 62).

his convictions, he knows that it is a departure. The conscience provides this revelation. But problems are not always painted white or black; they are often, or sometimes, an unrecognizable hue. When we lost the brined onions in 1984 my conscience spoke, but I didn't listen.

For a long time I struggled with the situational ethics argument. But the concept didn't hold water. The argument denies the existence of absolutes.

But if there are no absolutes then every question about right and wrong becomes a matter of opinion, and belongs to the best debater. Every moral question in life has an "absolute" for an answer. "Situational ethics" is an absurdity. If not, then right and wrong are nothing more than a matter of interpretation. Morality would centrifuge down into a mass of opinions rather than one irrefutable truth.

The Ten Commandments are a simple and to the point list of absolutes. "Thou Shalt Not Lie" came to us without any qualifiers. These four words in this one commandment provided the answer when the debate about overstating the inventories on our financial statement came along.

The Bible was clear, common sense only pointed in one direction—for a clear mind—and even good business sense pointed away from inflating the inventories.

An argument can easily be made that MS caused the poor judgment, and I will die believing that. But regardless of the MS connection, it is glaringly obvious that I failed in 1984 when I insisted that we file a false financial statement.

But when we lost our business in 1985, the blame cannot be shared. MS gets full billing.

In Closing

It seems that I have lived life in reverse. I left academia prematurely and ventured into the "real" world—not cautiously with fear, and without consciousness of my ignorance of what was out there, but rather with an unfettered leap, certain that I was larger than any problem life could recruit from its legion of uncertainties.

I think that by the writing of this book I believed that I would find a closure to the tragedies that MS had imposed on my life and on the lives of those dearest to me—hoping that by telling the story I would no longer be haunted by ghosts from any part of my past.

As time passed, my acceptance of the way life had turned out came easier. My spiritual growth helped me to put everything in perspective. It helped me to get my priorities straight, and it reminded me of how insignificant this life is, relative to eternity. I saw the bigger picture, and MS wasn't part of it.

I believe that we are all brought to this world for a purpose. I had a view of what I wanted that purpose to be for me. Early on, I made a blueprint for my life. But it was my blueprint. I never asked God about his. And there were no provisions for the unexpected.

I told God to take control and to do things the way he wanted to, and then I got mad because he didn't choose the way I wanted him to choose. When MS sent all my plans and dreams cascading into nothingness, I blamed God. I was wrong.

Danny S. New

The most difficult of times now are memories of the simplest of times long ago—those early days of growing onions, when the unexpected routinely knocked at the door. In farming, the unexpected always lurks in the shadows, and it's usually an unwanted guest.

I remember a particularly dreary day in 1976. We finished transplanting onions that day, and irrigating was an absolute necessity. At least we thought so then. In those days, everything seemed like a matter of life or death. We pitched a tent, built a fire, and "toted" pipe in the freezing cold for most of the night. What I remember is the peaceful sound of the water under extreme pressure as it surged from the guns. I close my eyes and see the fine mist as it settles on the onions in the dimness of night.

On early spring mornings, now, I often awake to the sounds of robins and bluejays chirping outside my window. And I almost get out of bed, anxious to tour the onion fields, or to rush to the plant to check out the onion ring line or the bottling line. And then I remember that I have no onion fields or onion ring lines or bottling lines. And I lie back down and pray.

It's strange what specific memories haunt me—things from the past, once taken for granted and suddenly gone. Simple things, like the clanking of jars on the production line late at night, or my name called on the PA system, or the sound of a forklift shuffling product. It is the more routine things of life that we take for granted, and that we miss the most when they are gone.

Life is a continuum, I have come to believe. It is not a series of unrelated events. Every experience flows from and is modified by all the rest of the events in our past. The sum total of these experiences makes us who we are and what we are. The Vidalia Onion, medical school, multiple sclerosis, the wrong choices, the right choices, and my relationship with God—they have all been forever integrated into my soul.

If, in the end, the gains outnumber the losses, then I will judge life to have been good. Maybe it didn't take me as far as I wanted to go, or as far as I thought it should have taken me, but it had to be enough, because it was all that had been chosen for me. What I have to do now is to squeeze out any remaining drops of happiness that may have survived the trip. There is no further point in calculating consequences.

Ralph Waldo Emerson said in his essay on Power, "It is not what they do to you, but it is what you do with what they do to you that matters." And Emerson says, "...Above all, we must put what we know into practice. And first, last, middle, and without end honor every truth by use." I commit myself to a search for truth, and when I find it, I will use it.

I hope that this will not be my last writing. I plan to record the progression of this disease for as long as I can. Now I am legally blind, but that does not mean totally blind. There are aids that enable me to keep writing and reading—for now at least. At this point, walking is difficult, and falling is routine, but of much more concern to me are the intellectual problems. When and if my mental state deteriorates to the point that my thoughts are no longer coherent, then I will stop. Until then, and forever thereafter, I will put my trust in God.

Treatments Aimed at Altering Course of Disease

MS treatments basically fall into two categories—those directed at altering the natural course of the disease, and those intended to alleviate specific symptoms.

FDA approved the first drug intended to alter the course of the disease in 1993. Betaseron® (interferon beta-1b) was approved for use on relapsing-remitting MS. Its effectiveness on chronic-progressive disease has not yet been determined.

A multicenter, randomized, double-blind, placebo-controlled trial indicated that interferon beta-1b was well tolerated and had a beneficial effect on relapsing-remitting MS. Interferon beta-1b is a genetically engineered product produced by a strain of the bacteria Escherichia coli (E. coli) whose DNA has been altered so that it contains the gene for human interferon.

Interferons are a family of naturally occurring proteins, three of which have been identified (alpha, beta, and gamma interferon). Betaseron® has both antiviral and immunoregulatory activities.

In a 2-year controlled study there was a 31% reduction in annual relapse rate in a group treated with Betaseron® compared to a placebo group (from 1.31 to 0.9). The number of patients free of relapses was 16% IN THE placebo group compared to 25% in the Betaseron® group. There was a significant reduction in the median percent increase in lesion load as determined by MRI for the treated group (1.1%) as opposed to the placebo group (16.5%).

In a study of frequent MRI scans (every 6 weeks) 29% of the placebo group had new or expanding lesions as compared to only 6% in the treated group.

The 2-year study was continued for a third year, but with only 80%% of the original patients participating. The third year MRI data did not show a trend toward additional benefit for the treated patients as opposed to those on placebo. This may be the result of the production of antibodies against Betaseron®, which occurs in approximately 45% of patients receiving the treatment. But the relationship between clinical efficacy and antibody production is not known.

The mechanism of action remains unknown. Several possible mechanisms have been considered. One possibility might be interferon beta's ability to inhibit interferon gamma synthesis (292 293). Downregulating tumor necrosis factor (TNF) is another possible mechanism (292). Studies strongly suggest that TNF may be toxic to oligodendrocytes (294), the myelin producing cells of the central nervous system.

According to a study by the National Institute of Health, the drug inhibits infiltration of damaging immune substances across the blood-brain barrier.

Avonex® is the second drug approved as a treatment for MS, that altered the natural course of the disease. Avonex®, like Betaseron®, is an interferon beta produced through recombinant DNA technology. But Avonex® (interferon beta-1A) is produced in mammalian cells whereas bacterial cells produce Betaseron®. A 30-mg dose of Avonex® is administered once a week, opposed to the 250-mg dose of Betaseron® that is administered every other day. Both of these drugs have been shown to reduce the frequency of attacks.

A third drug, Copaxone® (glatiramer acetate), formerly called copolymer I, soon followed. The March 1998 issue of Neurology reported that the results of a study indicated sustained effects of Copaxone® after 32 months, and that mean relapse rate was reduced 29%.

A study published in the April 1998 issue of neurology showed MRI evidence that Copaxone® reduces the frequency, the number, and area of new lesions. This study showed that treatment with Copaxone® reduced the frequency of new enhancing lesions by 57%. Evidence indicates that the drug has a clear beneficial effect on relapse rate.

The mechanism(s) of action is (are) unknown, but it is thought to act by modifying immune processes that are thought to be involved in the disease process in MS. One concern in using any drug that modifies the immune response is the possibility that it could interfere with useful immune function. For example, it could interfere, in theory, with the immune systems ability to recognize foreign antigens and thus interfere with the body's defenses against infection and tumor surveillance. But at this point there is no evidence that this occurs, but the risk has not been evaluated.

It is known that glatiramer acetate reduces the intensity and severity of experimental allergic encephalomyelitis (EAE), an experimental animal model for MS. But how this works is not clearly understood.

REFERENCES

(1) Fischer C, Joyeux O, Haguenauer J P, Maugiere F, Schott B 1984 Surdite et acouphenes lors de poussees dans 10 cas de sclerose en plawues. Revue Neurologique 140: 117-125.

(2) Quine D B, Regan D, Berverley K I, Murray T J 1984 Patients with multiple sclerosis experience hearing loss specifically for shifts of tone frequency. Archives of Neurology 41: 506-508.

(3) Quine D B, Regan D, Murray T J 1984 Degraded discrimination between speech like sounds by patients with multiple sclerosis and Friedreich's ataxia. Brain 107: 1113-1122.

(4) Sanders E A C M, Arts R J H M 1986 Paraesthesiae in multiple sclerosis. Journal of the Neurological Sciences 74: 297-305.

(5) McDonald W I, Sears T A 1970 The effects of experimental demyelination on conduction in the central nervous system. Brain 93: 583-598.

(6) Freal J E, Kraft G H, Coryell J K 1984 Symptomatic fatigue in multiple sclerosis. Archives of Physical Medicine and Rehabilitation 65: 135-138.

(7) Krupp L B, Alvarez L A, LaRocca N G, Scheinberg L C 1988 Fatigue in multiple sclerosis. Archives of Neurology 45: 435-437.

(8) Canadian MS Research Group 1987 A randomized controlled trial of amantadine in fatigue associated with multiple sclerosis. Canadian Journal of Neurological Sciences 14: 273-278.

(9) Shibasaki H, McDonald W I, Kuroiwa Y, 1981, Racial modification of clinical picture of multiple sclerosis: comparison between British and Japanese patients. Journal of the Neurological Sciences 49: 253-271.

(10) Kurtzke J F 1970 Clinical manifestations of multiple sclerosis. In: Vinken P J, Bruyn G W (eds) Handbook of clinical neurology, Vol 9. North Holland, Amsterdam, pp 161-216.

(11) Kurtzke J F 1970 Clinical manifestations of multiple sclerosis. In: Vinken P J, Bruyn G W (eds) Handbook of clinical neurology, Vol 9. North-Holland, Amsterdam, pp 161-216.

(12) Uhthoff W 1890 Untersuchungen uber die bei der multiplen Herdsklerose vorkommenden Augenstorungen. Archiv fur Psychiatrie und Nervenkrankheiten 21: 55-116 and 303-410.

(13) Brown M R, Putnam T J 1939 Remissions in multiple sclerosis. Archives of Neurology and Psychiatry 4

(14) National Multiple Sclerosis Society, New York, N. Y.

(15) Bradley W. G., Whitty C W M 1966 Acute optic neuritis: prognosis for development of multiple sclerosis. Journal of Neurology, Neurosurgery and Psychiatry 31: 10-18.

(16) Sandberg H O 1972 Acute retrobulbar neuritis — a retrospective study. Acta Ophthalmologica 50: 3-8.

(17) Davis F A, Bergen D, Schauf C, McDonald W I, Deutsch W 1976 Movement phosphenes in optic neuritis: a new clinical sign. Neurology 26: 1100-1104.

(18) Earl C J, Martin B 1967 Prognosis in optic neuritis related to age. Lancet 1: 74-76.

(19) Matthews W. B., McAlpine Multiple Sclerosis. Second Edition. 1991

(20) Reagan D, Silver R, Murray T J 1977 Visual acuity and contrast sensitivity in multiple sclerosis-hidden visual loss. Brain 100: 563-579.

(21) Carroll F D 1940 Retrobulbar neuritis. Observations on one hundred cases. Archives of Ophthalmology 24: 44-54.

(22) Perkin G D, Rose F C 1979 Optic neuritis and its differential diagnosis. Oxford University Press, Oxford.

(23) Uhthoff W 1889 Untersuchen uber die bei der multiplen Herdsklerose vorkommenden Augenstorungen. Archiv fur Psychiatrie und Nervenkrankheiten 21: 55-116.

(24) Schauf C L, Davis F A 1974 Impulse conduction in multiple sclerosis: a theoretical basis for modification by temperature and pharmacological agents. Journal of Neurology, Neurosurgery and Psychiatry 37: 152-161.

(25) Brenneis M, Harrer G, Seizer H 1979 Zur Temperaturempfindlichkeit von Multiple-Sklerose-Kranken. Fortscfhritte der Neurologie-Psychiatrie 47: 320-325.

(26) Zweifach P H 1978 Studies of hyperthermia in optic neuropathy. Archives of Ophthalmology 96: 18361-1834.

(27) Waxman S G, Geschwind N 1983 Major morbidity related to hyperthermia in multiple sclerosis. Annals of Neurology 13: 348.

(28) Brickner R M 1950 The significance of localized vasoconstrictions in multiple sclerosis. Research Publications of the Association for Research in Nervous and Mental Diseases 28: 236-244.

(29) Geller M 1974 Appearance of signs and symptoms of multiple sclerosis in response to cold. Mount Sinai Journal of Medicine 41: 127-130.

(30) Honan W P, Heron J R, Foster D H, Snelgar R S 1987 Paradoxical effects of temperature in multiple sclerosis. Journal of Neurology, Neurosurgery and Psychiatry 50: 1160-1164.

(31) Charcot J M 1898 In: Bourneville (ed) Lecons sur les maladies du system nerveux, Vol 1. Louis Bataille, Paris, pp 237-238.

(32) Ombredane A 1929 Sur les troubles mentaux de la sclerose en plaques. These de Paris.

(33) Van den Burg W, van Zomeren E A, Minderhoud J M, Prange A J A, Meijer N S A 1987 Cognitive impairment in patients with multiple sclerosis and mild physical disability. Archives of Neurology 44: 494-501.

(34) Rao S M, Hammeke T A, McQuillen M P, Khatri B O, Lloyd D 1984 Memory disturbance in chronic progressive multiple sclerosis. Archives of Neurology 41: 625-631.

(36) Grigsby J, Ayarbe S D, Kravcisin N, Busenbark D, Working memory impairment among persons with chronic progressive multiple sclerosis. J Neurol (1994) 241: 125-131.

(37) Staples D, Lincoln N B 1979 Intellectual impairment in multiple sclerosis and its relation to functional abilities. Rheumatology and Rehabilitation 18: 153-160.

(38) Grant I, McDonald W I, Trimble M R, Smith E, Reed E 1984 Deficient learning and memory in early and middle phases of multiple sclerosis. Journal of Neurology, Neurosurgery and Psychiatry 47: 250-255.

(39) Gilman S, Bloedel J R, Lechtenberg R. Disorders of the cerebellum. Philadelphia: FA Davis, 1981.

(40) Diener H C, Bichgans J, Guschlbauer BV, Bacher M, Rapp H, Langenbach P. Associated postural adjustments with body movement in normal subjects and patients with parkinsonism and cerebellar disease. Rev Neurol (Paris) 1990; 146: 555-63.

(41) Kurtzke J F. Clinical manifestations of multiple sclerosis. In: Vinken P J and Bruyn G W, eds. Handbook of clinical neurology, vol 9, Multiple sclerosis and other demyelinating diseases. New York: Elsevier, 1970: 161-216.

(42) Beatty WW, Goodkin D E, Beatty P A, Monson N (1989) Frontal lobe dysfunction and memory impairment in patients with chronic progressive multiple sclerosis. Brain Cogn 11: 73-86.

(43) Friedman H R, Janas J D, Goldman-Rakic P S (1990) Enhancement of metabolic acitivity in the diencephalon of monkeys performing working memory tasks: a 2-deoxyglucose study in having rhesus monkeys. J Cogn Neurosci 2: 18-31.

(44) Rao S M, Hammeke T A (1984) Speech: Winsconsin Card Sorting Test performance in relapsing-remitting and chronic-progressive multiple sclerosis.

(45) McAlpine's Multiple Sclerosis, Churchill Livingstone, Edinburgh, London, Melbourne, New York - 1991

(46) Amato, M.P., M.D.; Ponziani, G., M.D.; Pracucci, G., M.D.; Bracco, L., M.D.; Siracusa, G., M.D.; Amaducci, L., M.D.; Cognitive Impairment in Early-Onset Multiple Sclerosis. Arch Neurol/Vol 52, Feb. 1995.

(47) Young A C, Saunders J, Ponsford J R, Mental change as an early feature of multiple sclerosis. J Neurol Neurosurg Psychiatry. 1976; 39: 1008-1013.

(48) Grant C M, McDonald W I, Trimble M R, et al. Deficient learning and memory in early and middle phases of multiple sclerosis. J Neurol Neurosurg Psychiatry. 1984; 47: 250-255.

(49) Lyon-Caen O, Jouvent R, Hauser S, et al. Cognitive function in recent-onset demyelinating diseases. Arch Neurol. 1986; 43: 1138-1141.

(50) Beatty W W, Goodkin D E, Beatty P A, Monson N. Frontal lobe dysfunction and memory impairment in patients with chronic progressive multiple sclerosis. Brain Cogn. 1989; 11:73-86.

(51) Kurtzke J F. A proposal for a uniform minimal record of disability in multiple sclerosis. Acta Neurol Scand. 1981; 64(suppl 87): 110-129.

(52) Heaton R K, Nelson L M, Thompson D S, et al. Neuropsychological findings in relapsing-remitting and chronic-progressive multiple sclerosis. J Consult Clin Psychol. 1985; 53: 103-110.

(53) Beatty W W, Goodkin D E, Hertsgaard D, et al. Clinical and demographic predictors of cognitive performance in multiple sclerosis: do diagnostic type, disease duration, and disability matter? Arch Neurol. 1990; 47: 305-308.

(54) Peyser J M, Edwards J R, Poser C M, Filskov S B 1980 Cognitive function in patients with multiple sclerosis. Archives of Neurology 37: 577-579.

(55) Rao S M, Leo G J, Bernardin L, Unverzagt F, (1991a) Cognitive dysfunction in multiple sclerosis. I. Frequency, patterns, and prediction. Neurology, Cleveland, 41, 685-691.

(56) Rao S M, Leo G J, Ellington L, Nauertz T, Bernardin L, Unverzagt F, (1991b) Cognitive dysfunction in multiple sclerosis. II. Impact on employment and social functioning. Neurology, Cleveland, 41, 692-696.

(57) Ivnik R J, (1978) Neuropsychological test performance as a function of the duration of multiple sclerosis-related symptomatology. Journal of Clinical Psychiatry, 39, 304-312.

(58) Marsh G G, (1980), Disability and intellectual function in multiple sclerosis patients. Journal of Nervous and Mental Disease, 168, 758-762.

(59) Rao S M, Leo G J, Haughton V M, St Aubin-Faubert P, Bernardin L, (1989), Correlation of magnetic resonance imaging with neuopsychological testing in multiple sclerosis. Neurology, Cleveland, 39, 161-166.

(60) Feinstein A, Karsounis L D, Miller D H, Youl B D, Ron M A, (1992) Clinically isolated lesions of the type seen in multiple sclerosis: a cognitive, psychiatric, and MRI follow up study. Journal of Neurology, Neursosurgery, and Psychiatry, 55, 869-876.

(61) Fuster J M (1989) The prefrontal cortex: anatomy, physiology, and neuropspychology of the frontal lobe, 2nd edn. Raven Press, New York.

(62) Luria A R (1980) Higher cortical functions in man, 2nd edn. BVasic Books, New York.

(63) Schumacher GA, Beebe G, Kibler RF, Kurland LT, Kurtzke JF, McDowell F, Nagler B, Sibley WA, Tourtellotte WW, Willmon TL. Problems of experimental trials of therapy in multiple sclerosis: report by the panel on the evaluation of experimental trials of therapy in multiple sclerosis. Ann NY Acad Sci 1965; 122:P 552-68.

(64) Poser CM, Paty DW, Scheinberg L. New diagnostic criteria for multiple sclerosis: guidelines for research protocols. Ann Neurol 1983;13:227-31.

(65) Nuwer MR. Evoked potentials. In: Cook SD, ed. Handbook of multiple sclerosis. New York: Marcel Dekker, 1990: 271-90.

(66) Allen I V, Millar J H D, Kirk J, Shillington R K A 1979 Systemic lupus erythematosus clinically resembling multiple sclerosis and with unusual pathological and ultrastructural features. Journal of Neurology, Neurosurgery and Psychiatry 42: 362-401.

(67) Alexander G/E, Provost T T, Stevens M B, Alexander E L 1981 Sjogren syndrome: central nervous system manifestations. Neurology 31: 1391-1396.

(68) Alexander E L, Malinow K, Lejewski J E, Jerdan Sjogren's syndrome with central nervous system disease mimicking multiple sclerosis. Annals of Internal Medicine 104: 323-330.

(69) Fadli M E, Yousef M M 1973 Neuro-Behcet's syndrome in the United Arab Republic. European Neurology 9: 76-89.

(70) Schotland D L, Wolf S M, White H H, Dubin H V 1963 Neurologic aspects of Behcet's disease. American Journal of Medicine 34: 544-553.

(71) Epperson LW, Whitaker JN, Kapila A. Cranial MRI in acute disseminated encephalomyelitis. Neurology 1988;38:332.

(72) Hemachuda T, Phanuphjak P, Johnson RT, Griffin D, Ratanovongsiri J, Siriprasomsup W. Neurologic complications of Semple-type rabies vaccine. Neurology 1987; 37:550-6.

(73) Toro G, Vergara I, Roman G. Neuroparalytic accidents of antirabies vaccination with suckling mouse brain vaccination. Arch Neurol 1977;34:694-700.

(74) Rousseau J J, Lust C, Zangerle P F, Bigaignon G 1986 Acute transverse myelitis as presenting symptom of Lyme disease. Lancet 2: 1222-1223.

(75) Kohler J, Kasper J, Kern U, Thoden U, Rehse-Kupper B 1986 Borrelia encephalomyelitis. Lancet 2: 35.

(76) Pachner A R, Steere A C, 1986 CNS manifestations of third stage Lyme disease. Zentralblatt fur BVakteriologie, Mikrobiologie und Hygiene. Series A. 263: 301-306.

(77) Kohler J, Kern U, Kasper J, Rhese-Kupper B, Thoden U 1988 Chronic central nervous system involvement in Lyme borreliosis. Neurology 38: 863-867.

(78) Ashworth B, Emery V 1963 Cerebral dysrhythmia in disseminated sclerosis. Brain 86: 173-18.

(79) Macrae D, Aird R B 1954 The electroencephalogram in multiple sclerosis. Electroencephalography and Clinical Neurophysiology 6: 669-670.

(80) Goldstein N M, Satran R 1974 Serial electroencephalographic observations in chronic multiple sclerosis. Archives of Internal Medicine 134: 1055-1058.

(81) Danielczyk W 1978 Das EEG im Verlauf der multiplen Sklerose. Wiener Klinische Wochenschrift 90: 377-380.

(82) Mushlin AI, Detsky AS, Phelps CE, et al. The accuracy of magnetic resonance imaging in patients with suspected multiple sclerosis. JAMA 1993; 269:3146-3151.

(83) Paty DW, Oger JJF, Kastrukoff LF, Hashimoto SA, Hoops? Eisen AA. MRI in the diagnosis of MS: a prospective study with comparison of clinical evaluation, evoked potentials, and CT. Neurology 1988;38:180-185.

(84) Bartel DR, Markand ON, Kolar OJ. The diagnosis and classification of multiple sclerosis: evoked responses and spinal fluid electrophoresis. Neurology 1983;33:592-601.

(86) Magnetic Resonance Imaging Of The Brain And Spine Second edition, edited by Scott W. Atlas, Lippincott-Raven Publishers.

(87) Prineas J W 1985 The neuropathology of multiple sclerosis. In: Koetsier J (ed) Handbook of clinical neurology - demyelinating disease, Vol 3 (47). Elsevier, Amsterdam, pp 213-257.

(88) Esiri M M 1987 Macrophage populations associated with multiple sclerosis plaques. Neuropathology and Applied Neurobiology 13: 451-465.

(89) Hartung H-P, Heininger K 1989 Non-specific mechanisms of inflammation and tissue damage in MS. Annals of the Institute Pasteur 140: 226-233.

(90) Camma W, Blume B R, Norton W T, Gordon S 1978 Degradation of basic protein in myelin by neutral proteases secreted by stimulated macrophages; a possible mechanism for inflammatory demyelination. Proceedings of the National Academy of Sciences of the USA 75: 1554-1558.

(91) Selmaj K W, Raine C S 1988 Tumour necrosis factor mediates myelin and oligodendrocyte damage in vitro. Annals of Neurology 23: 339-346.

(92) Spoor T C, Rockwell D L 1988 Treatment of optic neuritis with intravenous megadose corticosteroids. A consecutive series. Ophthalmology 95: 131-134.

(93) Litvan I, Grafman J, Vendrell P, Martinez J M, Junque C, Vendrell J M, et al, Multiple memory deficits in patients with multiple sclerosis. Exploring the working memory system. Arch Neurol 1988; 45: 607-10.

(94) Ruchkin D S, Johnson R Jr, Canoune H. Ritter W. Short-term memory storage and retention: an event-related brain potential study (published erratum appears in Electroencephalogr Clin Neurophysiol 1991; 78: 324). Electroencephalogr Clin Neurophysiol 1990; 76: 419-39.

(95) Ruchkin D S, Johnson R Jr, Grafman J, Canoune H, Ritter W. Distinctions and similarities among working memory processes: an event-related potential study. Cogn Brain Res 1992; 1: 53-66.

(96) McCarthyR A, Warrington E K. Cognitive neuropsychology: a clinical introducrtion. San Diego: Academic Press, 1990.

(97) Paulesu E, Frith C D, Frackowiak R S J. The neural correlates of the verbal component of working memory (see comments). Nature 1993; 362: 342-5. Comment in: Nature 1993; 363: 583-4.

(98) Drake W E, Macrae D 1961 Epilepsy in multiple sclerosis. Neurology 11: 810-816.

(99) Elian M, Dean G 1977 Multiple sclerosis and epilepsy. In: Perry J K (ed) Epilepsy, the 8th International Symposum. Raven Press, New York, p341-344.

(100) Boudouresques J, Khalil R, Cherif A A et al 1975 Epilepsie et schlerose en plaques. Revue Neurologique 131: 729-735.

(101) Cendrowski W, Makowski J 1972 Epilepsy in multiple sclerosis. Journal of the Neurological Sciences 17: 389-398.

(102) Kinnunen E, Wikstrom J 1986 Prevalence and prognosis of epilepsy in patients with multiple sclerosis. Epilepsia 27: 729-733.

(103) Hopf H C, Stamatovic A M, Wahren W 1970 Die cerebralen Anfallen bei der multiple Sklerose. Journal of Neurology 198: 256-279

(104) Trouillas P, Courjon L 1972 Epilepsy with multiple sclerosis. Epilepsia 13: 325-333.

(105) Andermann F, Cosgrove J B R, Lloyd-Smith D, Walters A M 1959 Paroxmysmal dysarthria and ataxia in multiple sclerosis. A report of tow unusual cases. Neurology 9: 211-216.

(106) Netsell R, Kent R R 1076 Paroxysmal ataxic dysarthria. Journal of Speech and Hearing Disorders 41: 93-109.

(107) Perks W H, Lascelles R G 1976 Paroxysmal brain stem dysfunction as presenting symptoms of multiple sclerosis. British Medical Journal 2: 1175-1176.

(108) Voiculescu V, Pruskauer-Apostol B, Alecu C 1975 Treatment with acetozolamide of brain-stem and spinal paroxysmal disturbances in multiple sclerosis. Journal of Neurology, Neurosurgery and Psychiatry 38: 191-193.

(112) Brownell B, Hughes J T 1962 The distribution of plaques in the cerebrum in multiple sclerosis. journal of Neurology, Neurosurgery and Psychiatry 25: 315-320.

(113) Ulrich J, Waltraut G-L 1963 The optic nerve in multiple sclerosis. Neuro-opthalmology, Vol 3, part 3. Aeolus Press, Amsterdam, pp 149-159.

(118) Shepherd D I, 1979, Clinical features of multiple sclerosis in north-east Scotland. Acta Neurologica Scandinavica 60: 218-230.

(119) Leibowitz U, Alter M, Halpern L 1964 Clinical studies of multiple sclerosis in Israel III: Clinical course and prognosis related to age. Neurology 14: 926-932.

(120) Poskanzer D C, Schapira K, Miller H, 1963, Epidemiology of multiple sclerosis in the counties of Northumberland and Durham. Journal of Neurology, Neurosurgery and Psychiatry 26: 368-376.

(121) Boutin B, Esquivel E, Mayer M, Chamet S, Ponsot G, Arthuis M 1988 Multiple sclerosis in children: report of clinical and paraclinical features of 19 cases. Neuropediatrics 19: 118-123.

(122) Duquette P, Murray T J, Pleines J et al 1987 Multiple sclerosis in childhood: clinical profile in 125 patients. Journal of Pediatrics 111: 359-363.

(123) Birley J L, Dudgeon L S 1921 A clinical and experimental contribution to pathogenesis of disseminated sclerosis. Brain 44: 150-212.

(124) Muller R 1949 Studies in disseminated sclerosis. Acta Medica Scandinavica 133 (suppl 222): 1-214.

(125) Weinshenker B G, Bass B, Rice G P A et al 1989 The natural history of multiple sclerosis. Journal of the American Medical Association 146: 1367-1369.

(126) Muller R 1949 Studies in disseminated sclerosis. Acta Medica Scandinavica 133(suppl 222):1-214.

(127) Bonduelle M, Albaranes R. 1962 Etude statistique de 145 cas de la sclerose en plaques. Semaine des Hopitax de Paris 38: 3762-3773.

(128) Poser S, 1978 Multiple Sclerosis: an analysis of 812 cases by means of electronic data processing. Springer, Berlin.

(129) Confavreux C, Aimard G, Devic M 1980 Course and prognosis of multiple sclerosis assessed by the computerized data data processing of 349 patients. Brain 103: 281-300.

(130) Verjans E, Theys P, Belmotte P, Carton H. 1983 Clinical parameters and intrathecal IgG synthesis as prognostic factors in multiple sclerosis. Part I. Journal of Neurology 229: 155-165.

(131) Cazzullo C L, Ghezzi A, Marforio S, Caputo D, 1978, Clincial picture of multiple sclerosis with late onset. Acta Neurologica Scandinavica 58: 190-196.

(132) Poser C M, 1985, The course of multiple sclerosis. Archives of Neurology 42: 1035.

(152) McAlpine D, 1972 In: Multiple sclerosis: a reappraisal, 2nd edn. Churchill Livingstone, Edinburgh, p 197.

(153) Thygesen P 1953 The course of multiple sclerosis: a close-up of 105 attacks. Rosenkilde and Bagger, Copenhagen.

(154) Alexander L, Berkeley A W, Alexander A M 1958 Prognosis and treatment of multiple sclerosis - quantitative nosometric study. Journal of the American Medical Association 166: 1943-1949.

(155) Gudmundsson K R 1971 Clinical studies of multiple sclerosis in Iceland. Acta Neurologica Scandinavica 47 (suppl 48): 1-78.

(156) Broman T, Andersen O, Bergmann I 1981 Clinical studies on multiple sclerosis I: Presentation of an incidence material from Gothenburg. Acta Neurologica Scandinavica 63: 6-33.

(157) McAlpine D 1972 In: Multiple sclerosis: a reappraisal, 2nd edn. Churchill Livingstone, Edinburgh, p 197.

(158) Kurtzke J F, Beebe G W, Nagler B, Auth T L, Kurland L T, Nefzger M D 1968 Studies on the natural history of multiple sclerosis 4: Clinical features of the onset bout. Acta Neurologica Scandinavica 44: 467-494.

(159) Kurtzke J F, Beebe G W, Nagler B, Auth T L, Kurland L T, Nefzger M D 1973 Studies on the natural history of multiple sclerosis and correlates of clinical change in an early bout. Acta Neurologica Scandinavica 49: 379-395.

(160) Brown M.R, Putnam T J, 1939 Remissions in multiple sclerosis. Archives of Neurology and Psychiatry 41: 913-920.

(161) Alexander L, Berkeley A W, Alexander A M, 1961, Multiple sclerosis: prognosis and treatment. Thomas, Springfield.

(162) Kurtzke J F, 1956, Course of exacerbations of multiple sclerosis in hospitalized patients. Archives of Neurology and Psychiatry 76: 175-183.

(163) Franklin G M, Nelson L M, Heaton R K, Burk J S, Thompson D S 1988 Stress and its relationship to acute exacerbations in multiple sclerosis. Journal of Neurological Rehabilitation 2: 7-11.

(164) Sibley W A 1987 Risk factors for multiple sclerosis- implications for pathogenesis. In: Crescenzi G S (ed) A multidisciplinary approach to myelin diseases. Plenum Press, London.

(165) Acheson E D 1977 Epidemiology of multiple sclerosis. British Medical Bulletin 33: 9-14.

(166) Hammond S R, McLeod J G, Millingen K S et al. The epidemiology of multiple sclerosis in three Australian cities: Perth, Newcastle and Hobart. Brain 111: 1-25.

(167) Hader W J, Elliot M, Ebers G C 1988 Epidemiology of multiple sclerosis in London and Middlesex county Ontario, Canada. Neurology 38: 617-621.

(168) Skegg D C G, Corwin P A, Craven R S, Malloch J A, Pollock M 1987 Occurrence of multiple sclerosis in the north and south of New Zealand, Journal of Neurology, Neurosurgery and Psychiatry 50: 134-139.

(169) Phadke J G, Downie A W 1987 Epidemiology of multiple sclerosis in the north-east (Grampian region) of Scotland- an update. Journal of Epidemiology and Community Health 41: 5-13.

(170) Baum H B, Rothschild B B 1981 The incidence and prevalence of reported multiple sclerosis. Annals of Neurology 10: 420-428.

(171) Kurland L T 1952 The frequency and geographic distribution of multiple sclerosis as indicated by mortality statistics and morbidity surveys in the United States and Canada. American Journal of Hygiene 55: 457-476.

(172) Poskanzer D C, Prenney L B, Sheridan J L, Kondy J Y 1980 Multiple Sclerosis in the Orkney and Shetland Islands I: Epidemiology, clincial factors, and methodology, Journal of Epidemiology and Community Health 34: 229-239.

(173) Kuroiwa Y, Igata A, Itahara K, Shinzaburo K, Tsubaki T, Toyokura Y, Shibasaki H 1975 Nationwide survey of multiple sclerosis in Japan. Neurology 25: 845-851.

(174) Vassallo L, Elian M, Dean G 1979 Multiple Sclerosis in southern Europe II. Prevalence in Malta 1978. Journal of Epidemiology and Community Health 33: 110-13.

(175) Alter M, Liebowitz U, Speer J 1966 Risk of multiple sclerosis related to age at immigration to Israel. Archives of Neurology 15: 234-237.

(176) Alter M, Kahana E, Loewenson R 1978 Migration and risk of multiple sclerosis. Neurology 28: 1089-1093.

(177) Miller H, Ridley A, Shapira K 1960 Multiple sclerosis. A note on social incidence. British Medical Journal ii: 343-345.

(188) Rao S M, Leo G J, St Aubin-Faubert P. Information processing speed in patients with multiple sclerosis. J Clin Exp Neuropsychol. 1989; 11: 471-477.

(189) Litvan I, Graffman J, Vendrell P, Martinez J M. Slowed information processing in multiple sclerosis. Arch Neurol. 1988; 45: 281-285.

(194) Ruge D, Brochner R, Daris L 1958 A study of the treatment of 637 patients with trigeminal neuralgia. Journal of Neurosurgery 15: 528-536.

(195) Rushton J G, Olafson R A 1965 Trigeminal neuralgia associated with multiple sclerosis. Archives of Neurology 13: 383-386.

(196) Read C F 1932 Multiple sclerosis and Lhermitte's sign. Archives of Neurology and Psychiatry 27: 227-228.

(197) Ekbom K 1971 Carbamazepine: a new symptomatic treatment for the paraesthesiae associated with Lhermitte's sign. Zeitschrift fur Neurologie 200: 341-344.

(199) New England Journal of Medicine, January 19, 1998.

(200) Pentajen, Dr. Jack H., M.D. PhD., University of Utah, Published in the Annals of Neurology, Vol 39, #4.

(221) Van den Burg W, van Zomeren E A, Minderhoud J M, Prange A J A, Meijer N S A 1987 Cognitive impairment in patients with multiple sclerosis and mild physical disability. Archives Neurology 44: 494-501.

(291) Arnason, Barry G.W., MD. Interferon beta in multiple sclerosis. Neurology 1993;43:641-643.

(292) Noronha A, Toscas A, Jensen MA. IFN-beta downregulates T cell activation and IFN-alpha production:implications for MS. J Neuroimmunol (in press).

(293) Ling PD, Warren MK, Vogel SN. Antagonistic effect of interferon-beta on the interferon-gamma-induced expression of Ia antigen in murine macrophages. J Immunol 1985;135:1857-1863.

(294) Maimone D, Gregory S, Arnason BG, Reder AT. Cytokine levels in the cerebrospinal fluid and serum of patients with multiple sclerosis. J Neuroimmunol 1991;32:67-74.

(295) Paty DW, Li DKB, The IFNB Multiple Sclerosis Study Group. Interferon beta-1b is effective in relapsing-remitting multiple sclerosis: MRI results of a multicenter, randomized, double-blind, placebo-controlled trial. Neurology 1993;43:662-667.

GLOSSARY

Acute — Having sharp, severe symptoms, a rapid onset and a short course; not chronic.

Akinesia — Difficulty in beginning movement.

Amyotropic Lateral Sclerosis (Lou Gerig's disease) – A progressive spinal muscular atrophy characterized by muscle wasting. Sensory abnormalities, common in MS, are absent. Death usually occurs within 2 to 5 years.

Ataxia - Trouble coordinating muscles in the execution of voluntary movements.

Audiometry — A method of objectively testing hearing, based on changes in electroencephalogram by perceived sound, without the requirement of a behavioral response.

Autoimmune disease — An inappropriate response by the host's own immune system to its own tissue, instead of to an invading antigen.

Avonex® - Interferon beta 1A; one of three immunotherapies approved by FDA for use in the United States to modify the disease process in multiple sclerosis.

Axons — The single nerve cell process that conducts impulses away from the nerve cell body. It is normally enveloped in a myelin sheath, produced by oligodendrocytes in the central nervous system, and by Schwann cells in the peripheral nerves.

Betaseron® (Interferon beta 1B) - One of three immunotherapies approved by FDA for use in the United States to modify the disease process in multiple sclerosis.

Blood-brain barrier — A term used to describe a composite of permeability barriers between the blood and the brain and between the blood and the cerebrospinal fluid. These barriers prevent the movement of damaging elements into the CNS.

Brainstem — The portion of the brain that connects the spinal cord to the rest of the brain. It includes the pons, midbrain, and medulla oblongata.

Central nervous system — Includes the brain, optic nerve, and spinal cord.

Cerebellum — The cerebellum affects balance, eye movements, and coordinates the planning of limb movements. It is the large posterior part of the brain lying above the pons and medulla and beneath the posterior portion of the cerebrum.

Cerebrospinal Fluid — A liquid cushion that literally bathes the brain and spinal cord. The buoyant force reduces the weight of the brain from 1400 ounces in air to less than 50 ounces immersed in the CSF. Analysis of this fluid is often helpful in diagnosing many central nervous system diseases, including multiple sclerosis.

Cerebrum — The largest part of the brain, consisting of two hemispheres.

Chronic — A disease of slow progression and long duration.

Controls — A standard used to check observations and conclusions in order to establish their validity.

Cortex — The outer portion of an organ.

Corticosteroids — A steroid produced by the adrenal cortex. Although these medications do not prevent MS exacerbations, they may result in quicker resolution.

Cranial nerves — The 12 pair of nerves that originate in the brain.

Diplopia — Double vision

Double blind — A reference to medical research where neither the patient nor the doctor knows who is receiving the experimental drug or treatment and who is receiving a placebo.

Dysarthria — Trouble speaking

Dysphagia — Trouble swallowing. A speech/language pathologist can assess these patients.

Exacerbation — An increase in the severity of a disease.

Evoked Potentials — A diagnostic test that measures slowed or blocked conduction along central nervous system pathways. This can be caused by demyelinating lesions.

Emotional lability — A symptom in several neurological diseases, including MS. It is marked by exaggerated emotional expressions that do not fit the situation—laughing or crying when inappropriate for the circumstance.

Extended disability status scale (EDSS) — A 10 point scale ranging from 0 to 10 that provides a measure of overall disability.

Extracerebral - Outside the brain.

Frontal lobe - One of the four lobes of the brain, associated with mood, personality, and emotion.

Gamma globulin — A protein formed in the blood, and important in resisting infection.

Gait — Manner of walking.

Gait ataxia — An unsteady or irregular gait.

Gray Matter — That portion of the brain composed of cell bodies, as opposed to the white matter, where the nerve fibers are covered by myelin.

Incidence of disease — The ratio of the number of new cases in a given period of time, usually one year, and the total number of people at risk for developing the disease.

Interferon — A family of naturally occurring proteins, three of which have been identified (alpha, beta, and gamma interferon). Two interferon drugs have been approved by FDA as a treatment for MS [Betaseron and Avonex (Rabif is another Interferon widely used, but not approved in the U.S.)]

Internal Rectus Muscle — One of the muscles that move the eye. In MS, problems with this muscle can result in an INO which may result in diplopia.

Intraaxial — Within the brain stem

Ion — A charged particle, having lost or gained an electron.

Lassitude — A special type of fatigue, often experienced by MS patients. It can occur in the morning or later in the day, and is independent of the degree of exertion.

Lhermite's sign — A neurological symptom of a pain that is often described as a sudden electric shock passing down the back to the legs when the neck is flexed. Sometimes the sensation is described as tingling or pins and needles. The sensation is always brief, lasting only a few seconds (196). MS is the most common cause of this symptom.

Macrophage — A component of the immune system that destroys foreign microorganisms and "eats" debris left by other cells in the immune system.

Medulla — The central portion of an organ, as opposed to the outer cortex.

Midbrain — Along with the pons, and medulla oblongata, these comprise the brainstem.

Movement Phosphenes — Bright flashes, sometimes noticed when moving the eyes in the dark. These can occur during the acute stage of optic neuritis, but may occur during recovery.

Multiple sclerosis — A progressive, inflammatory, demyelinating disease effecting the white matter of the central nervous system. It can cause physical disability and mental impairment.

Muscular dystrophy — A genetic disease that causes muscle weakness and muscle wasting, but does not cause neural degeneration as occurs in multiple sclerosis.

Myelin — The insulating material that surrounds the axons of nerve fibers. It is critical in the conduction of impulses in the nervous system.

Myelin Basic Protein — A component of myelin that is elevated in the CSF during an acute attack, indicating that demyelination has occurred.

Neuro-ophthalmologist — A neurologist that specializes in visual problems.

Neurotransmitter — A chemical agent released by a presynaptic cell that stimulates a postsynaptic cell (a synapse is the junction between two neurons).

Nystagmus — A rapid, involuntary, "jerking" movement of the eyes, a classical sign of MS.

Oligodendrocytes — Cells that produce myelin in the central nervous system.

Ophthalmoscope — A device for studying the interior of the eye through the pupil.

Optic Neuritis — Optic neuritis is inflammation of the optic nerve, usually resulting in blurred vision.

Oscillopsia — An illusory sensation of swaying of the visual field; can sometimes be partly compensated for with converging prisms.

Palsy — Paralysis

Paraparesis — A slight paralysis afflicting the lower extremities.

Paresthesia — An abnormal sensation such as burning, prickling, tickling, or tingling—sometimes described as pins and needles. Persistent paraesthesia is extremely common in MS, occurring in 84% of the subjects in one study (4). In MS, this symptom usually persists for about six weeks—a period of time that is similar to many transient symptoms of multiple sclerosis.

Paroxysmal symptoms — Symptoms appearing suddenly with recurrent manifestations and brief episodes occurring frequently, often triggered by movement or sensory stimuli.

Paroxysmal ataxia — Ataxia occurring frequently with recurrent manifestations and brief episodes.

Pathologic — Resulting from disease.

Periventricular — Around the ventricles, hollow cavities within the brain filled with circulating cerebrospinal fluid.

Percutaneous rhizotomy — Removal of section of spinal nerve root, for relief of pain.

Placebo — An inert substance, given as a medicine for its suggestive effect. When used in medical trials where neither the doctor nor the patient knows who is getting the experimental drug and who is getting the placebo, the trial is referred to as double blind.

Prevalence of disease — The ratio of the total number of cases alive in the given population and the total size of the population.

Primary progressive — MS disease that is progressive from the onset, as opposed to secondary-progressive that begins as relapsing-remitting disease and later develops into the progressive form.

Psychometric tasks — Tasks requiring mental and cognitive control. MS patients showing an increase in lesion load as determined by MRI either showed a worsening in performance on some of these tasks or a reduced ability to improve with practice on some tests having to do with attention and information-processing speed.

Radiation — The direct emission of heat into the surrounding environment.

Relapse — The appearance of a new symptom or tithe reappearance of a previous symptom at any time after the initial attack.

Verbal-phonological short-term memory (What you hear) — Studies have shown that this aspect of memory is more vulnerable to disruption by MS than visuo-spatial short-term memory (what you see).

Printed in the United States
759200003B